Withdrawn for Sale

2

SPECIAL FORCES HEROES

Also by Michael Ashcroft:

Victoria Cross Heroes
Dirty Politics, Dirty Times:
My Fight with Wapping and New Labour

Smell the Coffee: A Wake-Up Call for the Conservative Party

www.lordashcroft.com

Visit the Special Forces Heroes website at
www.specialforcesheroes.com
and also
www.helpforheroes.org.uk

Special Forces Heroes

Extraordinary true stories of daring and valour

MICHAEL ASHCROFT

FOREWORD BY
ANDY McNAB

headline
review

First published in Great Britain in 2008
by HEADLINE REVIEW

An imprint of Headline Publishing Group

4

Michael Ashcroft would be happy to hear from readers with their comments
on the book at the following e-mail address: info@lordashcroft.com

Cataloguing in Publication Data is available from the British Library.

HB ISBN 978 0 7553 1807 0
TPB ISBN 978 0 7557 1893 3

Text design by Janette Revill
Typeset in GaramondThree by Avon Dataset Ltd, Bidford on Avon, Warwickshire
Printed and bound in Great Britain by CPI Mackays, Chatham ME5 8TD

Headline's policy is to use papers that are natural, renewable and recyclable products and
made from wood grown in sustainable forests. The logging and manufacturing processes
are expected to conform to the environmental regulations of the country of origin.

HEADLINE PUBLISHING GROUP
An Hachette Livre UK Company
338 Euston Road
London NW1 3BH

www.headline.co.uk
www.hachettelivre.co.uk

This book is dedicated to those who lost their lives in British 'Special Forces' operations – both before and after the SAS and SBS were actually formed. I salute the 'cold courage' of those who knew in advance that they were taking incredible risks for their country.

CONTENTS

ACKNOWLEDGEMENTS

I will start by thanking the forty-four brave men featured in this book. Without their courageous deeds and their medals, I would have nothing to write about. Many of these servicemen have been kind enough to cooperate with me and many have been willing to check the accuracy of their entry, while others have agreed to help me more fully, either by being interviewed about their careers or by jotting down a few lines about their experiences. I am grateful to all those who have given up their time to improve this book. I have decided to donate all my author's royalties to Help for Heroes, a charity providing support for the servicemen and women wounded in Afghanistan and Iraq. I hope this will go some way to showing my gratitude and admiration for what they do.

My appreciation goes to a military hero turned best-selling author, Andy McNab, for agreeing to write the foreword. Andy was Britain's most highly decorated serving soldier before he left 22 SAS Regiment in 1993 having been awarded the Distinguished Conduct Medal (DCM) and the Military Medal (MM). He agreed to contribute when I met him for lunch at the House of Lords. I am honoured that such a distinguished former SAS man should put his name to *Special Forces Heroes*.

I am grateful to Angela Entwistle, my corporate communications director, and her team, for helping to get this project off the ground and for their assistance during the preparation of the book.

I would like to thank Michael Naxton, my medals consultant, for playing such a crucial role in helping to build up the medal collection that forms the basis for *Special Forces Heroes*. Michael, who is a veteran of the medals' world, also gave me some invaluable advice, and carefully read and corrected the proofs.

For a second time, I am grateful to Wendy McCance, Emma Tait and their colleagues at Headline for enabling me to bring a subject that is dear to my heart – bravery – to a wider audience. As with my book *Victoria Cross Heroes*, they have been thoroughly professional and it has been a delight to deal with them.

My appreciation goes to Mark Souster, of Empire Media Productions, and Richard Dale and Mike Kemp, of Dangerous Films, for enabling this book to be linked to a four-part television series on channel *five*. Mark Hedgecoe, Nick Green, James Leigh, Vanessa Tovell, Verity Jackson and others grafted at the 'coalface' to make the project such a success. I commend the series, also called *Special Forces Heroes*, to readers of this book.

Fellow author General Sir John Wilsey has been particularly kind to me. When I tracked down Peter Jones, the recipient of two gallantry medals, he informed me that he was going to feature prominently in Sir John's book, *Ulster Tales*, due to be published in 2009. Sir John not only let me read the relevant chapter from his forthcoming book, but also allowed me to quote from it. I am grateful for his generosity of spirit and the thoroughness of his research.

I would also like to thank those other authors and publishers who have allowed me to quote from their books, particularly when their manuscripts contained interviews with one or more of the forty-four men featured here.

Many of the gallantry and service medals highlighted were purchased at auction. I would therefore like to thank the cataloguers who researched the background to the medal recipients and the circumstances that led to the decorations being awarded. I have relied heavily on their work for some of the accounts in this book but, because their work is compiled anonymously, it is impossible to thank each one by name. However, Dix Noonan Webb, in particular, was responsible for many splendid write-ups and I salute the quality of the firm's website.

Finally, I am grateful to senior officials at the Ministry of Defence for giving me expert guidance on what was – and was not – permissible to put in my book from a security point of view. Their advice has been invaluable and I have sought to follow it to the letter.

FOREWORD
by Andy McNab

I have little doubt that the private collection of British Special Forces medals that Lord Ashcroft started to assemble in 1988 now forms the largest of its kind in the world. The collection, however, is remarkable not just for its size but also its variety and the number of years that it spans.

Even though I served in the Regiment (the SAS) for a decade until 1993, I was unaware that there were Special Forces-style operations going on as early as the Crimean War. After all, this conflict is traditionally renowned, not for its intelligence-led forays behind enemy lines, but for conventional warfare that led to the needless loss of life in the Charge of the Light Brigade. Yet, the very first medal highlighted in this book – a VC for Lieutenant (later Rear Admiral) John Bythesea – is for a typical SAS operation in which a two-man undercover team slipped unnoticed deep into enemy territory during the Crimean War to ambush a party delivering mailbags containing Russian secrets. This was all happening in 1855 – almost a century before the SAS was even formed.

In his book, Lord Ashcroft uses the medals and the men who were awarded them to recount how the Special Forces developed over the next 150 years. He tells some remarkable stories of valour throughout the Second World War and involving a series of conflicts and incidents right up to the two Gulf Wars. This is a book full of accounts of outstanding bravery in the face of incredible hardship. Having carried out covert operations with the Regiment in Northern Ireland, I particularly enjoyed the accounts of courage behind the medals that were awarded to some of the men whom I served with during the Troubles. Many of these stories have had to remain shrouded in mystery for years for security reasons. Only now that we have peace in the province are tales of the bravery that took place in the fight against the IRA beginning to emerge.

Today the Regiment, which evolved from the 1st Special Air Service and other specialist fighting units formed during the Second World War, remains the most élite fighting force in the world. No other military unit uses the combination of highly trained men, brilliant intelligence and serious firepower with such devastating consequences against those who confront it.

Having met with Lord Ashcroft to discuss his book, I know that he has pursued a lifelong fascination with bravery and has a real passion for medals that are associated with great deeds of courage. His decision to put the trust's collection of VCs – the largest in the world – on public display shows, too, his commitment to creating a centre of excellence for bravery at the Imperial War Museum that can be enjoyed by the nation.

When I wrote *Bravo Two Zero* and *Immediate Action*, the two books about my career in the Regiment, I hoped to bring the skilled and daring work of the SAS to a wider audience but without compromising its security. As someone who has served proudly with the Regiment and who has been fortunate enough to be twice awarded gallantry medals for my actions, I am certain that *Special Forces Heroes* will also bring the achievements of Special Forces soldiers to a larger, and appreciative, audience. I commend Lord Ashcroft for his diligence in researching this book so carefully. I have no doubt that it is a labour of love that will be enjoyed and cherished by those who read it.

PREFACE

It is less than straightforward to divide bravery into subsections. However, as someone with a lifelong interest in the subject, I would argue there are broadly two types of valour – spur-of-the-moment bravery and cold courage, the latter involving advanced planning.

I have nothing but admiration for those who have been decorated for spur-of-the-moment bravery, perhaps a serviceman who, in the heat of battle and with his blood up, risked his life to save a wounded friend and/or comrade. Many such men have rightly been awarded the Victoria Cross, Britain's most prestigious military bravery award, and other decorations for their sterling actions.

This book, however, deals primarily with premeditated cold courage. It takes a truly special sort of valour to go undercover behind enemy lines, or to be part of a small, élite unit on a hit-and-run raid against a far larger force. The participant knows that he is putting his life on the line to a far greater extent than most servicemen do regularly in their line of duty. If the mission goes wrong, the serviceman knows that, at best, he might be captured and kept as a prisoner of war for months or even years. At worst, he might be seized, tortured, mutilated and killed. The more difficult and daring the operation becomes, the less are the chances that those on it will return.

Special Forces Heroes is not intended to be a history of the British Special Forces – history books have been written with great success by others. Neither is it meant to be the definitive book detailing all the heroes of Britain's Special Forces over the years. Instead, the book deals solely with the collection of gallantry medals that I started to build up two decades ago. These medals were generally awarded to servicemen for Special Forces or Commando-style operations – even though some of the recipients were not members of the Special Air Service (SAS) or Special Boat Service (SBS).

Today, these medals – which form the largest private collection of such British decorations in the world – are owned by a trust, which was set up to care for and protect them. It is also responsible for preserving the collection of Victoria Crosses – at more than 150, once again the largest in the world – that I first began to amass in 1986. This VC collection formed the basis for my book *Victoria Cross Heroes*, which was first published in 2006 to mark the 150th anniversary of the VC. Incidentally, the collection will go on public display from 2010, following my donation to the opening of a new gallery at the Imperial War Museum in London.

The first VC I bought was at auction and had been awarded to Leading Seaman James Magennis, a submariner, for his astonishing bravery towards the end of the Second World War. Originally intended as a one-off, this first purchase led me to want to build a collection of bravery medals that would do justice to their recipients, outstanding servicemen from Britain and the Commonwealth who had risked their lives, and in many cases given their lives, in being awarded the official honours. At first I thought I would collect VCs only, because there are so many stories of bravery in our armed forces that I feared, otherwise, it would be difficult to know where to start and where to stop.

However, my first purchase of a medal for Commando or

Special Forces-type operations came in the summer of 1988 when I learnt that the medals of Corporal William 'Bill' Sparks were being auctioned at Sotheby's. Sparks, a Royal Marine, was one of the famous Cockleshell Heroes, who had carried out a daring raid behind enemy lines in December 1942. I found it astonishing that a group of men had undertaken such a difficult and dangerous assignment when they knew there was an incredibly high chance they would either die or be captured. The Cockleshell Heroes and the Dambusters were two missions that had enthralled me since childhood. I had seen the film *The Cockleshell Heroes* – in all its black-and-white glory – shortly after it came out at the end of 1955 when I was just nine years old, watching open-mouthed, and at the end I felt totally in awe of the bravery of those who had participated in the operation.

Twelve men were taken across the Channel in a submarine and then left to paddle up one of occupied France's largest estuaries in their small canoes with their faces blackened. Before they set out, they were warned by their commanding officer – who had come up with the idea for the operation – that their own safety came second to the success of the mission. They were even told that if they succeeded in blowing up their targets – enemy ships – they would be on their own because it was too difficult and dangerous for anyone to come to fetch them. In short, they were told they should try to get from near Bordeaux in south-west France to Spain, using their own initiative in an unfamiliar country swarming with German soldiers and their informants. Yet still these men – motivated by a desire to fight for their country, for freedom and for their comrades – unhesitatingly agreed to climb out of their submarine into canoes and embark on a mission that would cost eight of them their lives. I find such raw courage utterly astonishing and deeply moving.

After successfully bidding for Sparks's medals, I decided that

I would occasionally expand my collection to include bravery medals in general – not just VCs. So now and again, when a medal with a fascinating story comes up – perhaps one with a quirk of history, an unusual location for a battle, an outstanding piece of team work or an incredible example of courage – I'll bid for it. This buying process has generally accelerated over the years and I have developed a particular interest in SAS and Special Forces-style operations. One thing led to another, and now there is this second collection of gallantry and service medals, which is separate from the VC collection. Today, the second collection involves the medals of forty-four men.

History books rightly record that the immediate origins of the British Special Forces lie in the early years of the Second World War. I make no apology, however, for applying the term and the title of the book, *Special Forces Heroes*, more loosely – to medals won for daring hit-and-run raids against a far bigger military force, for missions deep behind enemy lines and the like. I am therefore, in some cases, writing about incidents that go back to the mid-nineteenth century, when some of the basic tactics later adopted by the SAS and the SBS were first used by British servicemen.

I also make no apologies for once again recounting a handful of the stories that appeared in *Victoria Cross Heroes* because they involve Special Forces-type operations. In each case, the stories are told differently. If the two books very occasionally overlap, so be it. Frankly, the accounts of derring-do are so incredible that they are worth telling at least twice. Neither do I apologise for including a handful of medals that have no obvious link with Special Forces: for incidents which took place in Northern Ireland at the height of the work in the province carried out by the SAS and other British security and intelligence groups.

I have gone to great lengths not to reveal sensitive information about national security or to endanger the safety of individual former servicemen, notably those who operated in Northern Ireland. In certain cases, I have changed the names of some of the men who feature in this book, either at their request or because I have been unable to trace them and do not want to put them at risk. For security reasons, too, I am not giving the dates of birth of men who served after the Second World War, or the towns or villages in which they now live. Furthermore, in a small number of instances, I have chosen not to reveal the date the gallantry awards were gazetted, or an individual's rank or regiment. This has, once again, been done so that there can be nothing that leads to them being identified. In short, I have erred on the side of caution on anything to do with personal safety, but without holding back from telling the men's sensational stories.

I have been deeply moved by many of the stories I have researched. I also share the sense of anger of many SAS men that the bravery of soldiers during the Battle of Mirbat in Oman has never been properly recognised. As a result, I have now sponsored the Battle of Mirbat Memorial, at the National Memorial Arboretum in Staffordshire, to commemorate the courage of the men from 22 SAS on 19 July 1972.

Finally, some of the language used by the former servicemen in their interviews is a little colourful. I have chosen not to censor their words, other than to insert some asterisks in place of appropriate letters so as not to cause unnecessary offence.

When you go home, tell them of us and say,
For your tomorrow, we gave our today.

Epitaph at the Kohima Memorial in Burma, which marks the loss of Allied lives in repulsing the Japanese 15th Army towards the end of the Second World War. The words are attributed to John Maxwell Edmonds (1875–1958), an English classicist.

1

ORIGINS OF THE BRITISH SPECIAL FORCES

According to Greek legend, as narrated by Homer and others, the Trojan War was waged against the city of Troy in around 1200 BC. At one point during the war, it was said that Troy was besieged by the Acheaens (Mycenaean Greeks) for almost a decade. In the Greeks' determination to end the war, they devised a ruse, and a giant hollow wooden horse, an animal that was sacred to the Trojans, was built. It was filled with soldiers and left outside the besieged city, while the rest of the Greek army appeared to retreat. The Trojans, believing the war was over, dragged the wooden horse into the city and drunkenly celebrated their apparent victory. At night, up to 3,000 men crept out of the horse and opened the gates of the city to their comrades, who were by now waiting outside. After a fierce battle, the Greeks won control of Troy and later burnt it to the ground.

The story of the Trojan Horse is, of course, largely, if not wholly, fictitious but, if there was ever an early inspiration for the modern-day Special Forces, surely this was it. Given the success of the plan, however, I find it surprising how few real-life Commando or Special Forces-style operations there were around the world between 1200 BC and the Second World War. This was partly because military leaders over the centuries – even fearless, ruthless warriors such as Ghengis Khan – had a bizarre sense of fair play. It was one thing to decapitate, bludgeon or, latterly, shoot a rival dead – even to rape and pillage – but it was considered cowardly and lacking in glory to deceive the enemy, or to mount devious hit-and-run raids against him.

It is true that Alexander the Great, the Greek king who conquered the world in the fourth century BC, had his élite forces that enabled him to remain undefeated on the battlefield. So, too, did the Romans and the Persians as they built their great empires, but even such formidable armies still lacked the element of stealth that is associated with modern-day Special Forces operations.

As recently as the nineteenth century, only isolated examples of what might be loosely described as Commando or Special Forces-style operations can be found in the records of the British military. In 1800, Colonel Coote Manningham raised an Experimental Corps of Riflemen, which later became a regiment in the regular Army. The soldiers were armed with a new precision rifle, and the Experimental Corps of Riflemen was considered a force of sharpshooters and scouts who were taught to think for themselves rather than simply follow orders. Even in a traditional armed conflict they were unconventional, going into battle not in line, but in skirmishing formations ahead of the main infantry. Despite their variations to the norm, however, they were not so different from the regular Army and cannot be looked upon as anything approaching a modern-day Special Forces unit.

Just a few years later, towards the end of the Napoleonic Wars, the Russian officer Denis Davidoff was in charge of a small, but effective, force of Hussars and Cossacks that repeatedly took on the might of Napoleon's army. His partisan unit raided and harassed the French force all the way to Moscow and back with a series of hit-and-run raids and the occasional more conventional confrontation.

It is ironic, perhaps, that the Crimean War of 1854–6 – famous for the crass stupidity of the Charge of the Light Brigade, resulting in dreadful loss of life – also provides an early and successful example of a Commando or Special Forces raid. The earliest medal in the trust's Special Forces collection is a VC awarded to Lieutenant (later Rear Admiral) John Bythesea that was purchased at auction in 2007.

Yet after the Crimean War, no push to develop special operations further is evident. The First World War of 1914–18, which claimed the lives of more than ten million military personnel and civilians, will always be remembered for its trench warfare. On the Western Front, tactics were employed that are the antithesis of Commando and Special Forces operations. Day after day, military commanders sent thousands of men 'over the top' and to their deaths just to make minuscule advances along a narrow battlefield. It is true there were some premeditated activities during land battles in the Great War that loosely had a Special Forces theme – including trench raids by small units to gather documents and to capture prisoners – but these were the exception rather than the rule.

In the years between the two world wars, little thought was given to the development of special operations. H.E. Fox-Davies, a subaltern in the Durham Light Infantry, did, however, write a paper in which he highlighted the need for small bodies of specially trained men to be used against specific targets. The paper, seen and admired by at least one general, argued that the force would be able to create significant damage to the enemy, out of proportion to the number of men it required. General Wavell gave Fox-Davies the chance to try out his scheme on manoeuvres but nothing really came of the idea.

More important was the development of the Special Night

3

Squads (SNS) established by Charles Orde Wingate, a British Army officer, in 1936. The joint force of British soldiers and Jewish Settlement Police was used during the Arab revolt of 1936–9. Wingate used a group of hand-picked men to carry out surprise ambushes. The force was highly successful in halting attacks by Arab guerillas on the pipeline of the Iraqi Petroleum Company. The effectiveness of the force was matched only by its brutality – Wingate personally lined up suspected terrorists and rioters and shot them in cold blood, and his men were equally ruthless. Martin van Creveld, the Israeli military historian, wrote that the men's training included 'how to kill without compunction; how to interrogate prisoners by shooting every tenth man to make the rest talk; and how to deter future terrorists by pushing the heads of captured ones into pools of oil and then freeing them to tell the story'. The ferocity of the tactics earned criticism as well as praise and in 1938 the SNS – forerunner of the SAS – was disbanded and Wingate was ordered out of Palestine.

It was only after the start of the Second World War, however, that Britain started to give serious consideration to the idea of forming small élite forces – specially trained and equipped – to carry out special operations. This new line of thinking was not prompted by the fact that other nations, notably the Germans, had surged ahead in this type of warfare, leaving Britain lagging behind. Far from it, Britain led the way and proved that there was – and, of course, still is – a place for such units on the modern-day battlefield.

In his book *British Special Forces*, William Seymour writes of special operations: 'These demand a particular skill, exceptional courage, a certain amount of imagination (but not too much), and the will-power to go on to the end, come what may; all of which are well suited to the British character with its love of adventure, willingness to accept hardship and risk, and propensity for individualism.'

Seymour, a full-time soldier who served in the Special Forces during the war, added: 'Perhaps it is an island race whose men have the blood of seafaring folk coursing through their veins – and thickened over the centuries by some successful buccaneering – who are the most likely to respond to the call of maritime adventure than those who have never had to look to their moat for salvation.'

Possibly because of Seymour's theory, the Germans and the Italians, on the other hand, were not inclined to use Special Forces during the Second World War. The only German military commander to use such tactics successfully was Otto Skorzeny, who mounted a series of brilliant Commando-style operations against Allied forces. In 1943, Skorzeny was personally selected by Adolf Hitler to lead the operation to rescue Italian dictator Benito Mussolini, who had been overthrown and imprisoned by the Italian government. Skorzeny took part in Operation Oak, a daring glider-based assault on the Campo Imperatore Hotel at Gran Sasso. Mussolini was rescued without a bullet being fired. Skorzeny, who sported a formidable facial scar from a pre-war fencing duel, escorted Mussolini to Rome and later Berlin. This adventure earned Skorzeny fame, promotion to major and the Knight's Cross, Germany's prestigious gallantry award. Skorzeny eventually wrote a book, *Skorzeny's Special Missions: The Memoirs of the Most Dangerous Man in Europe*, in which he detailed many of his wartime exploits. The Italians did occasionally use 'human torpedoes', or manned torpedoes, in naval operations against specific targets in the Second World War, but even such courageous individual feats did not inspire others to develop additional special operations against their enemy.

By the spring of 1940, the British Army had formed ten Independent Companies, each comprising some twenty officers and 270 men. They were trained and equipped to carry out sabotage raids on the enemy's lines of communications, but in reality most of the companies – due to a shortage of troops – were asked to carry out conventional infantry roles. In November 1940, the companies were disbanded and many of the specially trained men volunteered for – and were accepted into – the new Special Service battalions that had come into existence from June of that year.

After the evacuation of most of the British Expeditionary Force from Dunkirk, Winston Churchill had ordered his military commanders to form a 'butcher and bolt' raiding force to continue the war against Nazi Germany. The format of the new force – and indeed the name 'Commando' – was put forward by Lieutenant Colonel Dudley Clarke, who at the time was serving as Military Assistant to General Sir John Dill, the Chief of the Imperial General Staff (CIGS). Clarke had admired some of the guerrilla tactics of the Boer Commando units fighting the British during the Boer War of 1899–1902. Like Clarke, Churchill favoured the word 'Commando' but other military leaders preferred the phrase 'Special Service'. For the remainder of the war, both were used and were considered ideal for bolstering the confidence of the British public after the setback of Dunkirk. Britons liked the idea of a superior, specially trained force defending our shores.

Commando troops received extra money from which they had to fund their own accommodation whenever in Britain. They were trained in physical fitness, survival, orienteering, close-quarter combat, silent killing, signalling, amphibious and cliff assault, vehicle operation, weapons and demolition. Initially, each Commando was to consist of a headquarters unit plus ten troops of fifty men, including three officers, but later in the war the sizes of the force varied.

In *British Special Forces*, William Seymour, who served during the war in 52 (ME) Commando, writes:

> A good Commando had to be a protean figure. Every worthwhile soldier has to have courage, physical fitness and self-discipline, but those who served in the Commandos needed these virtues more abundantly, for they would be called upon to perform feats well above the normal run of duty, and often to work longer hours and enjoy less rest than their counterparts in a regiment. A high standard of marksmanship had to be attained, as did the ability to cross any type of country quickly, to survive a rough passage of sea in a small boat and arrive on the other side ready to scale a cliff, to use explosives, to think quickly and if needs be to act independently, and to be prepared to kill ruthlessly. A man would learn some of these skills in his training, but vitality and a zest for adventure must be the well-spring of every one of his actions.

Of course, not all volunteers made the grade and they had to return to their units. The system generally worked well but some commanders resented the fact that many of their best men were being whisked away to join the Commandos. Much of the early training was carried out – using fast landing craft – in Inveraray, Scotland.

The first Commando in the field was No. 3, which was under the leadership of John Durnford-Slater, a regular gunner who went on to become a brigadier. He took just days, from late June 1940 to 5 July, to raise the Plymouth-based fighting unit. On the night of 14 July, No. 3 Commando took part in a raid on German-occupied Guernsey that was led by Durnford-Slater, but the party failed to make contact with the German garrison. This was not, in fact, the first Commando raid of the war. On the night of 23 June that year, 120 men from No. 11 Commando/Independent Company took part in an offensive reconnaissance manoeuvre on the French coast south of Boulogne-sur-Mer and Le Touquet. In a skirmish, two German soldiers were killed while Dudley Clarke – who was there as an observer – received a bullet graze to one of his ears.

Clarke was now asked to expand the Commando force and in doing so he worked closely with the Royal Navy through Captain G.A. Garnons-Williams. Over the summer of 1940, six more Commandos were formed: Nos 4, 5, 6, 7, 8 and 9. Furthermore, a small secretariat was set up in Admiralty to ensure the raids were coordinated properly. This task fell to Lieutenant General Sir Alan Bourne, the Adjutant General of the Royal Marines.

In October 1940, Brigadier J.C. Haydon was appointed to command the Special Service Brigade. This led, under his guidance, to the Commandos being amalgamated into Special Service Battalions. However, Nos 1 to 5 Special Service Battalions proved unwieldy and were disbanded in March 1941. The Commandos had kept their own identity within the battalions and they were now re-formed and expanded to create eleven Commandos (numbered from 1 to 12 with No. 10 missing).

In February 1942, the Commandos were given their own training headquarters – later to be called Commando Basic Training Centre – in Achnacarry, Scotland. The new volunteers – all trained soldiers – underwent a twelve-week course that was said to be the toughest the British Army had ever devised. The aim was to create a formidable soldier who was confident in the art of amphibious warfare. It was essential that he be able to land on a hostile beach and be ready for immediate, fast and furious fighting. To ensure maximum reality, every training exercise was carried out with live ammunition and explosives. In *British Special Forces*, William Seymour writes:

> A man was expected to march seven miles in the hour, climb a cliff, fire a gun accurately on the run and know how to kill silently with knife or garrotte. The assault course – part of which was known as the Death Slide – became legendary, and training included living off the land (cooking and eating rats!). Much of a Commando's work would be done in darkness, and training at Achnacarry was aimed to produce a creature of the night and mist who would strike swiftly and silently at the foe.

Those who founded the Commandos decided the units should have no administrative 'tail'; instead, every member was a front-line fighter. This was possible when the Commandos were used for their original aim of short, swift raids on specific targets. However, from 1943 onwards the Commandos were given tasks not that dissimilar to ordinary infantry battalions and that meant they had to develop some transport and a non-combatant 'tail'.

As the Second World War intensified, the Commandos became the basis for even more specialist military units, including the Special Air Service (SAS), the Special Boat Squadron (SBS), the Parachute Regiment and the Long Range Desert Group (LRDG). The SAS was raised by the then-Lieutenant David Stirling, although he always modestly suggested he was one of its five founders. Stirling, 6ft 7in. tall, solidly built and athletic, was a formidable, but unassuming, character who had a great sense of adventure. He had been keen to learn to parachute and was not deterred when his first jump using faulty equipment left him paralysed from the waist down for weeks and in hospital for months. It was as he lay recuperating that he contemplated a new type of strategic warfare. Like the early Commando raids, it would seek to destroy specific targets but with far fewer – just one twentieth – of the men. He believed that four-man airborne units operating behind enemy lines in the Middle East, where he was serving, could cause havoc using surprise, guile and judgement. The idea quickly came to fruition and on 24 August 1941, Stirling formed L Detachment of the Special Air Service Brigade. He recruited sixty-five Commandos and was given five aircraft from which to drop them two nights before the Eighth Army's then planned offensive in four months' time. The men were given a rapid but rigorous training programme and were dropped on the night of 16 November with the aim of destroying enemy airplanes on five airfields in the Gazala-Timimi area.

Appalling weather – including winds of up to Force 8 – scuppered the plan. Just twenty-one of the fifty-four men reached the pick-up point agreed with the LRDG. Five men died, twenty-eight were taken prisoner and one aircraft was lost. Yet from this inauspicious start, the SAS was born. During the desert war, the SAS performed many successful and daring long-range insertion missions and destroyed aircraft and fuel depots. When the Germans stepped up security, the tactics were changed to hit-and-run raids. Later in the war, the SAS were used in numerous other successful operations, including the invasion of Italy. Before and during the Normandy invasion, the SAS was used to help the French Resistance and to strike at targets.

Today, of course, the SAS – with its motto of 'Who Dares Wins' – is one of the most respected and feared fighting units in the world. The SAS is the principal Special Forces unit of the modern British Army and it serves as a model for similar units in other countries. The other parts of the British Special Forces in existence today are the SBS, the Special Reconnaissance Regiment (SRR), and the Special Forces Support Group (SFSG).

The origins of the SBS were laid in June 1940 when Roger Courtney, a powerful man with a thirst for adventure, was given authority to form the first Special Boat Section (it did not become the Special Boat Squadron until 1977). The force was hived off and initially known as the Folbot Troop, a folbot being a folding boat or kayak. Courtney, who did not believe that enough was being done to target German shipping, initially chose just twelve men and, using ten canoes, he began intensive training off the Isle of Arran. Courtney believed that small parties could operate out of submarines using small landing craft to land and carry out reconnaissance and sabotage on enemy targets. He believed that the reconnaissance parties could obtain useful data on top of the kind that was available from aerial photographs. Courtney also believed that sabotage parties should be used to disrupt inland communications, destroy ammunition dumps and blow up enemy shipping with limpet mines. Furthermore, he believed the SBS could be used to drop off and recover agents. The Folbot Troop was attached to No. 8 Commando, which had provided it with most of its servicemen.

It was decided that the Folbot Troop's first operation in November 1940 should target German operations on the Dutch coast. As with the first mission for the SAS, the SBS got off to a troubled start due to adverse weather. The men were taken close to their targets on motor torpedo boats (MTBs), but their folbots could not be launched. Eventually, the mission had to be aborted but Courtney learnt a useful lesson, namely that submarines were preferable to MTBs as carriers. Three months later, the section sailed with No. 8 Commando for the Middle East. During 1941 and for the rest of the war, it began to make its mark through exactly the sort of reconnaissance and sabotage work that Courtney had intended. The Special Boat Squadron was renamed the Special Boat Service in 1987. Today the SBS – with its motto 'By Strength and Guile' – remains a formidable and respected fighting force, having taken part in operations all around the world.

There is no doubt that, even in recent years, Britain has continued to make more use of Special Forces than any other major military power. The national psyche seems more drawn to such tactics than other nations. In 1985, three years after the Falklands War, David Stirling, the founder of the SAS, wrote: 'The British have . . . demonstrated a unique aptitude for Special Forces.' Stirling, who was known fondly as the 'Phantom Major', died shortly after being knighted in 1990, but his reputation and his legacy live on. In his foreword to Alan Hoe's book *David Stirling: The Authorised Biography of the Creator of the SAS*, General Sir Peter de la Billière pays tribute to Stirling's qualities. De la Billière, who commanded the British forces during the First Gulf War, wrote: 'David Stirling was a legend in his time and eccentric in his day. Tough physically and mentally, he was essentially a visionary. Of course, he was a man of action. He was a leader of the greatest distinction whose personality inspired others.' Furthermore, de la Billière wrote of Stirling that he was 'a great man who might well be described as the Robin Hood of the twentieth century'.

Since the SAS was formed, its members have seen action in far-away locations such as Malaya, Oman, Borneo, Aden, Radfan, Northern Ireland, the Gambia, the Falkland Islands, Bosnia, the Gulf, Somalia, Sierra Leone and Afghanistan. Despite astonishing incidents of bravery from countless Special Forces men, only one member of the SAS has won the Victoria Cross (VC). This is because so many of their heroics are carried out in secret and unseen by officers who have to recommend bravery awards. Also, the award of the VC to a serving SAS soldier would turn him into an instant celebrity and make it difficult, or impossible, for him to do his job properly afterwards.

However, Major Anders Lassen, a Dane serving in the Special Forces during the Second World War, was awarded the VC. He was an exceptional soldier and ideally suited to Special Forces operations because he was cool, fearless and quick-witted. He took part in numerous SBS and SAS missions from 1943–5 but it was when fighting around Lake Comacchio in Italy that he entered SAS legend. He killed and captured several Germans and his individual presence even affected enemy strategy in the area. He was eventually killed attempting to destroy a number of German pill-boxes, but his raw courage was recognised with the award of a posthumous VC. Lassen's unique Special Forces VC is in the collection of the Resistance Museum in Copenhagen but, shortly before this book went to press, I was thrilled to acquire an outstanding Military Medal (MM) won on that Italian raid in April 1945. Private Stanley Hughes, of the SBS, was awarded his MM for his actions as a 'fearless and outstanding leader' at the taking of St Vito. Sadly, he was killed during the operation and his body now lies next to Lassen's in the Argenta Gap cemetery in Italy.

Many men have died while serving in the SAS. In his book *The Complete History of the SAS: The Story of the World's Most Feared Special Forces*, Nigel McCrery writes:

> An average of three SAS soldiers die every year, on a bad year it can be as high as twenty. The SAS is not a large Regiment and the death of an individual soldier is a great loss. It is an unfortunate part of SAS life that many soldiers do die, some while in training, others during operations. One only has to take

a look at Saint Martin's church in Hereford to see the cost. Here lie many young men, good men, men full of life and promise, dead before their time. It is not that the Regiment is careless or 'Gung-Ho', on the contrary it is because these men dared to face foe and adversity head on – they 'Dared to Win'.

It is on the clock tower at the SAS's Hereford headquarters that they engrave the names of those servicemen who have died carrying out their duties. Hence, when an SAS man retires, and leaves the Regiment, he is said to have 'beaten the clock'.

2

EARLY 'SPECIAL FORCES' OPERATIONS

The Crimean War

The Crimean War was fought between 1853 and 1856, but did not involve Britain for the first year of the conflict. It is often described as the first 'modern war'. It is therefore perhaps appropriate that this is where my story about Special Forces-style operations begins. Queen Victoria had been on the throne for seventeen years when Britain entered the conflict. The main fighting took place on the Crimean peninsula in the Black Sea, but there was also conflict in the Baltic. The war developed into a confrontation between, on the one hand, Imperial Russia, and, on the other, the Ottoman Empire, Britain, France and Sardinia.

Tensions in the area, already in existence from the 1840s, grew further in the 1850s, especially after Tsar Nicholas I sent troops into Moldavia and Walachia. Russia and the Ottoman Empire went to war in 1853 and the following year the conflict grew after the former ignored an ultimatum from Britain and France to withdraw from Moldavia and Walachia. Both countries declared war on Russia on 28 March 1854.

For the next two years, there were fierce battles and grim sieges. Significantly, this was the first major war to be covered by a corps of war correspondents. The work of William Howard Russell, of The Times, *among others meant the British public was made aware of the horrors of war and the inadequate planning by the country's leaders.*

Despite harsh winters, British troops lacked adequate clothing and conditions in the hospitals were shocking despite the efforts of Florence Nightingale and others. Cholera and typhoid alone claimed 20,000 British lives compared to the 3,400 killed in battle.

The Battle of the Alma on 20 September 1854 was the first major combat between the two sides. The following month, the Russians were driven back at the Battle of Balaclava and, early in November, heavy casualties were sustained by both sides at the Battle of Inkermann. Then, on 11 September 1855, the British and French forced the fall of Sebastopol and the next year peace was concluded in Paris. The conflict had marked the introduction into warfare of railways and the telegraph, the use of trenches and the development of modern nursing methods.

As well as leading to the creation of the Victoria Cross in 1856, the war became infamous for military and logistical incompetence. During the Battle of Balaclava, Lord Cardigan sent 673 men into the Valley of Death in a foolhardy cavalry charge – the Charge of the Light Brigade – that left 118 of his men dead and 127 wounded. Yet, paradoxically, the Crimean War was the occasion of an early Special Forces-style operation. It is interesting to note, too, that it was always intended that every VC ever awarded should be made from the two bronze cannon captured from the Russians at Sebastopol.

LIEUTENANT (LATER REAR ADMIRAL) JOHN BYTHESEA

Royal Navy

AWARD: VICTORIA CROSS (VC)
DATE OF BRAVERY: 12 AUGUST 1854
GAZETTED: 24 FEBRUARY 1857

The first Special Forces-style raid of the Crimean War resulted from a mild rebuke delivered by one senior Royal Navy officer to another more junior one. Early in the conflict – in the summer of 1854 – the British fleet was stationed off the Russian-occupied island of Wardo, close to Finland, in the Baltic. Captain Hastings Yelverton, from HMS *Arrogant*, which was one of the larger warships in the area and had already seen action against Russian forces, paid an official visit to Admiral Sir Charles Napier, the commander of the British fleet. Yelverton was gently ticked off for the fact that despatches from the Russian Tsar were being constantly landed on Wardo and forwarded from there to the Commanding Officer at Bomarsund. Napier's gripe was that the British forces had taken no action to prevent this.

Upon returning to his ship, Yelverton mentioned this state of affairs to his men and one of them, Lieutenant John Bythesea, became determined to please Napier by doing something to disrupt the flow of mail that British intelligence sources had identified. Bythesea came up with an ambitious plan to slip on to Wardo and try to intercept the Russian mail as it was being moved across the island. He suggested that a foreign national, Stoker William Johnstone, whom he had discovered spoke Swedish, should accompany him on the mission. Yelverton's initial reaction was that a much larger force should accompany Bythesea but – in true Special Forces fashion – it was eventually decided that a larger party was more likely to draw unwanted attention.

At this time, Bythesea was twenty-seven. He had been born in Bath on 15 June 1827 and was the youngest of five sons of the Reverend George Bythesea, the rector and patron of Freshford, Somerset. Bythesea's eldest brother, Lieutenant G.C.G. Bythesea, of the 81st Foot, had been killed in action at Ferozeshuhur (also spelt Ferozeshah), a hard-fought battle in the Punjab in 1845 when the British defeated the Sikhs. John

Bythesea had broken with the family tradition of joining the Army by entering the Royal Navy in 1841 as a Volunteer First Class. After passing the necessary examination, he was promoted to mate in February 1848. Between February and June 1848, he served on HMS *Victory*. Then for the next year he served on HMS *Pilot* in the East Indies, and was promoted to Lieutenant on 12 June 1849. He was appointed to HMS *Arrogant* in September 1852 and saw action in the spring of 1854. On 18 May, the *Arrogant*, together with HMS *Hecla*, had come under fire from a force of Russian troops situated behind a protective sandbank. The Russian troops were, however, soon dispersed and the next morning the two ships proceeded up a narrow channel to the town of Ekness. Here they faced determined opposition from two batteries. The *Arrogant* suffered two killed and four wounded before the enemy's guns were silenced.

It was on 7 August 1854 that Napier and Yelverton had the conversation about the former's desire to disrupt the Russian mail service. Just two days later, and clearly with minimal planning, Bythesea and Johnstone rowed ashore on their own. Fortunately, luck was on their side. They made their way to a local farmhouse, where the owner had been forced to hand over all his horses to the Russians and was therefore only too willing to help them. He not only gave them food and lodgings but informed them about how the Russians had improved a nine-mile stretch of local road to make it easier and quicker for messengers carrying the despatches to Bomarsund. However, the two men had not managed to arrive on the island unnoticed. Informants had told the Russians that a small shore party from the British fleet was on the island and search parties had been sent out to capture them. Bythesea and Johnstone were able to avoid capture only because the farmer's daughters gave them old clothes so that they were disguised as Finnish peasants.

On 12 August, having been on the island for three long days, Bythesea was told by the well-informed farmer that the Russian mail boat had landed and the despatches were to be sent down to the fortress at Bomarsund at nightfall, with a military escort to accompany them part of the way. That night, Bythesea and Johnstone hid in bushes along the way. They watched from a safe distance as the military escort, reassured that the route was clear, turned back leaving five unarmed messengers on their own. Bythesea and Johnstone knew the moment had come to strike. Armed with just a single flintlock pistol, they ambushed the five men. Two fled into the night, while the other three were captured along with the despatches. Bythesea and Johnstone returned to the hidden boat on which they had arrived and forced the three men to row to the *Arrogant*. Johnstone steered the craft as Bythesea held the pistol and ordered their prisoners to row. On their arrival at the ship, the prisoners were taken on board while the despatches were taken to Admiral Sir Charles Napier and General Baraguay d'Hilliers, the French commander. Napier was thrilled by their actions, while d'Hilliers' admiration for the men was said to be 'unbounded'.

Bythesea's reward for the daring and successful mission was to be given command of the three-gun steam vessel HMS *Locust*, which was present at the fall of Bomarsund, as well as at the bombardment of Sveaborg in August 1855. He was promoted to commander on 10 May 1856. Neither Bythesea nor Johnstone expected their bravery to be officially recognised. Both modestly considered they had just been doing their duty. However, at Queen Victoria's behest, the VC was instituted on 19 January 1856 for extreme bravery in the face of the enemy and the awards were able to be backdated to the early conflicts of the Crimean War. The first VC to be won was the decoration given to Lieutenant Charles Lucas, who served in HMS *Hecla*, for throwing a live shell overboard on 24 June 1854. However, the second and third VCs to be won – although, in fact, the twenty-second and twenty-third to be announced officially in the *London Gazette* – were awarded to Bythesea and Johnstone. Bythesea's VC, which was the result of recommendations from Napier and d'Hilliers, was gazetted on 24 February 1857.

The first investiture, intended for the first ninety-three recipients of the medal, took place amid great fanfare in Hyde Park, London, on 26 June 1857. At the occasion, sixty-two servicemen received their medal from the Queen. The remaining thirty-one were serving overseas and received their medals at a later date. Bythesea was the second man – after Commander Henry Raby – to have his VC pinned on him by the Queen, who remained mounted on her horse, Sunset, while conferring each award. Johnstone was one of those serving overseas and his medal was sent out for presentation aboard his ship.

Bythesea went on to serve at sea around the world, including the operations against China from 1859–60. For his final seagoing command, in 1870, he was appointed to the battleship HMS *Lord Clyde*. However, this command ended in disgrace for the courageous commander. In March 1872, *Lord Clyde* went to the aid of a paddle steamer that had run aground off Malta. However, in doing so, *Lord Clyde* also ran aground and had to be towed off by her sister ship, HMS *Lord Warden*. This episode led to Bythesea and his navigating officer being court martialled and severely reprimanded, with instructions that neither were to be employed at sea again. It was a sad end to Bythesea's previously distinguished and unblemished military career.

However, typical of the man, Bythesea bounced back from his humiliation. In 1874, the same year that he married, aged forty-seven, he took up the post of Consulting Naval Officer to the Indian Government. This enabled him, over the next six years, to restructure – from the old Indian Navy – the Royal Indian Marine. Further honours followed – the Most Honourable Order of the Bath in 1877 and a Companion of the Most Eminent Order of the Indian Empire the following year. He retired from the active list on 5 August 1877 – only to be promoted to rear admiral seventeen days later. He died at his home in South Kensington, London, on 18 May 1906, aged seventy-nine. A guard of honour, made up of petty officers from HMS *Victory*, was mounted at the funeral. Bythesea is buried in Bath Abbey cemetery in his home city, while a memorial was erected to him and his brothers in his father's old church at Freshford.

Incidentally, little is known about Stoker William Johnstone, Bythesea's fellow VC recipient. At the time of the incident on Wardo, there was a Leading Stoker John Johnstone serving on board the *Arrogant*, who had been born in Hanover, Germany. However, the first name is different and there is nothing to suggest that he spoke Swedish. It is, perhaps, more likely that the recipient of the VC was one of the foreign nationals that Napier recruited in Stockholm on the way to the Baltic because he felt his crew was too small. If this explanation is correct, Johnstone is probably an anglicised version of Johanssen.

There was a great sense of anticipation when Bythesea's medal came up for auction at Spink in London in April 2007. Not only was it the second VC ever won but, for me, with a dual passion for the VC and Special Forces medals, it was in many ways the ultimate military decoration from this period. Bythesea's VC had been awarded for an early Special Forces-style operation, using a small, undercover force against a larger army for a specific target. I was therefore absolutely thrilled when the trust became the successful bidder for Bythesea's VC, albeit saddened that his other medals and awards had been stolen some thirty years earlier and never recovered.

BOATSWAIN HENRY COOPER
Royal Navy
AWARD: VICTORIA CROSS (VC)
DATE OF BRAVERY: 3 JUNE 1855
GAZETTED: 24 FEBRUARY 1857

When Boatswain Henry Cooper arrived in the Crimea in 1854, he was a formidable and colourful figure. He sported a bushy beard and moustache and, aged twenty-nine, had already earned a reputation for bravery and derring-do. In the preface to this book, I broadly divided bravery into spur-of-the-moment courage and cold courage, which is planned and calculated. Cooper was one of those extraordinary men who displayed both sorts of courage on numerous occasions. In short, he was undoubtedly the sort of man whom any serviceman would want on his side in the heat of battle – strong and fearless, yet also thoughtful and cunning.

Born in Devonport, Devon, in 1825, Cooper joined the Royal Navy when he was fifteen. When not at sea, however, he was a committed family man living in Torpoint in east Cornwall with his wife Margery, who eventually bore him seven children. In 1848 and aged twenty-three, Cooper was serving in HMS *Philomel* on the west coast of Africa. The ship and its crew became involved in a serious confrontation with a pirate-slaver during which the *Philomel* was riddled with shot, leaving one man dead and nineteen injured. Cooper excelled himself in battle and was among the boarding party that subsequently overran the slaver and imprisoned its sixty-strong crew. Some years later, Cooper was serving in HMS *Miranda* when there was an explosion as the ship was leaving Plymouth for the Black Sea. The blast ripped off the hands of one of the seamen and sent him overboard. Cooper did not hesitate. He leapt into the sea, swam to the seriously injured man and kept him afloat until they were both rescued.

In 1854, *Miranda* was sent to the White Sea and Cooper was present at the capture of the town and forts of Kola, the capital of Russian Finland. In 1855, a large British force was sent across the Black Sea to seize the Straits of Kertsch and to operate beyond them in the Sea of Azov. When the Russians refused to challenge the British fleet at sea, the British were forced to change tactics. Military leaders came up with a plan for the Azov operation, which involved a series of Commando-style raids on enemy positions on shore. On 29 May, Cooper was part of a supporting crew for three volunteers who landed at a beach near the heavily fortified town of Genitchi. The volunteers torched corn stores, ammunition dumps and other Russian equipment despite encountering a volley of enemy fire. As they retreated, they encountered a party of Cossacks, but they still managed to return to their waiting boat and escape to safety. All three men in the raiding party were awarded the VC for their actions, although not Cooper who was deemed merely to have played a supporting role.

Lieutenant Cecil Buckley, one of the three volunteers, was on the rampage again just three days later. On this occasion, he landed with just Cooper at the town of Taganrog in the northeast corner of the Sea of Azov. As they came ashore, the town – defended by some 3,000 Russian troops – was under heavy bombardment from the Allied forces. Time and time again, the daring pair landed their small boat – a four-oared gig manned by other volunteers – whenever they saw a likely target. In a series of hit-and-run missions, they destroyed government buildings and stores, as well as arms and other equipment. Each time, they escaped back out to sea, often under fire from the shore. Today military experts see this phase of the war as a turning point. The effectiveness of the raids had a devastating effect on the enemy. The Russians, who could not match the power of the Allied fleet and so preferred land battles, ultimately learned there was sometimes no substitute for the speed and flexibility provided by sea power.

Cooper was awarded his VC for his bravery at Taganrog on 3 June 1855 – rather than for any of his many other acts of courage. As further battles raged, *Miranda* was hit two weeks later by heavy fire from the fort of Sebastopol, and Captain Lyons was mortally wounded. Cooper picked up the injured captain and carried him below deck, where he died from his injuries the following week. Cooper's final act of bravery came when he took charge of the ship's boats during an attack on the fortress of Kertsch. He was the first man to take the British flag ashore and set it flying.

At Hyde Park in June 1857, Cooper was present at the initial VC investiture to receive his decoration from Queen Victoria. The French had got to hear of Cooper's courage and exceptional record and he was one of the few men of junior rank to receive a Legion of Honour for his bravery during the Crimean War. Cooper settled in his Cornish home town of Torpoint after retiring from the Royal Navy and died there on 15 July 1893, aged sixty-eight.

COMMANDER (LATER ADMIRAL OF THE FLEET AND SIR) JOHN EDMUND COMMERELL

Royal Navy

AWARD: VICTORIA CROSS (VC)
DATE OF BRAVERY: 11 OCTOBER 1855
GAZETTED: 24 FEBRUARY 1857

QUARTERMASTER (LATER CHIEF OFFICER OF COASTGUARDS) WILLIAM THOMAS RICKARD

Royal Navy

AWARD: VICTORIA CROSS (VC)
DATE OF BRAVERY: 11 OCTOBER 1855
GAZETTED: 24 FEBRUARY 1857

John Commerell, William Rickard and George Milestone were responsible for one of the most successful Commando-style raids of the Crimean War. The VCs of the former two men are owned by the trust. The reluctance of the Russians to take on the might of the British fleet resulted in a change of tactics and, of all the hit-and-run raids on the Russian forces, those carried out by Commerell, Rickard and Milestone were perhaps the most audacious. At the time, Commerell was twenty-six, Rickard was twenty-seven and Milestone is understood to have been of a similar age.

Commerell was born in London on 13 January 1829. He entered the Royal Navy in 1842 after being educated at Clifton and the Royal Naval School. Rickard was born in Stoke Damerel, near Devonport, Devon. He joined the Royal Navy as a Boy 2nd Class in 1845, aged seventeen, and first saw active service on board HMS *Britomart* in West African waters. Although he was invalided home with a foot injury in 1847, he later served in the Crimean War.

Commerell was a lieutenant when the war started but had been promoted to commander within a year. In February 1855, he was ordered to sail to the Black Sea in the six-gun paddle sloop HMS *Weser*, which was to be accompanied by a gunboat. However, the ship caught fire, struck a rock and ran aground entering the Dardanelles in April 1855. The *Weser* was left with nineteen holes in her hull, but was refloated and repaired.

Within a month, a force of fifty-six ships and 15,000 men was sent to seize the Straits of Kertsch and operate in the Sea of Azov. The Russians were soundly defeated at sea and their warships ran into harbour for cover. This enabled the Allied forces to destroy two hundred Russian supply ships in seven days. After this success, British military operations took the form of Commando-style hit-and-run raids aimed at enemy stores and supply lines on the Spit of Arabat and the mainland.

It was in the dead of night on 11 October 1855 that Commerell, Rickard, Milestone and two other men launched a rowing boat from the *Weser*. The plan was for the two support crew to wait with the boat and keep watch while the others went ashore to cause maximum mayhem to the Russian supplies. After landing at 4.30 a.m., the three men made their way under cover of darkness to their target two and a half miles away – a large fodder store containing 400 tons of corn. Throughout their journey, Commerell used a hand-held compass to guide them to their destination. The three men, however, had to wade, sometimes neck high, through two canals to reach it. On arrival at the store, they set fire to it, but this alerted twenty or thirty Cossack guards, who gave chase on horseback. The three Britons made it across the first canal but Milestone became so exhausted that he urged the other two to go on without him. Commerell and Rickard refused to abandon their comrade and instead helped him to the next canal, where they swam alongside him. Milestone had to be half carried, half dragged towards the boat. By now, the Cossacks were close behind, firing on them and, once again, Milestone faltered as he got stuck in the mud. Rickard went back and dragged him to safety as the Cossacks drew ever closer. As they reached their rowing boat, Commerell turned and shot dead the closest Cossack with his revolver at a distance of some sixty yards. It was only after they reached the

Weser, that they learnt their mission had been a success. The fodder store had burnt to the ground.

Commerell and Rickard were each awarded the VC and were due to be among the first group of recipients to get their awards from Queen Victoria. However, neither were able to attend the presentation in Hyde Park in June 1857. Commerell was distinguishing himself again – this time in China. He went on to have a brilliant naval career. Eventually, he was elected MP for Southampton from 1885 to 1888, and used his position to champion the need to maintain a formidable Navy. In 1889, he was made commander-in-chief at Portsmouth, and in this role he hosted a visit from the Kaiser. The German monarch insisted on honouring his host and gave him a magnificent diamond-hilted sword and the Prussian Order of the Red Eagle. In 1891, Commerell became a groom-in-waiting to the Queen and he was appointed Admiral of the Fleet the next year. He finally retired in 1899 and died two years later at his home in London, aged seventy-two. His formidable collection of medals, including the Order of the Bath (Civil Division), was sold at auction in 1994. The medals were accompanied by the sword given to him by the Kaiser.

It is thought that Rickard probably received his VC some time in 1857 from his commanding officer. He, too, was on active service at the time of the Hyde Park ceremony. However, Rickard, a formidable, bearded man, may have celebrated his award too vigorously, for he was reduced to the rank of able seaman at the end of 1857 with the loss of a good-conduct badge. Yet, the following July, he was restored to the rank of quartermaster. His final appointment was aboard HMS *Impregnable* and afterwards he was employed with the Coastguard. He ended up as Chief Officer of Coastguards and settled on the Isle of Wight with his wife. He died at the Royal Infirmary at

Ryde on 21 February 1905, aged seventy-seven. Rickard is one of the few recipients of a VC also to be awarded the Conspicuous Gallantry Medal (CGM). He also received the French Legion of Honour.

The First World War

The Great War, fought between 1914 and 1918, was 'total war' and led to more than ten million military personnel and civilians being killed. It was eventually won by the Allied powers of Britain, France, Russia and, latterly, the United States of America. They defeated the Central powers, led by Germany, Austria-Hungary and the Ottoman Empire.

Before America entered the war in 1917, the Allied powers were sometimes referred to as the Triple Entente, and the Central powers as the Triple Alliance. These pre-war diplomatic alliances were intended to make war less likely because no country would relish taking on three major powers. However, once the conflict broke out, the alliances made it more widespread. The spark that started the war was the assassination of Archduke Franz Ferdinand, the heir to the Austrian throne, in Sarajevo on 28 June 1914, which set off a rapid chain of events. Austria-Hungary declared war on Serbia, Russia mobilised its forces in defence of the Serbians, Germany declared war on France and Russia, and invaded (officially neutral) Belgium en route *to France, and Britain declared war on Germany.*

The war took place in many theatres but much of it was fought on the Western Front, with both sides dug in along a meandering line of fortified trenches stretching from the Channel to the Swiss frontier with France. The conflict is perhaps best remembered for its trench warfare. Advances in military technology meant that defensive firepower outweighed offensive capability, yet military commanders persisted in using nineteenth-century tactics against twentieth-century technology. Millions of men were sent 'over the top' to face barbed wire that slowed their advance, artillery that was far more lethal than ever before and machine-guns that were deadly against an advancing infantry. The Germans began using poison gas in 1915, and soon the Allies followed suit. Yet still thousands of men were sent to their deaths while military leaders desperately tried to break the stalemate. On 1 July 1916, the first day of the Battle of the Somme, the British Army suffered the bloodiest day in its history, sustaining 57,470 casualties, of whom 19,240 were killed. Battles such as Ypres, Vimy Ridge, the Marne, Cambrai, Verdun and the Gallipoli campaign also resulted in horrific levels of casualties.

America joined the war on the Allied side in 1917 – the same year as the Bolshevik Revolution occurred in Russia. The United States had been angered by the fact that German U-boats had attacked its merchant ships, sinking three of them, so Congress declared war on Germany on 6 April 1917. The Americans' participation eventually proved decisive, more than making up for the withdrawal of Russia from the Allied side. The Allies managed to withstand the German spring offensive of 1918, and countered with their own hundred days' offensive from 8 August, during which they gradually gained the upper hand. The Central powers collapsed in the autumn, and on 11 November the opposing armies on the Western Front agreed to a ceasefire. The fighting did not start again, although a formal state of war persisted between the two sides until 1919, when the Treaty of Versailles was the first in a series of peace treaties to be signed between the various combatants.

Trench warfare is about as far removed from Special Forces warfare as it is possible to get. However, one medal in the collection – a VC – was awarded for a classic undercover operation, not by the Army but the Royal Navy.

PETTY OFFICER (LATER CHIEF PETTY OFFICER) ERNEST HERBERT PITCHER

Royal Navy

AWARD: VICTORIA CROSS (VC)
DATE OF BRAVERY: 31 JULY – 1 AUGUST 1917
GAZETTED: 6 SEPTEMBER 1917

During the second half of the First World War, the British Q-ship fleet was seen as the answer to German U-boats, which had caused terrible damage to the Allies' merchant fleets in the early stages of the conflict. The U-boats had proved their supremacy at sea and, because of this, a pattern emerged whereby a U-boat, to preserve costly torpedoes and allow it to plunder its target's valuables, would surface close to a merchant ship and accept the soft target's surrender. This enabled the merchant crew to leave the ship. The German submarines would then take any valuables they wanted before scuttling the abandoned ship. In order to combat this practice, a Q-ship – a gunship disguised to look like a merchant ship – was devised as a sort of Trojan Horse of the seas. The plan was that as the U-boat surfaced after the surrender, the British gunship would blow it out of the water. Of course, war being war, it was not always quite so simple.

Ernest Pitcher was born in Mullion, Cornwall, on 31 December 1888, the son of a coastguard. He joined the Royal Navy at the age of fourteen and by August 1914 was serving on the super-Dreadnought *King George V*. Aged twenty-six, Pitcher volunteered for the expanding Q-ship fleet in 1915. He served on the ex-collier *Loderer*, also known as HMS *Farnborough*, or *Q.5*. Built in 1904, *Loderer* was fitted out at the naval dockyard in Devonport with the typical devices of a Q-ship – five twelve-pounder guns variously concealed by a steering house aft, hinged flaps on the main deck and dummy cabins on the upper deck; two six-pounder guns hidden at either end of the bridge; and a Maxim gun in a dummy hencoop amidships. There were eleven officers and fifty-six men on board, with Pitcher one of the few regular Royal Navy ratings. *Loderer* was commissioned under her original name on 21 October 1915 but was renamed *Farnborough* after the Admiralty received an anonymous tip-off that her new role as U-boat bait had been leaked to the Germans.

Farnborough made the fourth Q-ship U-boat kill of the war on 22 March 1916, when she sank Kapitan Leutnant Guntzel's *U.68* with all hands. This success led to the Q-ship's captain, Lieutenant Commander Gordon Campbell, being promoted to commander. *Farnborough* accounted for her second kill, *U.83*, on 17 February 1917, to the west of Ireland. The target was sunk with the loss of all hands bar an officer and one seaman.

In March 1917, Pitcher and most of the rest of *Q.5*'s crew elected to follow Campbell to his next Q-ship. This was another former collier, which was renamed *Pargust*. She had improved equipment and armaments, including a four-pounder gun, and went to sea in May. In June, *Pargust* was torpedoed by Kapitan Leutnant Rose's *UC.29*. The decoy panic party left the ship and when the U-boat surfaced the remaining crew fired thirty-eight shells at it causing it to blow up and sink. Under the thirteenth rule of the VC Royal Warrant, an officer and a rating were each given a medal on behalf of the whole crew, while Campbell, as commander, received a Bar to the Distinguished Service Order (DSO) he had won for his second kill. On that occasion, Pitcher was awarded one of eight Distinguished Service Medals (DSMs).

Flushed by their further success, most of *Pargust*'s crew now followed Campbell on to another Q-ship, *Dunraven*. At 10.58 a.m. on 8 August 1917, their new ship, disguised as a British merchant vessel, was zigzagging some 130 miles off Ushant when a U-boat was sighted on the horizon. *Dunraven* maintained her course as the U-boat, *UC.71*, closed. At 11.17, the enemy submarine dived, then resurfaced 5,000 yards away on the starboard quarter. The U-boat opened fire at 11.43. Acting in the manner of a panicking merchant captain, Campbell sent out a distress signal giving the ship's position. He also fired off some token rounds from the ship's little two-and-a-half-pounder gun, trying to indicate that it was the only weapon he possessed. The U-boat closed again and, when a torpedo almost hit *Dunraven*, the crew generated a cloud of steam to simulate boiler trouble. At the same time, Campbell despatched a panic party to make it look as if the ship was being abandoned. The submarine now scored three quick hits on *Dunraven*'s poop. The first detonated a depth charge, which wounded three men and cut communications between Pitcher, the captain of the four-inch gun crew, and the bridge. Pitcher's team now had a potentially life or death decision to make. They decided not to move, since leaving the ship would have given the game away. They felt that it was imperative that the Germans should remain convinced that the ship had already been abandoned. The second and third shells started a major fire, which meant Pitcher and several others were now concealed on a red-hot deck. They lifted boxes of cordite off the deck and on to their knees in a bid to stop them exploding, but still they did not flee.

At that point, *UC.71* was obscured by black smoke to *Dunraven*'s stern, which presented Campbell with a dilemma. He knew an explosion on his own vessel was inevitable, but if he delayed in giving the order to abandon ship he might get a clear shot at the submarine. Writing later about the dilemma he faced, he said, 'To cold-bloodedly leave the gun's crew to their fate seemed awful, and the names of each of them flashed through my mind, but our duty was to sink the submarine. By losing a few men we might save thousands not just of lives but of ships and tons of the nation's requirements. I decided to wait.'

The inevitable explosion on *Dunraven* came at 12.58 p.m., before the U-boat could be fired upon. It blew out the stern of the ship and propelled the four-inch gun and its crew into the air. The gun landed on the well-deck and one man was thrown into the sea, while Pitcher and another crewman landed on mock railway trucks made of wood and canvas, which cushioned their falls and saved their lives.

UC.71 immediately crash-dived as two shots were fired at her but without any telling effect. Pitcher and the other wounded men were now removed to the cabins, where they stayed for the rest of the action with 'shells exploding all around them'. As Campbell was preparing a torpedo attack, *Dunraven* was shelled abaft the engine room. Then the U-boat resurfaced and for twenty minutes torpedoed the Q-ship until diving again at 2.50 p.m. Campbell responded by firing two torpedoes. Both missed but, fortunately for *Dunraven*'s crew, the U-boat had now exhausted its own supply of torpedoes and fled the scene. A British destroyer, *Christopher*, towed the battered Q-ship towards Plymouth but, as the weather deteriorated, she sank at 3 a.m. Many bravery awards were made to the crew of the *Dunraven*, with the VC assigned specifically to Pitcher's gun crew. Pitcher himself eventually received the medal after a ballot.

This action involving *Dunraven* was a turning point. Three weeks later it was agreed that there was a stalemate in this form of warfare and the Q-service was wound down. Furthermore, the use of Q-ships had caused submarine commanders to start sinking ships without giving crews the chance to leave, in case the vessels were not all they appeared to be.

Pitcher received the gun crew's VC from George V at Buckingham Palace on 5 December 1917, as well as the French

Medaille Militaire and the Croix de Guerre. He was promoted to chief petty officer on 1 August 1920. Seven years later he retired from the Royal Navy after a quarter of a century's service, and went to work as a woodwork teacher in a boys' preparatory school in Swanage, Dorset. He also ran a pub, the Royal Oak in nearby Herston, for a time. However, he rejoined the Royal Navy on 5 August 1935, and served on shore for five years at Poole, Portland and Yeovilton. He died on 10 February 1946 at the Royal Naval Auxiliary Hospital in Sherborne, Dorset, aged fifty-seven.

3

THE SECOND WORLD WAR

The Special Air Service (SAS) and the Special Boat Service (SBS – originally the Special Boat Section and later the Special Boat Squadron) came into being during the Second World War. The worldwide conflict lasted from 1939 to 1945 and the extent of the casualties was without precedent. It is estimated that at least 62 million people died, which equated to two per cent of the world's population at the time. Of these, some 25 million were military casualties, perhaps 37 million civilian (some estimates put the civilian death total as high as 47 million, which would mean the war claimed the lives of 72 million in total). Disease, starvation, massacres, aerial bombing and genocide caused the civilian casualties. It is thought that the Holocaust alone claimed the lives of nine million people, most of them Jews.

The Second World War was essentially the amalgamation of two conflicts, one beginning in Asia in 1937 as the Second Sino-Japanese War and the other beginning in Europe in 1939 with Germany's invasion of Poland. Eventually, the Allied powers, led by the British Empire, the Commonwealth, the United States and the Soviet Union, defeated the Axis powers of Germany, Italy and Japan. The war was largely caused by the imperial ambitions of Japan in Asia and the expansionist aggression of Nazi Germany in Europe. The largest and deadliest war in history ended with the dropping of two atomic bombs on Japan.

A desperate desire to avoid another world war had caused Britain and France to pursue a policy of appeasement in an attempt to placate Hitler. Neville Chamberlain, the British prime minister, famously returned from Munich in 1938 with an 'agreement' that supposedly guaranteed 'peace in our time'. Yet, on 1 September 1939, just nine days after agreeing a secret pact with the Soviet

Union, Germany invaded Poland. Britain and France declared war on Germany two days later.

The war spread rapidly, particularly in the first six months of 1940. As a result of its secret alliance with Germany, the Soviet Union attacked Finland and occupied Latvia, Lithuania and Estonia. It then annexed Bessarabia and Northern Bukovina from Romania. Germany went on a 'roll', invading Denmark, Norway, Luxembourg, Belgium, the Netherlands and France, before making preparations to invade Britain. Italy declared war on Britain in June 1940, before invading British Somaliland. Attempts by Italy to overrun Greece were, however, thwarted.

In 1941, the war spread fast and furiously further around the globe. Germany invaded Greece, then betrayed the Soviet Union by sending in troops – Operation Barbarossa, the largest invasion in history, got underway on 22 June. As the war spread to North Africa and the Middle East, America showed its support for the Allies by signing a treaty – the Atlantic Charter – with Britain in August. The Japanese then launched a surprise air attack on the US Pacific Fleet in Pearl Harbor, Hawaii, on 7 December 1941. The US declared war on Japan the following day and China followed suit. On 11 December, Germany declared war on the United States.

There were several theatres for the war in 1942 and 1943 – Europe, the Soviet Union, the Pacific, North Africa, China and south-east Asia. By 1944, the tide of the war had started to turn. A Soviet offensive relieved the siege of Leningrad and soon the Allies started to gain ground elsewhere. On D-Day – 6 June 1944 – the Allies, mainly forces from Britain, America and Canada, invaded German-held Normandy. Within three months, Paris had been liberated. By April 1945, the Allies had advanced into Italy and the Western Axis powers knew the war was lost. On 8 May, the Allies celebrated VE (Victory in Europe) Day, while the Soviets celebrated their Victory Day the following morning.

America wanted a swift end to the war against Japan but the enemy held out until US President Harry Truman used a new 'super weapon' to end the hostilities. A nuclear bomb was dropped on Hiroshima on 6 August 1945, *thereby destroying the city. The US called on Japan to surrender but got no response and so three days later a nuclear bomb was dropped on Nagasaki. The Japanese finally surrendered on 15 August (VJ Day), while Japanese troops in China formally surrendered on 9 September. The Second World War was finally at an end.*

During the six years of war, weapons and technology had been transformed and with them came a change of tactics, including the development of Commando and Special Forces units. As well as nuclear weapons, radar, jet engines and computers were used in war for the first time. Boats and vehicles that had been considered cutting edge in 1939 were virtually obsolete by 1945, while aircraft, battleship and tank designs made huge advances in just six years. By 1945, world leaders realised there had been a shift of power away from the British Empire and Western Europe to the new 'super powers' of the US and the Soviet Union. This led to the creation of the United Nations in 1945, which was intended to succeed, where the League of Nations had failed, in preventing another world war.

SERGEANT FRANK GORDON WORRALL

Army

AWARD: MILITARY MEDAL (MM)
DATE OF BRAVERY: 9 JUNE 1941
GAZETTED: 2 DECEMBER 1941

The Litani River raid involved some of the great early exponents of Special Forces tactics. They included Major (later Lieutenant Colonel) Geoffrey Keyes, who received the Military Cross (MC) for his role and who later was awarded a posthumous Victoria Cross (VC) (see page 44), and Paddy Mayne, a co-founder of the SAS and subsequently a legend within the Regiment. Following the allied invasion of Syria on 8 June 1941, No. 11 Commando was sent to cross the Litani River in Lebanon where they fought, highly successfully, against troops from the French Vichy regime, who had allowed the Luftwaffe to use their air bases in

Syria. On 9/10 June, the Commando made two landings on the north of the Litani, fell upon the enemy rear, cut communications and put much of the enemy artillery out of action. Unfortunately, a third force under Keyes landed on the south of the river in error.

During twenty-four hours of intense action, few men emerged with greater credit than Frank Worrall, of the Royal Artillery, who was in C Battalion Layforce (11 Commando) when the raid took place. Worrall was a member of the centre party, which comprised his own No. 1 Troop, together with Nos 7 and 8 Troops, with eight officers and 145 men. They embarked in four landing craft and came under heavy machine-gun fire as they approached the beach. Due to the intensity of fire, the landing-craft went hard astern as quickly as possible after grounding and most of the men were wading up to their chests when they jumped into the water. Despite this, they struggled ashore and quickly cleared the beaches suffering, at this early stage, just one fatality.

The full story of Worrall's bravery was recalled by Lieutenant Gerald Bryan of No. 1 Troop, his section leader:

> I raced madly up the beach and threw myself into the cover formed by a sand dune. The men behind me were still scrambling out of the landing-craft and dashing over the twenty yards of open beach. Away on the right we could hear the rattle of a machine-gun and the overhead whine of bullets, but they seemed fairly high. I was just beside a dry stream bed and so started to walk along it, at the same time trying to untie the lifebelt attached to my rifle. Colonel Pedder was shouting to us to push on as quickly as possible. Soon the ditch that I was in became too narrow and there was nothing for it but to climb out into the open. The ground was flat with no cover. The machine-

guns were now firing fairly continuously but were not very worrying. When I got out into the open – rather like moorland – I started shouting 'A Section No.1 Troop,' which represented my command. Before long we were in pretty good formation, with myself, batman [officer's orderly] and tommy gunner in the centre.

We came to the main road and saw, on the other side, a trench showing clearly in the white chalk. It was empty, but behind it were two caves in a little cliff. I fired a rifle shot into the left-hand cave. There were sounds of commotion inside. We stood ready with grenades and tommy guns and shouted to them to come out. Seven sleepy French emerged in pyjamas and vests. We had certainly caught them sleeping. My batman remained with them to hand them over to the colonel who was coming up behind. It was now quite light, the time being about 04.45 hours. The rest of the section had pushed on, so I followed, and came on a wire running along the ground. This I cut with a pair of wire cutters. I found the section held up and under fire from snipers. Also, which was more to the point, they had found a 75mm gun. It was about thirty yards away and firing fairly rapidly. We flung some grenades and it stopped. However, we had three casualties, which wasn't so good. A corporal was shot through the wrist and was cursing every Frenchman ever born. As he couldn't use a rifle, I gave him my Colt automatic pistol, and he carried on.

We crawled through some scrub to get closer to the gun. Here we met B Section officer Alastair Coade and a few men, also attacking the gun position, so we joined forces. The gun itself was deserted, the crew being in a slit trench. We bunged in a few more grenades and then went in ourselves. It was rather bloody. My section comprised mostly RA [Royal Artillery] blokes, who knew how to handle the gun, and in a few minutes the sergeant

[Worrall] had discovered which fuses to use from one of the original gun crew. This gun was the right-hand gun of a battery of four, the others being anything from about 100 yards to 300 yards away. They were still firing. Our gun was pointing away from the battery, so we grabbed the tail piece and heaved it right round so that it was pointing towards the nearest gun. The sergeant took over command of the gun, shoved a shell in and sighted over open sights, then fired. The result was amazing. There was one hell of an explosion in the other gun site and the gun was flung up into the air like a toy. We must have hit their ammo dump. No time to waste. The sergeant traversed on to the next gun, sighted rapidly and fired. There was a pause. Where the devil had the shell gone? Then there was a flash and a puff of smoke in the dome of a chapel about half a mile up the hillside. A thick Scottish voice said, 'That'll make the buggers pray!' The sergeant hurriedly lowered the elevation and fired again, this time a bit low. However, the gun crew started to run away and our Bren [gun] opened up and did good work. Just then a runner turned up with orders from the colonel to report to him with as many men as possible when we had finished off the battery. It did not take long to get a good hit on each of the two remaining guns. The sergeant then broke off the firing pin of our gun with the butt of a rifle.

We had to cross about 300 yards of open ground to reach the colonel so we just ran like hell, and although there were a few bullets flying around, I don't think we had a single casualty. When I arrived at Commando HQ and reported to the colonel, he explained that he was pushing in some men and wanted our section to support them and pick off snipers. We took up what positions we could but there wasn't much cover. I left the colonel and went over to a Bren-gun post about fifty yards away, but it took me a good ten minutes to get there as I had to crawl the whole way. The French had spotted us and were putting down a lot of small arms fire – very accurate. The whole time bullets spat past my head and sounded very close. It was most unpleasant and hard to think correctly. When I reached the Bren posts, they were stuck. Every time they tried to fire, an MG [machine-gun] opened up and they couldn't spot it. Suddenly, the B section officer said he had spotted it and grabbed a rifle, but as he was taking aim he was shot in the chest and went down, coughing blood. Then the sergeant [Worrall] was shot in the shoulder, from a different direction, which meant we were being fired on from two fronts.

I crawled back to Commando HQ but when I was about ten yards away, I heard someone shout, 'The colonel's hit. Get the medical orderly.' I shouted to the adjutant and he replied that the colonel was dead and that he was going to withdraw the attack and try his luck elsewhere. So I shouted to my men to make for some scrub about a hundred yards away and started crawling towards it. All the time bullets were fizzing past much too close for comfort and we kept very low. The sergeant [Worrall], who had been wounded, decided to run for it, to catch us up, but a machine-gun got him and he fell with his face covered with blood. As I was crawling I suddenly felt a tremendous bang on the head and I knew I had been hit. However, when I opened my eyes I saw that it was in the legs and decided not to die. I dragged myself into a bit of a dip and tried to get fairly comfortable, but every time I moved, they opened up on us. I could hear an NCO yelling to me to keep down or I would be killed. I kept down. After a time (when the initial shock had worn off) the pain in my legs became hellish. My right calf was shot off and was bleeding, but I could do nothing about it, and the left leg had gone rigid. By now the sun was well up and it was very hot lying there. I was damned thirsty but could not get a drink as I had to expose myself to get my water bottle, and each time I tried I got about twenty rounds all to myself, so I put up with the thirst and lay there, hoping I would loose consciousness.

After about two hours, a lot of fire came down and the next thing was twenty-five French advancing out of the scrub with fixed bayonets. The four men left from my section were captured. I raised my arm and one of the French came over and gave me a nasty look. I was carrying a French automatic pistol that my sergeant had given me in exchange for my rifle. It had jammed at the first shot but like a fool I had held on to it. Anyway, he just looked at me for a while and away he went and I was left alone. I had one hell of a drink and felt better. About half an hour later my four men were back with a stretcher, under a French guard. Both the colonel and B Section officer were dead, so they got me on to the stretcher and carried me down to a dressing station, where a British medical orderly gave me a shot of morphia. While we were lying there, a machine-gun opened up and the French medical fellows dived into a cave, but the bullets were right above our heads and they were obviously firing over us at something else. Some time later an ambulance turned up, and we were taken to a hospital in Beirut. In the ambulance were two wounded French, two sergeants from our side, and myself. We remained as prisoners of war in Beirut until the British entered the town six weeks later.

Lieutenant Gerald Bryan subsequently had a leg amputated and was awarded the Military Cross (MC).

It was Lieutenant Colonel Geoffrey Keyes who recommended Worrall for his bravery award, concluding: 'The dash and efficiency of this NCO in silencing the battery had consider-able effect on the successful crossing of the river, as the guns covered the approaches and crossings at very short range.'

Worrall's bravery had also been noticed by others. In a biography of her brother, Elizabeth Keyes writes:

> Farmiloe [Captain] and Tavendale, the regimental sergeant major, climbed the ridge to the north of the gully to see what was happening to No.1 Troop, as a battery of four French 75mm guns was putting down a very heavy barrage on to the beach. This was at 7.15 a.m., and they were in time to see five or six men, led by Sergeant Worrall, from Lieutenant Bryan's section, 'throw at least three well-directed hand grenades' on to a French 75mm gun position, rush and capture it, and then turn the captured gun on to the other positions and destroy them. Farmiloe reported this feat to Colonel Pedder, and the advance continued.

The announcement of Worrall's award was made in the *London Gazette* of 2 December 1941:

> W/S Sergt. Frank Gordon Worrall, Royal Artillery, att. C Batt. Layforce. In the action at the Litani River in Syria on June 9th, 1941, this NCO was part of a force landed North of the river to disorganise enemy resistance from the rear. With Lt Bryan, RE, his section leader, he led a party of men against a French 75mm Battery, despite considerable opposition from concealed MGs. Having captured the nearest gun with hand grenades, Sgt Worrall layed the gun with such accuracy that the remaining three guns were rapidly silenced. When ordered to continue the advance, he put this gun out of action before moving on. Shortly afterwards he was severely wounded in the head, and taken prisoner, but has now been liberated.

It is not known the circumstances under which Worrall was freed so swiftly in 1941 or what happened to him after he left the Army.

TEMPORARY LIEUTENANT COLONEL GEOFFREY CHARLES TASKER KEYES

Army

AWARDS: MILITARY CROSS (MC) AND VICTORIA CROSS (VC)
DATE OF BRAVERY: 9 JUNE 1941 AND 17/18 NOVEMBER 1941
GAZETTED: 21 OCTOBER 1941 AND 19 JUNE 1942

By the second year of the Second World War, General Erwin Rommel, the commander of the Afrika Korps, had established himself as a formidable military leader. He was seen by the Allied commanders as a constant threat. Would it not be a wonderful, morale-boosting coup for the Allies if he could be killed? The difficulty, of course, was how to pull it off. Inevitably, given his role, Rommel was constantly surrounded by thousands of soldiers but did he have an Achilles heel? Geoffrey Keyes, from well-bred military stock, thought he had spotted Rommel's weakness.

Keyes was born in Aberdour, Fifeshire, Scotland, on 18 May 1917 – a much-wanted son after three daughters. Even his name gave him a lot to live up to. He was named Geoffrey after his uncle, who was killed in 1915 during the First World War, and Charles after his grandfather, who had commanded the Indian Frontier Force for several years, while Tasker was an Irish family name. As a baby, he was so quiet that his eldest sister was once caught sticking a pin into him to see if he was real. The young Keyes had hoped to follow his father into the Royal Navy but he failed the eyesight test. After going to Eton and

Sandhurst, he joined his uncle's regiment, the Royal Scots Greys, as a second lieutenant. The fact that he was the son of Sir Roger Keyes (later Lord Keyes of Zeebrugge and Dover), the Admiral of the Fleet, undoubtedly put him under pressure to succeed as a soldier. Perhaps, too, he had inherited his father's sense of adventure and derring-do. From October 1937, he served in Palestine but, while on leave in February 1940, he volunteered for special service. As an accomplished skier, he was picked for the Narvik Expeditionary Force two months later, but when the Allies had to relinquish their position in Norway, he was evacuated back to England and rejoined his regiment. He served briefly as liaison officer to the Chausseurs Alpins, and for his work in that role was awarded the French Croix de Guerre.

After his return from Norway, he delighted his father by volunteering for the newly formed Commando organisation. Indeed, on 25 July 1940, he received a letter from his father saying, 'I am so pleased you applied for that service – because I was going to apply *for you*. I am D.C.O. – Director of Combined Operations, all Commandos and Independent Companies come under my influence . . . Your loving Daddy.' Keyes was posted to the 11th Scottish Commando and, after a rigorous training programme, embarked for the Middle East in January 1941.

Following the allied invasion of Syria in early June 1941, No. 11 Commando, in which Keyes served, was sent to lead the crossing of the Litani River in Lebanon, fighting against troops of the French Vichy regime. Keyes played a leading part in this operation (see page 37) where the aim was to seize the bridge, preventing it from being blown up, and thereby enable the Australian 21st Infantry Brigade to advance into Syria along the coast road. It was at 3 a.m. on 9 June when eleven assault craft left HMS *Glengyle* destined for the shore and to attack the enemy forces. Keyes's party, in four assault craft, landed on a flat sandy shore overlooked by the enemy. He was quickly faced by a problem that had confronted the Australian forces for the past two days — a river thirty yards wide that was too deep to wade and too broad to swim with heavy equipment. As they waited, Keyes and his men came under heavy fire, first from well dug-in troops and then from two large French destroyers, which had steamed down the coast to bombard the beaches. Keyes's task was to carry out a classic infantry assault, one that was unsupported by air and in broad daylight. He used small boats to cross the river and, with the help of other British and Australian forces, pulled off a brilliant attack that, within less than six hours, led to the surrender of the Vichy French forces. It was for his leadership and courage that Keyes was awarded the MC. In his report of the raid, the ever-thoughtful Keyes recommended that, in future, Commandos should be as lightly equipped as possible, and that instruction in enemy guns (which they had seized) should be included in their training manuals.

The *London Gazette* of 21 October 1941 announced Keyes's MC:

Major Keyes commanded a detachment of C Bn. Layforce during the initial stages of the battle but later took over command of the battalion on learning that his Commanding Officer had been killed.

Major Keyes's detachment was landed in error by the RN [Royal Navy] on the south bank of the river instead of the north bank and Major Keyes found himself in consequence unable to carry out his task unless the crossing of the river was effected. In daylight and under heavy fire he organised the river crossing and succeeded in capturing the Redoubt [fort] on the far side which was strongly defended by machine-guns, mortars and artillery.

Although his task was actually completed when the Australian Brigade passed through the Redoubt, Major Keyes did not retire but remained in position until the next morning giving valuable support until the situation became stabilised. He then checked and re-organised his battalion which had suffered 25 per cent casualties.

Colonel Pedder, Commanding Officer of 11 Commando, was killed in the Litani River action and, as a result, Keyes took over command of the depleted unit; 24 years old, he was probably the youngest Lieutenant Colonel in the army (this acting rank was officially confirmed 20 July).

By the autumn of 1941, Keyes had formulated another daring plan and, after much persuasion, won over General Head-quarters Cairo to sanction an attempt to destroy the German HQ, 250 miles behind enemy lines at Beda Littoria, Libya. Furthermore, the intention was to capture General Erwin Rommel. The 'Rommel Raid' was timed to coincide with a British offensive – on 17/18 November 1941. Colonel Robert Laycock, the officer commanding Middle East Commando operations, had reservations about the mission but decided to accompany the force as an observer. He remained at the landing place throughout.

Laycock's own report – rather than the heavily edited version that appeared in the *London Gazette* – tells the extraordinary tale of the mission, and I would not try to improve upon it.

Lt. Col. Geoffrey Keyes, Royal Scots Greys, commanded a detachment of a force which landed by submarine some 860 miles behind the enemy lines to attack Headquarters, Base,

Installations and Communications. The original plan, formulated several weeks in advance at 8th Army Headquarters, included orders for attacks on various separate objectives. Although the whole operation was considered to be of a somewhat desperate nature, it was obvious that certain tasks were more dangerous than others.

Colonel Keyes, who was present at all the meetings and assisted in the planning, deliberately selected for himself from the outset the command of the detachment detailed to attack what was undoubtedly the most hazardous of these objectives – the residence and Headquarters of the General Officer Commanding the German Forces in North Africa. (When the plan was submitted to me as Commander of the Middle East Commandos, in which capacity I may be regarded as having some experience of this type of warfare, I gave it my considered opinion that the chances of being evacuated after the attack were slender and that the attack on General Rommel's house in particular appeared to be desperate in the extreme. This attack, even if initially successful, meant almost certain death for those who took part in it. I made these comments in the presence of Colonel Keyes, who begged me not to repeat them lest the operation be cancelled).

In the execution of the Operation, Colonel Keyes led his detachment ashore. The majority of the boats, including his own, were swamped on the passage to the beach but, whereas his officers and men were able to take advantage of the shelter of a cave in which they lit a fire, warmed themselves and dried their clothing, Colonel Keyes remained throughout the night on the beach to meet any men who managed to get ashore from the second vessel.

Shortly before first light the detachment moved to a Wadi [dry riverbed] in which they remained hidden during the hours of daylight. After dark on the second night, Colonel Keyes set off with his detachment towards the objective, but was deterred by his Arab guide, who refused to accompany the party as soon as the weather deteriorated. Without guides, in dangerous and precipitous country, faced with a climb of over 1,800 ft in pitch darkness and an approach march of 18 miles which they knew must culminate in an attack on the German Headquarters, soaked to the skin by continuous torrential rain and shivering from cold from half a gale of wind, the fast ebbing morale of the detachment was maintained solely by Colonel Keyes' stolid determination and magnetic powers of leadership.

Biding through the hours of daylight and moving only during darkness Colonel Keyes had led his detachment to within a few hundred yards of the objectives by 2200 hours on the fourth night ashore. Restricted by the depletion of his detachment through stragglers and through the fact that some of his men never reached the shore from the submarine, Colonel Keyes now found himself forced to modify his original orders in the light of fresh information elicited from neighbouring Arabs.

Having detailed the majority of his men to take up positions so as to prevent enemy interference with the attack on General Rommel's residence, Colonel Keyes was left with only one Officer (Captain Campbell) and one other Rank (Sgt Terry) with whom to break into the house and deal with the Guards and Headquarters Staff. At zero hours (2359 hours) having despatched the covering party to block the approaches to the house and to guard the exits from neighbouring buildings, he himself with Captain Campbell and Sergeant Terry crawled forward past the guards, through the surrounding fence and so up to the house itself.

Colonel Keyes hoped to be able to climb in through a window or enter by the back premises but these proved to be inaccessible.

He therefore, without hesitation, boldly led his party up to the front door and, taking advantage of Captain Campbell's excellent German, beat on the door and demanded entrance. As soon as the sentry opened the door Colonel Keyes and Captain Terry set upon him but, as he could not be overpowered immediately, Captain Campbell shot him with his revolver. The noise naturally but unfortunately roused the occupants of the house. Colonel Keyes, appreciating that speed was now of the utmost importance, posted Sgt Terry at the foot of the stairs to prevent interference from the floor above – a task which he accomplished satisfactorily by firing a burst from his Tommy-gun at anyone who attempted to reach the building.

Although the lights in the passage were burning, those inside the ground floor rooms were extinguished by the occupants. If the raiding party was to achieve any measure of success these rooms had to be entered. This could be done by stealth which would however have taken time, and had the enemy been bold enough to come into the passage, they would immediately have appreciated that they were attacked by three individuals only, whom they could easily have overpowered. The only alternative was to attempt to bluff the occupants by dashing into each room in turn with the minimum of delay. This latter course Colonel Keyes unflinchingly adopted although he undoubtedly realised that it was almost certain death for the man who first showed himself silhouetted by the passage lights against a darkened doorway.

Colonel Keyes, who instinctively took the lead, emptied his revolver with great success into the first room and was followed by Captain Campbell who threw in a grenade, but the inevitable result of such daring occurred on his entering the second room of the ground floor. He must have been perfectly aware that it was occupied, since Sgt Terry, who was a few yards away, reported to me later that he could hear the occupants breathing and moving about inside. Colonel Keyes was shot almost immediately on flinging open the door and fell back into the passage mortally wounded. On being carried outside by Captain Campbell and Sgt Terry he died within a few minutes.

It may be added that on several occasions before the expedition sailed I suggested to Colonel Keyes that he should detail a more junior officer to take his place in leading the actual assault on the German Headquarters and that he himself should remain at the Operational Rendezvous. I again made this suggestion to him after he got ashore just prior to his leaving my Headquarters south of Chescem-el-Chelb. On each occasion he flatly declined to consider these suggestions saying that, as Commander of his detachment, it was his privilege to lead his men into any danger that might be encountered – an answer that I consider [was] inspired by the highest traditions in the British Army.

From the conception of the operation, through the stages in which it was planned, during the weary days spent in waiting for the expedition to sail, and up to the last moment where I saw him 250 miles beyond the enemy lines, heading for almost certain death, I was profoundly impressed by his confidence and determination to face unlimited danger. Colonel Keyes' outstanding bravery was not that of the unimaginative bravado who may be capable of spectacular action in moments of excitement but that far more admirable calculated daring of one who knew only too well the odds against him. That he was aware of danger I have no doubt from previously discussing the operation with him and from his description of his former brilliant action at Litani River, but that he could ever allow fear to influence his action for one single second is unthinkable to anyone who knew Colonel Keyes.

Only Laycock and Terry made it back to British lines after thirty-seven days in the desert. The remainder were either taken prisoner or killed. To add insult to injury (and death), there had been a massive intelligence failure. Rommel had never used the building raided by Keyes. The German commander had, in any case, been in Rome at the time. It says much for Rommel's sense of chivalry – and his respect for Keyes's bravery – that he sent his personal chaplain to Libya to conduct Keyes's funeral. It was left to Sir Winston Churchill to comfort Admiral Keyes over the death of his son. 'I would far rather have Geoffrey live than Rommel dead,' the British prime minister said.

It was Keyes's younger brother Roger, who, as a sub-lieutenant, later went in search of and found Goeffrey's marked grave. Roger told his father that it had been situated 'in the kind of country Geoffrey likes'. Elizabeth Keyes, his sister, wrote a book about her brother's life, which was published in 1956. The biography, *Geoffrey Keyes*, ends with the words:

> Many wonderful things have been said about Geoffrey. His batman (who came home after a spell in Auswitz [sic] death camp) wrote: 'Our first Colonel used to say "You can't be a good soldier *and* a gentleman," and I think Colonel Keyes did more to disprove this saying than anyone else I ever met in the services. When I think of our little fleet of ships leaving England for the Middle East in 1941, with its list of names of sons of great men, there is only one that stands out in front on its own – Colonel G.C.T. Keyes, V.C., M.C.'
>
> In telling Geoffrey's story I have done my best as a tribute not only to my brother but to the men who served with him, many of whom have helped me to fill in the picture of the 11th Commando. With so much help from everyone concerned, I felt this book must be written, in the hope that others too may be

inspired to follow their star – no matter where it leads them – becoming, like Geoffrey, 'steadfast enduring soldiers' in the army of God.

Perhaps the important thing, however, was for the budding British Special Forces to learn lessons from the Rommel-assassination mission. The modest military gains – a handful of Germans dead – had not compensated for the loss of so many fine men, or the time and resources that the operation had taken up. It was good for Commandos to be ambitious in their choice of targets, but it was foolish to be wildly over-ambitious and to overestimate what could be achieved by the new Commando units. In his book *British Special Forces*, William Seymour astutely assessed the raid:

> The mission, in which many deeds of heroism were performed, had failed. It had been carried out with considerable dash and a degree of skill, and Colonel Keyes undoubtedly deserved the posthumous VC awarded to him. But it was wasteful. The lives of many valuable officers and men had been put at risk, and lost, in an attempt to achieve something which, through wrong information, could not have succeeded.

LIEUTENANT COLONEL AUGUSTUS CHARLES NEWMAN

Army

AWARD: VICTORIA CROSS (VC)
DATE OF BRAVERY: 27/28 MARCH 1942
GAZETTED: 19 JUNE 1945

TROOP SERGEANT MAJOR GEORGE ERNEST HAINES

Army

AWARD: DISTINGUISHED CONDUCT MEDAL (DCM)
DATE OF BRAVERY: 27/28 MARCH 1942
GAZETTED: 5 JULY 1945

SERGEANT WILLIAM ALBERT CHALLINGTON

Army

AWARD: DISTINGUISHED CONDUCT MEDAL (DCM)
DATE OF BRAVERY: 27/28 MARCH 1942
GAZETTED: 5 JULY 1945

ABLE SEAMAN (LATER PETTY OFFICER) PETER REEVES

Royal Navy

AWARD: DISTINGUISHED SERVICE MEDAL (DSM)
DATE OF BRAVERY: 27/28 MARCH 1942
GAZETTED: 30 JULY 1942

The Commando raid on the strategically important port of St Nazaire, in German-occupied France, was one of the earliest, most daring and most successful Special Forces operations of the Second World War – but it came at a price. In his book *British Special Forces*, William Seymour writes:

> The St Nazaire raid, brilliantly conceived and executed, had as its primary objective the blocking of what was at that time the largest dock in the world – the Forme Ecluse. Bombers having made life too uncomfortable for German battleships, St Nazaire was the only port left on the French coast capable of taking a ship like the *Tirpitz*, which could play a damaging part in the Battle

for the Atlantic. Subsidiary objectives were the destruction of various locks and bridges that controlled the entrances to the three harbours – Avant Port, Basin de St Nazaire and Bassin de Penhouet.

Altogether, three groups took part in the attack, comprising in total forty-four officers and 233 other ranks. The codename for the mission was Operation Chariot and each group was asked to land at a different point. The force – largely consisting of men from No. 2 Commando – was under the command of Lieutenant Colonel Augustus Charles Newman, known affectionately as 'Colonel Charles' to his men. The aim was to land using motor launches (MLs) and ships and, once the objectives had been achieved, to retreat in the craft that remained intact after the fighting.

In his book *Saint-Nazaire: Operation Chariot – 1942*, James Dorrian spelt out the varying tasks of the three groups:

Landing from six MLs at the heavily fortified Old Mole, Captain 'Bertie' Hodgson's GROUP ONE was tasked with seizing and holding the Old Mole itself, clearing the Avant Port and Old Town, destroying the Power Station complex and blowing all gates and bridges within the South Entrance. A little further to the north, another six MLs would put Captain 'Micky' Burn's GROUP TWO ashore in the deep indentation known as the Old Entrance. Burn's men in conjunction with *Campbeltown*'s [the ramming ship] parties, would seek to isolate the wedge of land between the two main basins and the 'Normandie' dock. For this purpose the Pont de la Douane [Bridge M] was to be destroyed and a blocking position established on the far side of the northern caisson. Storming ashore from *Campbeltown*, Major Bill Copland's GROUP THREE would complete the neutralization of the great dock by demolishing its pumping station, both winding houses and the northern caisson. A subsidiary task assigned to this group was the destruction of the underground fuel stores, immediately east of *Campbeltown*'s ramming point.

Nobody was in any doubt of the difficulty of the task or the fact that, faced with a far larger embedded German force, the chances of making it back alive and uninjured were slim. Most of the men in the party wrote their wills and last letters before departing for their mission. Few letters were penned more succinctly and thoughtfully than the one by Major Bill Copland to his wife, Ethel: 'My dearest, I have to write this letter although God knows I hope you never receive it – which you only will if I don't come back. We sail in a day or two on a somewhat desperate venture, but one of high purpose. If we succeed, and only the worst of ill luck will stop us, then we shall have struck a great blow for the cause of freedom. Remember too that if I do get blotted out I shall probably die in good company – for never did a finer crowd set out on a doughtier task. I shall always believe that Commandos are the real spirit of Britain at her best.'

Newman, who was born in Buckhurst Hill, Essex, on 19 August 1904, was thirty-seven at the time of the mission. It is hard to improve on the account provided by the *London Gazette*, which announced his VC on 19 June 1945:

On the night of 27/28 March 1942 Lieutenant Colonel Newman was in command of the military force detailed to land on the enemy occupied territory and destroy the dock installations of the German controlled naval base at St Nazaire. This important base was known to be heavily defended and bomber support had to be abandoned owing to bad weather. The operation was therefore bound to be extremely hazardous, but Lieutenant Colonel Newman, although empowered to call off the assault at any stage, was determined to carry to a successful conclusion the important task that had been assigned to him. Coolly and calmly he stood on the bridge of the leading craft, as the small force steamed up the estuary of the River Loire, although the ships had been caught in the enemy searchlights and a murderous cross fire opened from both banks, causing heavy casualties.

Although Lieutenant Colonel Newman need not have landed himself, he was one of the first ashore and, during the next five hours of bitter fighting, he personally entered several houses and shot up the occupants and supervised operations in the town, utterly regardless of his own safety, and he never wavered in his resolution to carry through the operation on which so much depended. An enemy gun position on the roof of a U-boat pen had been causing heavy casualties to the landing craft and Lieutenant Colonel Newman directed the fire of a mortar against this position to such effect that the gun was silenced. Still fully exposed, he brought machine-gun fire to bear on an armed trawler in the harbour, compelling it to withdraw and thus preventing many casualties in the main demolition area. Under the brilliant leadership of this officer the troops fought magnificently and held vastly superior enemy forces at bay, until the demolition parties had successfully completed their work of destruction.

By this time however, most of the landing craft had been sunk or set on fire and evacuation by sea was no longer possible. Although the main objective had been achieved, Lieutenant Colonel Newman nevertheless was now determined to try and fight his way into the open country and so give all survivors a chance to escape. The only way out of the harbour lay across a narrow iron bridge covered by enemy machine-guns and although severely shaken by a German hand grenade, which had burst at his feet, Lieutenant Colonel Newman personally led the charge which stormed the position and under his inspiring leadership the small force fought its way through the streets to a point near the open country when, all ammunition expended, he and his men were finally overpowered by the enemy. The outstanding gallantry and devotion to duty of this fearless officer, his brilliant leadership and initiative, were largely responsible for the success of this perilous operation which resulted in heavy damage to the important naval base at St Nazaire.

George Haines was born in Rosyth, Scotland, in February 1918 and enlisted in the East Surrey Regiment in 1935. The next year he was posted to the 2nd Battalion and he served in the Shanghai Defence Force, where he was promoted to lance corporal. On his return to the UK, he worked as an instructor but he became bored and applied for the Special Forces. He was accepted for training with the Commandos in the Highlands before being posted to No. 2 Commando. Promoted to sergeant, he took part in the Vaagso raid of 1941. When Newman was recruiting men for the St Nazaire raid, he told Haines that he had no more vacancies for men of his rank. Haines was so agitated by the prospect of missing out on the mission that he threatened to rip off his sergeant's stripes. Eventually, however, Haines was allowed to join his commanding officer on the raid – where his contribution was outstanding.

Haines, described as 'short and square' with enormous hands, was given command of a fourteen-strong Commando assault group. Their specific task was to attack enemy guns on the waterfront between the port's Old Mole and Old Entrance, both of which were heavily defended. Once that not inconsiderable task had been completed, their orders were to link up with Newman's HQ Reserve. But in order to fulfil his part in 'the sauciest job since Drake', Haines first had to get ashore from ML 177, commanded by Sublieutenant Mark Rodier. The craft was the sixth and rear-most in the column designated Group II. The ML was a little way astern of HMS *Campbeltown*, the lead ship. C.E. Lucas Phillips, in his book, *The Greatest Raid of All*, takes up the story:

> The scene that confronted Rodier's eyes as he followed close astern of Fenton was not one to be faced by the chicken-hearted. To port, to starboard and ahead motor launches were on fire and drifting out of control, for the spectacles that we have seen in the starboard column were being duplicated to port. Already the agonized cries of men trapped in the pools of burning petrol, which were to be one of the memories of that night for British and Germans alike, were beginning to be heard. Wreckage, corpses, flames and drifting palls of smoke were starkly clear in the cold glare of the searchlights. These, the sudden water-spouts of bursting shells and the swift streaks of coloured tracer, 'like red and green stitches on a piece of cloth', threatened the sixth launch with a like fate. Last of the troop-carrying boats in the starboard column, all that had gone before her seemed to have gone only to destruction.
>
> Yet Rodier held firmly on his way. He saw Tillie blow up ahead, Stephens and Platt on fire to port, Fenton sheer away to starboard immediately ahead. Hit several times, but nowhere vitally, he sailed through the maelstrom, past the guns of the Old Mole blazing at him at a hundred yards range, past the wrecks of his friends, through the stream of projectiles that

seemed to bar the way in to the Old Entrance. This he slightly overshot, as Burt and Beart [his comrades] had done, but, quickly discovering his mistake, turned short round, steamed into the Old Entrance, first of the troop-carrying MLs to enter, and came alongside on the southern quay at about 1.40 a.m. He gave Haines the order to disembark and the eager commandos climbed quickly ashore and, in the words of the watching Arkle [another comrade], 'passed rapidly into the shadows' . . .

In fact, Haines and his assault group failed to locate any operating enemy guns in the area designated to them, and instead they moved inland to join up with Newman and to strengthen his Reserve HQ. On reaching his embattled CO, Haines was said to have stood to attention 'as if on the parade ground' as he listened to his orders, which were to stay near his colonel for the remainder of the operation.

Lucas Phillips continues:

He [Newman] very soon did need him [Haines], for the fire from one of the 20mm guns beyond the Submarine Basin and from machine-guns mounted on the roof of the pens began to harass them. Newman called up Haines and said: 'We have simply got to stop those guns. What have you got you can take them on with?'

'I've got a 2-inch mortar, sir. No sights, but it's the only thing we've got.' With extraordinary unconcern, Haines took forward in his great hands a little 2-inch mortar, siting it slap in the open near the quayside of the Submarine Basin just beyond the end of one of the warehouses. Here he knelt down and, taking the small bombs that were passed to him by a chain of hands, including Newman's, from behind the cover of the building, dropped them down the barrel of the mortar, to go soaring high into the air and on to the enemy positions only two hundred yards away. With the enemy fire plunging down on the very spot where he knelt, but with 'unsurpassable coolness', he successfully silenced one position after another, if only temporarily.

There then came against him one of the armed vessels in the Basin, the flash of his mortar and the crump of its bombs being only too audaciously apparent. Coming close in, the ship made his position a 'veritable death trap'. Quite unperturbed, however, Haines leaped over to a Bren-gun that some fallen comrade had left, and, although the fire from the ship's machine-guns was 'cascading' in the very place where he was now lying, he sent a series of bursts so devastating and so well directed that the ship ceased fire and sheered away . . .

Before too long Newman realised that he and his surviving Commandos – about a hundred of them, many wounded – were facing hopeless odds, a realisation made all the more bitter to accept when he discovered that virtually all the MLs assigned for their re-embarkation were burning hulks. Sublieutenant Mark Rodier, who had delivered Haines and his team to the Old Entrance, had been killed, and his command, *ML 177*, sunk with heavy loss of life.

Lucas Phillips writes:

Newman himself, with the responsibility for the men's lives on his shoulders, alone had a moment's doubt. They had, he reflected, accomplished the major part of the mission. They could do no more. Though the idea of giving themselves up was entirely repugnant to him, he knew there could be no dishonour now in doing so. To satisfy his mind, he sought a second opinion, calling Bill Copland into a short conference. Did Copland think, he asked, that they ought to 'call it a day'? 'Certainly not,

Colonel,' replied the old warrior of the Great War, who was as cool and unexcited as though on a church parade. 'We'll fight our way out.'

It was shortly after this pleasing discussion that Newman ordered a breakout from the dockyard, in a final desperate bid for freedom, Haines being placed in command of the rearguard. Lucas Phillips continues:

> Sometime after 3 a.m. this extraordinary column, encumbered with wounded, short of ammunition, with little hope but for a faint chance of vagrant freedom, began its inspired and defiant dash through the serried rows of buildings thronged with enemies firing from every window and lying in wait at a few yards' range at every corner. Little finesse was possible now. Like an old-time garrison sallying out to cut their way through a besieging army, they moved forward at the double with spirits high . . . They moved by bounds, keeping to the shadowed ways at the edges of the long warehouses and halting from time to time to squat in some dark patch and collect together – sometimes to rush some open stretch by parties under covering fire, or to overcome some point of enemy resistance, or to give time for the straggling wounded to catch up . . .

The responsibility for clearing one of these points of enemy resistance fell to Haines. Ordered by Major Bill Copland, also of 2 Commando, 'to crash on with all speed', but nonetheless invited to ask whether he had any questions, Haines replied in a steady but quiet voice, 'None, sir.' Newman's column was soon on the move again. Once more, too, in the column's final effort to reach the town via Bridge D, his troop sergeant major excelled himself. Lucas Phillips continues:

There lay the girdered Bridge D, gaunt and ghostly in the curious light. It was barely seventy yards away. Beyond it the German machine-guns looked down from roof and window. Astride it on the far side, and stretching along the quayside, lay a line of enemy riflemen, last remaining elements of the German naval troops.

No means of indirect approach to the bridge was at hand, no cover to make use of against cocked and loaded weapons, no opportunity for finesse. Very coolly Haines, at his own suggestion, sited a Bren-gun to give a little covering fire. Then Newman called to his waiting soldiers: 'Away you go, lads!' Without hesitation the Commandos went for it, moving at a steady double as a hurricane of fire burst upon them from beyond the bridge. The astonished Germans, quite in the dark about the purposes of all these confounding occurrences, shot high and wide, as they had done all night. A violent storm of bullets swept over the Commandos' heads; others struck the steel girders of the bridge like hammers ringing on an anvil and, as the bullets ricochetted away, their tracers shot like sparks in all directions.

Disdainful of it all, Donald Roy made on right in the middle of the road, a splendid and inspiring figure, Newman now beside him. Close behind him were Sergeants Rennie, Denison, Montgomery and Haines. They saw the German riflemen athwart the bridge, scramble to their feet and retire. They passed the ships that Pritchard had sunk, passed Philip Walton's dead body and swept superbly over the Bridge of Memories, their rubber boots thudding on the hollow road while the bullets rang and sparked on the steelwork or whistled overhead into the night. They were a smaller party now, their route marked by a sprinkling of their dead and wounded, but marked too by the bodies of their enemies. To all those who took part it was the most inspiring moment of the night, like a charge of the olden times across fire-swept ground right into the heart of the enemy. In the stirring pages of British history there have been many glorious charges, many heroic assaults on battlemented walls and ramparts deemed impregnable, but, on its smaller scale and in its more modest intent, the breakout of the Commandos of St Nazaire ranks high among them as a manifestation of soldierly purpose and of the will and determination to defy odds ...

Haines was to the fore throughout this later stage of the fighting. He was last seen engaging an enemy machine-gun post. Yet, with Newman and most of the force out of ammunition and finally forced to surrender, Haines and five other members of 2 Commando holed up in the basement of a damaged building overnight.

Lucas Phillips continues:

To escape is honourable and the duty of all prisoners of war. To avoid capture and to fight again is still more honourable. Not all who landed at St Nazaire fell into enemy hands. Five Commandos, by their own determination and wit, by a great deal of luck and through the generous help of patriot Frenchmen given at the peril of their own lives, succeeded in avoiding capture and in obeying Newman's order to make their way to far distant Gibraltar.

These remarkable achievements were carried out by three separate groups, and two of them originated from the cellar of a bombed shop in St Nazaire, where a particularly gallant and resolute party of six men had concealed themselves. These were Troop Sergeant Major Haines, Sergeant Challington (Camerons), Lance Corporal Howarth (Grenadier Guards), Corporal Wright, the RE [Royal Engineers] diarist, Corporal Douglas (Liverpool

Scottish) and Private Harding (Gloucesters). All but Douglas and Harding were pretty sharply wounded, Wright bleeding profusely from a calf partly shot away, but that did not lessen their determination to seek freedom. Taking up a posture of defence, they stayed in the cellar all that Saturday, in considerable pain and with very little to eat, and narrowly escaping discovery as a German search party went through the ruins overhead. By good fortune some civilian trousers and a jacket were found for Challington, who had no chance of escape in a kilt, and a jacket for Haines.

Haines decided that that night they should make their way out in pairs, but Wright, knowing that he would seriously hold back other people and that he was too badly injured to go alone, walked out after dark and gave himself up. Haines and Challington, both with leg wounds, set off painfully together, the first to leave, and succeeded in making their way into the country but had the bad luck to run into a party of Germans.

For Haines and Challington, like Newman the previous night, their war was now over.

Challington, like Haines, received the Distinguished Conduct Medal (DCM). The *London Gazette* of 5 July 1945 formally recognised Challington's bravery from more than three years earlier:

On 28 March 1942 during the Commando raid at St Nazaire, France, Sgt Challington was in an assault group whose task was to destroy enemy coastal defence guns covering the Dry Dock Area. Disembarking from the burning bows of HMS *Campbeltown* on to the dock gates, Sgt Challington immediately engaged the enemy gun crews who were on the roof of the

Pumping Station and whose plunging fire was intense in the immediate area. Under his devastating covering fire, the assault onto the roof of the Pumping Station and the consequent destruction of the crews and guns was successfully completed. Later, when his assault group formed a covering force in the area in which the demolitions were taking place, this NCO, showing total disregard for his own safety, engaged and knocked out an enemy machine-gun position which was bringing heavy fire to bear on the Operational HQ. Continuing to display great courage and initiative, his group later became engaged in the street fighting in the town of St Nazaire and during the fighting he alone engaged an enemy motorcycle combination which approached at high speed firing an automatic gun from the sidecar. During this street fighting, this NCO's dash and initiative was outstanding and with a small group he managed to regain the open country through the town in an attempt to escape to Spain. He was captured only after organising other members of his party to set off in pairs to freedom.

Challington had been badly wounded by a bullet in his knee cap while crossing the main bridge. He was held prisoner in Stalag 383 at Hohen Fels, Germany.

Peter Reeves, who was born in 1919, followed his father into working for London Underground when he left school. He worked as a booking clerk at Hammersmith station in west London but, at the outbreak of war, joined the Royal Navy aged nineteen.

He was selected to take part in Operation Chariot and at 2 p.m. on 26 March 1942, the British force set sail from Falmouth, Cornwall. Reeves was attached to *ML 156*, which was commanded by Leslie Fenton, the Hollywood actor and director. The craft formed part of Group II, which was under the command of Captain Michael Burn and had been tasked with landing at the old port entrance. Along with *ML 177*, *ML 156* was intended to lead an assault on any guns operating between the Old Mole and the Old Entrance, to fire on any vessel in the dock and to come into the reserve.

The attack began at midnight on 28 March. Soon after arriving, the MLs came under heavy fire from *Sperrbrecher*, an anchored barrage breaker. *ML 192* was hit in the engine room, therefore forcing her to crash into the East Jetty. *ML 268* was also hit and exploded, killing fifteen of the seventeen Commandos on board. Fenton's *ML 156*, with Reeves on board, also came under attack and its engine and steering were put out of action. Unable to land, Fenton circled in mid-river for half an hour before withdrawing from the attack. *ML 156* was scuttled soon after the attack as she tried to limp back home and her crew were taken aboard the *Atherstone*. The sea was flat but it proved a difficult task transferring those wounded the day before. Fenton and his second in command, Temporary Sublieutenant Noel Machin, were awarded the Distinguished Service Cross (DSC). Reeves and two other crew each received the Distinguished Service Medal (DSM).

The primary aim of the mission – to block the port of St Nazaire – was achieved because the lead ship *Campbeltown* was well and truly rammed into the entrance and, in due course, her charges went off. Part of the dock was destroyed and the remainder was blocked. Indeed, the Germans were never able to repair the damage and the dock remained unserviceable until 1950. Success came at a price, however. There was heavy fighting and so many MLs were damaged – in the devastating cross fire as they made their way up the Loire – that many of the Commandos and sailors could not escape after carrying out their mission. Out of the total force committed, largely from No. 2

Commando, almost two-thirds failed to return. The Commando itself had fifty-nine men killed and 153 taken prisoner. Altogether the raid led to the awarding of five Victoria Crosses (VCs), four Distinguished Service Orders (DSOs), seventeen Distinguished Service Crosses (DSCs), eleven Military Crosses (MCs), four Conspicuous Gallantry Medals (CGMs), five Distinguished Conduct Medals (DCMs), twenty-four Distinguished Service Medals (DSMs) and fifteen Military Medals (MMs). Many other men were mentioned in despatches, some posthumously.

Newman, along with Haines and Challington, remained a prisoner until the end of the war. At one point, while being held in Spangenberg castle in western Germany, Newman had his fellow PoWs working on an unsuccessful tunnel designed to go into the foundation and under the moat. He died in Sandwich, Kent, on 26 April 1972, aged sixty-seven. Haines continued to serve after the war and his final appointment was in the Royal Pioneer Corps, with whom he served in the Brunei and Borneo operations, reaching the rank of major before retiring in 1973. He was last known living in Filey, North Yorkshire, and died on 4 March 1994, aged seventy-five. It is not known what happened to Challington after he left the Army. On the night of 15/16 March 1944, motor torpedo boat (MTB) 417, with Reeves on board, as part of a large force, attacked a convoy of French trawlers being escorted by the ships of the German 36th M-Flotilla. The convoy, travelling between Calais and Boulogne, was under the command of Kapitan Grosse. The British force torpedoed and sank *M 3610* and, later, off the coast of Dunkirk, did the same to the German minesweeper *M 10*. But soon after *MTB 417* was sunk by a German ship and all hands, including Reeves, aged twenty-four, were lost.

MAJOR GORDON GEOFFREY HENRY WEBB

Army

AWARDS: MILITARY CROSS (MC) AND BAR
DATE OF BRAVERY: 21/22 APRIL 1942 AND 19 AUGUST 1942
GAZETTED: 7 JULY 1942 AND 2 OCTOBER 1942

Major Gordon Webb was awarded his MC and Bar for two acts of bravery within the space of four months in raids on Boulogne and Dieppe in 1942. After being injured in the second incident, and when on a London station with his arm in a sling after returning from his mission, he was recognised by rail passengers from his photograph on the front of the *Evening News*. He later admitted to getting 'a little tight' because he was bought so many free drinks before being allowed to catch his train.

Webb was born in April 1920 and was educated at Trinity College, Glenalmond, Scotland, where he passed his Officer Training Course in November 1936. He worked for his family fruit-importing business in Glasgow after leaving school but, in August 1939, aged just nineteen, he enlisted in the Royal Artillery on the eve of hostilities. Next, Webb went to an Officer Training Unit at Filey, North Yorkshire, from where he emerged as a second lieutenant and was posted to 30 Field Regiment, Royal Artillery in France. He was mentioned in despatches for his work in the lead up to and the evacuation from Dunkirk. He volunteered to join the Commandos soon after returning to Britain and, in July 1940, he was selected for training in north-west Scotland. Here, among other activities, which included field craft under Lord Lovat, he was given demolition instruction by David Niven, the actor. It was said that Niven was popular for his generosity to the Commandos by way of laying on extra food and drink at a local hotel, but equally unpopular with his superiors because he kept disappearing to London to see his girlfriend.

Webb, who was intelligent with a fine sense of humour, thrived under the rigorous training and soon became a fully fledged member of No. 4 Commando. He quickly emerged as a right-hand man to Lord Lovat when he became commanding officer of No. 4 Commando. As part of Operation Claymore, he was selected to join the force bound for an attack on the German-held Lofoten Islands, off northern Norway, in March 1941. The raid proved a great success. The combined attacking force, which also included No. 3 Commando, destroyed eighteen cod-liver oil factories (capable of producing nitro-glycerine) and took around 215 prisoners, in addition to taking on board over 300 Norwegians. For Webb's role in the raid, his CO, Lieutenant Colonel D.S. Lister, MC, recommended him for the MC:

> Lieutenant Webb had been detailed to seize the Post Office and the only hotel in Svolvaer. This he did with incredible speed and thoroughness, thus stopping all communications to the mainland from the former, and taking a number of important enemy personnel prisoner in the latter. Had it not been for this quick action, news of the raid would undoubtedly have reached Narvik before it did, with consequences which might have been fatal to our forces. I recommend this officer for the Military Cross or other recognition of his valuable services during this operation.

However, Lister's appeal fell on deaf ears and Webb did not receive a bravery award for these actions.

Webb's next raid was on Hardelot, near Boulogne, in April

1942. No. 4 Commando had received orders to make a thorough reconnaissance of the beaches, to inflict as much damage as possible in the vicinity and, if possible, return with some prisoners. In preparation for the forthcoming raid on Dieppe, some Canadians from the Fusiliers Mont Royal also accompanied Lovat's force. However, they were put down on a sandbank where they remained stuck until the tide turned. Webb commanded B Troop. Each unit was set independent tasks to pursue once a path had been cleared for it off the beaches by C Troop. The raid was only a partial success and the party had an enemy searchlight to contend with. Charles Dunning recounted the events in his *The Fighting Fourth, No. 4 Commando at War 1940–45*:

> At our selected landing point, flat sandy beaches extended for some 400 yards and as we waded ashore there was a phosphorescent glow around our legs, which was most uncanny and we all thought it would warn the enemy. However, we got to the wire defences undetected and started to cut a way through for B Troop. Hardly had they reached us when all hell broke loose: the enemy machine-guns covering the beaches opened up. Not only was there tracer fire, but also illuminated flares and coloured light signals. The searchlight tried to light up the beach, but it couldn't depress sufficiently to succeed. However, it did manage to illuminate one of the LCAs [landing craft assaults] as lying off-shore. It was quite a spectacle. Fortunately, all the enemy machine-guns were on fixed lines and the fire whistled harmlessly overhead. B Troop went through on their various missions, reconnaissances were carried out and an attempt made to attack the searchlight, but it was found to be protected by two perimeter belts of wire, about 250 and 450 yards respectively from the searchlight post. The raiders had

insufficient time to deal with this unexpected defensive layout, so abandoned the attempt.

Eventually, after further adventures, including a brush with an enemy patrol, all were re-embarked. Webb was awarded the MC, which was gazetted on 7 July 1942. Due to the fact the war was still on, it contained few details of his action: 'In recognition of gallant and distinguished services in the successful Combined Operations on the enemy occupied coast in the Boulogne area.' It later emerged, however, that the original recommendation – submitted by Major the Lord Lovat – said:

> I have pleasure in recommending Captain Webb for a Military Cross or other suitable award, for his fine leadership when in command of a fighting patrol on the French coast between Hardelot village and Boulogne on the night of 21/22 April 1942. He led his patrol inland for a distance of half-a-mile despite heavy machine-gun fire from various strong points on the coast. He reached his objective – a searchlight battery – and having cut the wire and destroyed all the lateral telephone communications round it, was about to deliver a final assault when the Recall Signal from the beach compelled him to return. The information gained on this patrol was of great importance, and the enemy defences which encountered it were all driven out and forced to retire. He brought his patrol back without suffering any casualties, and I attribute the success of this patrol entirely to his good leadership.

Webb also received a personal, signed letter of congratulations from Louis Mountbatten (later 1st Earl Mountbatten of Burma) dated 7 July 1943. The Chief of Combined Operations wrote: 'Dear Webb, Many congratulations on your MC. I am so glad that your gallantry in the Hardelot raid has been recognised. Yours sincerely, Louis Mountbatten.'

The men of No. 4 Commando had received much of Lord Lovat's 'train hard, fight easy' philosophy before hitting the beaches near Dieppe in August 1942. At their training ground at Achnacarry, they repeatedly came under a hail of live ammunition in order to prepare them for the reality of war. This proved useful when they landed at Dieppe on 19 August – for their reception was hot. Indeed, Webb was hit before he even cleared his landing craft. A witness to the event was Second Lieutenant Donald Gilchrist:

> A mortar thumped as the LCA grated on the shingle. Webb cursed and clutched his shoulder, hit by a mortar fragment. The ramp clattered down and we swept up the beach, Webb still with us . . . we ran shoulder to shoulder as a solid stream of German machine-gun tracer bullets whizzed past at head height. We ran like half-shut knives, our bodies bent forward, as if we were forcing our way against a strong wind. The private panted, 'Jesus Christ, sir, this is as bad as Achnacarry!' . . . This was as bad as Achnacarry.

Despite his injuries, Webb continued to lead B Troop to their objective, the enemy Hess battery at Varengeville. Gilchrist continued:

> We were ready to go in. With fixed bayonets F Troop attacked, yelling like banshees. In too came B Troop, led by Gordon Webb. His right hand was dangling, useless – but he had a revolver in his left. Razor-sharp, Sheffield steel tore the guts out of the Varengeville battery. Screams, smoke, the smell of burning cordite. Mad moments soon over. A rifle shot from the buildings

behind the hedge. Laying in a yard was a wounded commando
soldier. From the gloom of a barn emerged the German who had
cut him down. He jumped up and crashed his boots on the prone
face. Our weapons came up. A Corporal raised his hand. We held
our fire. The Corporal took aim and squeezed the trigger. The
German clutched the pit of his stomach as if trying to claw the
bullet out. He tried to scream, but couldn't. Four pairs of eyes in
faces blackened for action stared at his suffering. They were eyes
of stone. No gloating, no pity for an enemy who knew no code
and had no compassion. We doubled across the yard to where the
two wounded lay side by side. For our comrade – morphine. For
the beast – a bayonet thrust.

Later Webb said that his men 'were asphyxiated by our own
bloody smoke and couldn't see a thing. Fifty of us lined up
abreast and went forward, disposing of Germans as we came
across them . . . we came across a dozen or fifteen Germans all
lying in firing positions, all facing the other way. Several of
them hadn't even had time to put their trousers on.'

An official communiqué summarised the action in the
following terms:

At daybreak, No. 4 Commando, consisting of 252 all ranks,
including Allied personnel, assaulted the six-gun battery
covering the west approaches to the port of Dieppe. The position
was defended by an approximately equal number of Germans
with all the advantages of concrete, wire and land mines,
concealed machine-gun posts, mortars, dual purpose flak guns
mounted in a high tower and full knowledge of the ground.
They had had two years to perfect these defences and when
the time came they fought with the greatest determination.
Yet within a hundred minutes of the landings, the position was

overrun, the battery and all its works totally destroyed and at least 150 Germans left dead or wounded in the path of the raiders and the scene of the fighting. Prisoners were also taken. British casualties numbered 45 all ranks, of whom twelve were back on duty within two months. Operation Cauldron is a classic example of the use of well-trained infantry soldiers, bold leadership and the thoroughness of the plan of attack and its swift execution.

Webb received an immediate Bar to his MC. It was gazetted on 2 October 1942 and again had minimum details: 'In recognition of gallant and distinguished services in the combined attack on Dieppe.' The original recommendation, however, later emerged which stated:

Captain Webb was wounded by mortar fire on the beaches [at Dieppe] during the initial landing. His right arm became useless but he insisted on going forward and led the whole of his force across country to the concentration area in the rear of the German battery. In the final assault Captain Webb led a bayonet charge, using a revolver and grenades with his left hand. His troops accounted for many of the enemy, including several officers.

Once again the Chief of Combined Operations wrote to congratulate this fine soldier on his actions in a letter dated 2 October 1942: 'Dear Webb, I am writing to offer my most sincere congratulations on getting the Bar to your Military Cross for the gallant part you played in the Dieppe raid, which I consider a particularly fine performance. Yours sincerely, Louis Mountbatten.'

Webb's wartime heroics were far from over and he took part

in the D-Day landing on 6 June 1944. The Commando's MO (Medical Officer), Captain J.H. Patterson, RAMC (Royal Army Medical Corps), travelled in the same landing craft as Webb, and recalled seeing him in the bows, 'peering forward, alert and tense'. Tense, no doubt, because in addition to his usual duties he also appears to have been given responsibility for the Commando's mortars – all of which could be called into support at any time. In the run-in to Sword Beach, Patterson recalled that 'bullets rattled against the craft and splinters whined overhead . . . There was thick smoke over the beach, and the tide low but flooding. There were many bodies in the water; one was hanging round one of the tripod obstacles. The shoals were churned with bursting shells. I saw wounded men among the dead, pinned down by the weight of their equipment.' Another witness recalled that 'bodies lay sprawled all over the beach, some with legs, arms and heads missing, the blood clotting the wet sand.'

As Webb and his comrades arrived on the beach and made their way to the enemy's wire at least one enemy pill-box was still very much in action. Soon No. 4 Commando had its own mounting casualties, estimated by this stage to be to the tune of forty men. After the battle on the beach, the survivors from No. 4 started fighting their way inland, in order to link up with the Airborne on the River Orne, an objective achieved after taking further casualties.

It had originally been intended that No. 4 Commando would be withdrawn from the frontline after a few days. However, the ferocity of the enemy's resistance was so formidable that Webb and his comrades in No. 4 remained on active service in France until early September – by D-Day plus four alone, the Commando's strength had been reduced from 455 officers and men to 160.

In the assault on Walcheren on 1 November 1944, No. 4 Commando was given the task of capturing Flushing. Webb went into battle as CO of No. 3 Troop, with his unit among those to land in the third wave of assault craft. This meant the enemy garrison was fully alert and their LCAs were subjected to heavy machine-gun fire in addition to 20mm cannon. Typically, the first man through the enemy's beach defences was Webb but No. 3 Troop quickly ran into severe opposition and fierce street fighting followed. Until reinforcements arrived, all they could do was to hold their ground. Webb, however, was ever conscious of the fact he had been assigned the task of clearing an enemy barracks and, when No. 1 Troop arrived at the scene, he was able to proceed as planned. By nightfall, much of the barracks had been cleared under the gaze of enemy snipers.

Following further fighting on D-Day plus one, the old port town was more or less in No. 4 Commando's hands, and the weary men were re-embarked. But the island of Walcheren still had a strong enemy garrison on its northern coastal strip and a plan was made for No. 4 to advance in the hours of darkness on D-Day plus six to clear it. Webb again handled things with distinction and, eventually, Walcheren was captured. No. 4's casualties amounted to one officer and twelve other ranks killed, and one officer and twenty other ranks wounded. In return, the enemy had suffered losses of around 200 men, in addition to some 1200 prisoners. The way had been cleared to march on Antwerp.

Webb was later awarded the Croix de Guerre for his bravery. After the end of the war, he was put in charge of a rehabilitation camp on Anglesey for former Japanese prisoners of war. He was demobbed in 1946 and returned to his family's fruit-importing business in Glasgow. He finally settled in Brighton where he worked as an insurance broker. He died in February 1991, aged seventy-one.

ACTING CAPTAIN FREDERICK THORNTON PETERS

Royal Navy

AWARD: VICTORIA CROSS (VC)
DATE OF BRAVERY: 8 NOVEMBER 1942
GAZETTED: 18 MAY 1943

During the Second World War, Frederick 'Fritz' Peters served with the so-called 'School of Spies'. Here, the Canadian worked with Guy Burgess and Kim Philby at a training centre in Hertfordshire that was geared to developing operations for the special services. In his book *My Silent Way*, Philby mentioned Peters: 'He often took Guy and me to dinner at the Hungaria to listen to our views on the new project. He had faraway naval eyes and a gentle smile of great charm.' Peters had won his place at the 'School of Spies' – more formally called the Directorate of Naval Intelligence – after a formidable military career, one that eventually resulted in him winning five bravery awards spanning two world wars.

He was born in Charlottetown, British Columbia, on 17 September 1889, the son of Frederick Peters, the prime minister and attorney general of Prince Edward Island. He joined the Royal Navy in 1905 and three years later, as a midshipman, helped in the rescue work after the hugely destructive Messina earthquake. He went on to serve with distinction as a naval officer during the First World War, being awarded the Distinguished Service Order (DSO) in 1915 and the Distinguished Service Cross (DSC) in 1918 for his achievements in the destroyer and torpedo flotillas. In the Second World War he served with more distinction, gaining a

Bar to his DSC in July 1940 for his role as commander of HMS *Thirlmere*.

However, it was a daring mission devised by the 'School of Spies' that led to him winning two more bravery awards, including the VC. The aim of the operation was to seize a vital point in the well-defended harbour of Oran, in French-held Morocco. The mission, it was decided, should be carried out by a small Anglo-American force. At the same time, members of the Special Boat Service were instructed to attack shipping in the harbour with top-secret 'mobile mines'. The force approached the boom of the harbour at 2.50 a.m. on 8 November 1942 with Peters in command of two Royal Navy ships, HMS *Walney* and HMS *Hartland*. The latter was spotted in the enemy's searchlights and came under heavy fire. It hit the jetty and eventually blew up at 10.15 a.m., after most of the crew and assault troops had abandoned ship.

Peters was on board *Walney*, which proceeded into the harbour and released three canoes manned by members of the SBS. It then rammed an enemy destroyer before being caught in searchlights and pummelled by heavy fire. Undeterred, Peters steered the ship through the boom and towards the jetty in the face of point-blank fire from the shore batteries, a destroyer and a cruiser. The *Walney* reached the jetty on fire and went down with her colours still flying. Peters was the only survivor of seventeen officers and men on the bridge, although the fighting left him blinded in one eye.

The *London Gazette* gave more details of his heroism when it announced his USA Distinguished Service Cross (Military) – awarded by the Americans and quite different from his earlier DSC and Bar from the British – on 19 January 1943:

> For extraordinary Heroism in Action. Captain Peters . . .
> remained on the bridge in the command of his ship in spite of
> the fact that the protective armour thereon had been blown in by
> enemy shell fire and was thereby exposed personally to the
> withering cross fire from shore defences. He accomplished the
> berthing of his ship, then went to the forward deck and assisted
> by one officer secured the forward mooring lines. He then with
> utter disregard of his own personal safety went to the quarter-
> deck and assisted in securing the aft mooring lines so that the
> troops on board could disembark. At that time the engine room
> was in flames and very shortly thereafter exploded and the ship
> turned on its side and sank.

He won his VC for the same act of bravery and it was gazetted on 18 May 1943: 'For Valour in taking HMS *Walney*, in an enterprise of desperate hazard, into the harbour of Oran on the 8th November, 1942.' Peters was taken prisoner after the attack and given medical treatment. Casualties on his ship had been high, with more than 50 per cent killed. *Walney* had destroyed one armed trawler and the SBS teams had damaged a destroyer, but the operation had failed because the harbour was too heavily defended. Yet, days later, Oran was in Allied hands after Operation Torch seized much of the Moroccan coast. Peters was then hailed as a hero by the French civilian population, carried shoulder high through the streets and showered with flowers in a bizarre 'victory parade'. However, in a tragic twist of fate, on 13 November – five days after exhibiting the bravery that won him the VC and the USA DSC (Military) – he was flying from Gibraltar to England when the plane crashed into the breakwater off Plymouth harbour, killing all five passengers.

Admiral Sir Andrew Cunningham, the task force commander

of Operation Torch, later said that Peters' 'courage and leadership achieved all that could be done against odds that proved overwhelming'. Winston Churchill went further, describing the *Walney*'s attack as 'the finest British naval engagement since Trafalgar'.

SERGEANT (LATER MAJOR) JOHN EDWARD ALMONDS

Army (SAS)

AWARDS: MILITARY MEDAL (MM) AND BAR
DATE OF BRAVERY: NOT SPECIFIC
GAZETTED: 26 NOVEMBER 1942 AND 27 APRIL 1944

'Jim Almonds always ran to the battle,' the late Earl (George) Jellicoe wrote in the foreword to a biography of this great soldier, written by Almonds' daughter. 'He was one of the first twelve men who joined David Stirling when he founded the SAS at Kabrit in early September 1941. Physically tough and with the self-discipline and mental strength never to give up whatever the circumstances, he yet showed that personal humility that led to his nickname.' 'Gentleman Jim' Almonds, as he was affectionately known, was a man who thrived on adversity and who relished any wartime challenge. Yet he was anything but headstrong and reckless. Instead, he was intelligent and disciplined. He wanted to survive his seemingly endless 'scrapes' – if only to embark on more adventures.

Almonds was born in Stixwould, Lincolnshire, on 6 August 1914, the son of a smallholder whose family had lost their farm due to foot and mouth disease. He made his first – but unsuccessful – attempt to join the Army on his fourteenth birthday in 1928. On his eighteenth birthday in 1932, however, he joined the Coldstream Guards. He soldiered at the Tower of

London and one of his duties was to guard the notorious Norman Baillie-Stewart, who had been jailed for passing secrets to his lover – a German Army officer's wife. He unofficially changed his first name out of convenience – if anyone called out 'John' half the barrack room looked up so, always practical, he volunteered to be called 'Jim'. The 'Gentleman' tag was added later because, although he was 6ft 4in. tall and deadly in the face of the enemy, he was gentle, calm and thoughtful in the company of his comrades.

Early in the Second World War, he volunteered for No. 8 Guards Commando, led by Lieutenant Colonel Bob Laycock, which together with other Commandos under his aegis became known as the 'Layforce'. It was typical of Almonds' methodical approach to life that as he set sail on the newly furbished HMS *Glenroy* – with such colourful characters aboard as David Stirling, Randolph Churchill, George Jellicoe and Evelyn Waugh – he started keeping a daily diary. This would eventually provide an invaluable account of his wartime exploits. Over the next four years, there were few dull moments.

Almonds and others were dive-bombed by enemy Stuka aircraft at sea off the North African coast in the Insect-class gunboat *Aphis*. Then with 8 Commando, Almonds took up position on the western side of Tobruk, the besieged natural seaport, which is today in Libya. With three comrades – Jock Lewes, Jim Blakeney and Pat Riley – he developed four-man tactics that would later be carried into the SAS. Operating largely at night, the team reconnoitred enemy positions in no man's land and made sporadic attacks on enemy forces.

His diary tells how a night attack on one enemy position was greeted with the usual thump of mortars and whine of shelling, which gradually became more intense until suddenly the enemy let fly with everything he had. Shells and mortars exploded everywhere, some just feet from the men's position. At one point, Almonds threw himself behind a stone wall and immediately afterwards a bomb burst on the other side.

By now, these undercover soldiers were known simply as the 'Tobruk Four'. Stirling brought the Tobruk Four into L Detachment on the basis of their formidable reputations, describing them affectionately as 'pure gold dust'. Almonds wrote in his diary after arriving at Kabrit in the Canal Zone on 5 September 1941: 'In camp and now belong to Special Air Service. Started training for a few operations to be carried out in enemy territory. To be dropped by parachute.' His matter of fact manner and economy of words masked the nature of formidable dangers that lay ahead.

His diaries chronicle his hazardous parachute and endurance training, experimental training missions and early raids behind enemy lines. The training itself was awesome, including practising parachute landings by rolling from the back of a truck at up to 30 mph. On 6 October 1941, he wrote: 'Afternoon spent jumping backwards from a lorry at twenty-five miles per hour. Three broken arms and a number of other casualties. Broken bones through training now six.' Quite apart from the training dangers and the times when he came under 'normal' enemy fire, he narrowly escaped death no less than nine times.

Such times – the early days of parachuting – were not for the faint-hearted. On 17 October, he noted: 'Two of the boys killed. Chutes never had a chance to open. Brought back across the canal by boat.' It was not the easiest preparation for the next day – when Almonds made his first parachute jump. By now, Gentleman Jim already had a fearsome reputation. It was no surprise that when Paddy Blair Mayne – later to be awarded the Distinguished Service Order (DSO) and three Bars – joined the clandestine unit at Kabrit, he chose Almonds as his troop sergeant.

Almonds and his comrades were prolific in their missions. For example, on 14 December, Almonds and Lewes carried out a successful enemy attack on the main Tripoli coastal road. After arriving at Mersa Brega, they spotted the lights of a large house and fort used as an enemy staging post. There were just the two of them but they pulled in and parked their captured lorry among the Italian and German trucks. They placed bombs on the parked enemy vehicles, while under fire from inside the fort, destroying several enemy transport and coming out of the 'beat up' uninjured.

At the end of 1941, Almonds took part in a raid on Nofelia aerodrome. He was machine-gunned from the air while lying motionless on the sand. Then later, he played 'ring a ring o' roses' round a rock while a Messerschmitt 110 aircraft shot at him and a member of the New Zealand Long Range Desert Group. The attack was successful but it cost Jock Lewes his life. Almonds' diary entry for 31 December 1941 ended with an affectionate tribute to his fallen friend: 'Yes, in many homes the Old Year is being watched die and new hopes rise with the prospect of the New Year ... I thought of Jock, one of the bravest men I have ever met, an officer and a gentleman, lying out there in the desert barely covered with sand. No one will ever stop by his grave or pay homage to a brave heart that has ceased to beat – not even a stone marks the spot.'

It was for this brave act and another similar raid that Almonds was awarded the MM. It was gazetted on 26 November 1942 when the original recommendation from David Stirling stated:

This NCO has at all times and under the most testing conditions shown great powers of leadership. After a raid on Nofelia aerodrome, he took command of his party after his officer had been killed. He showed great resource in managing to extricate this party with only one casualty, although all but one of his trucks had been destroyed. On another raid in the Agheila area, he led a party which destroyed five heavy enemy MT [military transport] and he participated in shooting up an enemy post in this locality. (It is requested that details of these operations should not be published owing to their secrecy.)

Almonds, aged thirty-six, learnt that his twenty-year-old wife had discharged their baby son from the Bristol Royal Infirmary, where he was receiving no treatment and was expected to die. The doctors said he would 'always be a weakling', yet after leaving hospital he quickly recovered at home. Eventually, he went on to pass the SAS selection and command one of the Regiment's squadrons at Hereford.

During a subsequent raid on Sidi Barrani in North Africa, Almonds and his section more or less ran out of water, eking out the tiny amount left – with typical Almonds self discipline – by taking just a teaspoonful each per day. They continued for three days under the burning sun with no expectation of finding water and then, against all the odds, they did find some at an abandoned supply dump, and survived.

Almonds had many talents, including being a naturally gifted engineer. Stirling was aware of this and soon had him building an extensive parachute training rig from spares and parts pilfered from Royal Engineers' dumps. Almonds used prisoners of war as his labour. He recorded that 'it was impossible to say no to David Stirling', such was his charisma and inspirational leadership. The combination of specialist training needs and the fact that his baby son was thought to be dying meant that he did not take part in the first major L Detachment parachute drops on Gazala and Timimi. In his diary, he recorded that twenty-one out of fifty-four men came back safely.

> After the massacre is over and the enemy's planes are blown up, there remains that terrible march back through the desert. No one who is sick or wounded could possibly make it and no one can afford to help. The weight already carried by each man is as much as he can bear . . . I am not there. I sit back here in the safety of the camp and wish I were with them. One more would have made the load lighter. A few words of encouragement when hard-pressed go a long way. In action before, when we've been up against it, I've managed to get a smile or a joke out of them . . . Reality beats fiction for sheer, cold, calculating courage. Some of these lads cannot be beaten. Films and books of daring and adventure fall far short of this, the real thing . . .

When the remnant of his comrades returned, he noted:

> It is difficult to get a story out of these people. They are a tight-lipped lot and never go into detail. But from their appearance . . . the last ten days in the desert must have been hell.

In July 1943, he took part in the raid on Sidi Haneish in enemy territory and then, while undercover, had to drive slowly through a convoy of German soldiers who had arrived to chase the departing SAS. In September 1943, against his better judgement, Stirling agreed with staff officers to mount a large raid on Benghazi. This was hardly in the style of the SAS because they had lost the element of surprise. In fact, they were late reaching the target and the enemy was expecting them. Mike Sadler, the famed Long Range Desert Group (LRDG) navigator, watched as Stirling beckoned Almonds in his jeep up to the front. Almonds immediately drove it, packed full of explosives, straight at the enemy with all guns blazing. As all hell let loose, the SAS group was forced to retreat. Almonds, however, was in a narrow lane and could not turn round. Instead, he and his comrade jumped clear just as the jeep blew up.

After a lengthy manhunt, Almonds was captured by the Italians and they paraded him round the town in the back of an open truck, his hands manacled to an ankle and a loaded gun to his head. He withstood later interrogation and several attempts at subversion through a planted double agent – an Italian 'Scotsman'. He then embarked for a second time on a sea voyage without knowing where he was going. The first time was with 8 Guards Commando *en route* to the Middle East in January 1941. This time it was in the hold of an enemy ship bound for Italy.

After masterminding a successful escape from his Italian PoW camp in February 1943, Almonds led a group of four, including an Australian, a New Zealander and a South African, towards the south coast. With typical style and understatement, he described this as 'the Italian picnic'. They faced atrocious weather and it sleeted for much of the thirteen days they were at large. The Australian developed pneumonia. All except Almonds were wearing cardboard-soled Italian boots and, when they burnt the bottoms out of them by a camp fire, it was the last straw. They gave themselves up, primarily to get the Australian some medical attention. As the ringleader, Almonds was told he would be executed. Instead, however, he was taken further north to another PoW camp at Ancona and placed in solitary confinement for seven months. Even then he was incapable of being idle or feeling sorry for himself. Showing astonishing resilience, he kept his mind alert by designing a thirty-two foot sailing ketch in his head, adding to the design each day and reciting the details until they were committed to memory.

His second chance to escape came when the Italian camp commandant asked him to go out and reconnoitre the positions of the approaching Germans. Almonds did so, reported in by phone and then – since he had not been asked to give his word to return – he walked the length of the Appenines. This time he was alone, which he felt increased his chances of success. He spent thirty-two days behind enemy lines – by this time the Italians had capitulated but the Germans fought on. Almonds headed south down the mountains towards the Allies and reached them after mapping an enemy minefield on the way. He was taken prisoner by the Americans, who did not believe his incredible story but eventually handed him over to the British.

It was for his two daring escapes from enemy hands that he was awarded a Bar to his MM, which was gazetted on 27 April 1944. The recommendation reads:

> Captured at Benghazi on 14 September 1942, this NCO was first taken to Campo 51 (Altamura). While here Almonds and three others, on 4 February 1943, bribed an Italian officer and sentry with coffee and remained working in the Red Cross hut till it was dark. The officer was decoyed by one PoW and the others then overpowered the sentry and gagged him. Almonds had a map stolen from a RC priest's Bible, and had constructed a compass. The four PoWs travelled over the hills by night through bad and rainy weather and reached the coast after twelve days. They could find no boat of any kind, were too weak to travel further and were therefore forced to give themselves up. At the time of the Armistice, Almonds was in Campo 70 (Monturano) and was sent out by the SBO to watch the coast

road. While out he was told by an Italian that the Germans had taken over the camp. He therefore made good his escape and set out westwards. He contacted American forces on 14 October 1942.

After successfully reaching England, Almonds was posted to the prime minister's residence at Chequers, which proved predictably unfulfilling for him. With the help of Paddy Mayne, he escaped again to rejoin the SAS, who were regrouping and training in Scotland. By now, the pressures of his astonishing war antics were beginning to take a toll. His appearance became gaunt and he had temporary difficulty in readjusting to normal family life. Once, out shopping, he turned on his wife and three-year-old son, whom he had not seen since he was three months old, and asked them why the hell they were following him. It was a temporary blip – his marriage survived fifty-seven years until his wife died in 1997.

Once back with his comrades, Almonds helped train the newcomers in preparation for parachuting behind enemy lines in German-occupied France. He was also asked to pass on his, by now, well-practised escape and evasion skills. In June 1944, Almonds and his section parachuted by night behind enemy lines into the Forest of Orleans. As part of Operation Gain, they wreaked havoc among the hard-pressed Germans by blowing up railway lines, bridges and ammunition dumps, and generally disrupting essential supply lines. In Almonds-speak, this became 'the French picnic'. Almonds even built a log cabin deep in the forest by notching and lashing saplings together and camouflaging the construction from the air with a dark green parachute. Never one to employ or permit unnecessary violence, he rescued a captured German from death at the hands of the French Maquis (resistance), named him Fritz and kept him during their two-month 'picnic' to do all the housework, cooking and washing-up. Jeeps and supplies were dropped by air at night and the local French resistance helped out. Almonds later said that it was all faintly comical, 'not a million miles away from the BBC television series *'Allo 'Allo*. As the US Third Army front line advanced towards the Operation Gain party, he judged it right to let Fritz slip away so that he would not be accused of fraternisation by his own side.

It was for his contribution behind enemy lines that the French awarded Almonds the Croix de Guerre with Silver Palm. On 12 March 1945, his commendation read:

> Squadron Sergeant Major (now war substantive Lieutenant) James Almonds, SAS, head of a section, parachuted with his men on the night of 16/17 June 1944, 300 kilometres behind enemy lines. Wounded on landing, he insisted on remaining in command and with his section ensured the destruction of all communication routes useful to the enemy. On 1 August 1944, despite being attacked by the enemy, he demonstrated magnificent personal courage and the indisputable qualities of a leader. Without any losses, he redeployed his unit and with no concern for the danger involved, led an attack on the Germans. He then returned alone to his old base headquarters to destroy his codebook and other secret documents. He did not cease during his mission to set a magnificent example to his men.

As the Allies advanced through France, he was mistakenly captured a second time by the Americans. Almonds was taken in front of General George S. Patton, who wagged his trademark pearl-handled pistol at him and snarled, 'If you're British, you'll be okay. If not, you'll be shot.' Eventually, he managed to convince the American liaison officer that he was British, and after making his way back to England, he was presented to Field Marshal Bernard Montgomery, who commissioned him inside his caravan.

Lorna Almonds Windmill, herself an ex-Army captain, published her book, *Gentleman Jim: The Wartime Story of a Founder of the SAS and Special Forces*, in 2001, ending it with this affectionate anecdote about her father from the last year of the war:

> After returning to the UK, he was out driving one day with Leslie Bateman [his comrade and friend] when they saw two Italian PoWs toiling in the fields, helping to bring in the harvest. 'Stop the car, Les,' he said. He patted his pockets and looked at his friend. 'Have you got any cigarettes?' Bateman said he had, and Almonds had some on him, too. He put them all together, got out of the car and picked his way across the field to the two PoWs. They stopped work, amazed and slightly apprehensive at the sight of a British officer coming towards them. 'This,' he said to them, 'is for you, because the Italian people were very kind to me and looked after me when I was an escaping prisoner of war in Italy.' The two men, at first stupefied, were quickly all smiles and responded with salutes and much bowing and scraping. 'Grazie, grazie, Il Capitano,' they said. It was a small gesture, but something about the simplicity of it brought tears to Bateman's eyes. It was not only for good manners and his lack of swearing that my father was known as 'Gentleman Jim'.

After the war, Almonds never lost his sense of adventure. He served in the British Military Mission to Ethiopia and with the Eritrean Police Field Force. He rejoined the SAS when it was reconstituted and commanded B Squadron 1st SAS, clearing terrorists from the Malayan jungle from 1953 to 1955. In 1956, while serving with the West African Frontier Force in Ghana, he began building by hand the boat he had designed and memorised while in solitary confinement in the Italian PoW camp. He sailed it back to England in 1961, accompanied by the chief regional officer and a young subaltern. He finally resigned his commission after four years in Ghana.

'Gentleman Jim' Almonds died in Lincolnshire on 20 August 2005, aged ninety-one. He was survived by his son and twin daughters, all of whom also served in the army. The trust bought his medals at auction in London in December 2007. The awards came with Almonds' original, shrapnel-damaged, handwritten wartime diary of over 20,000 words, consisting of daily entries kept by him from 28 January 1941 to 28 March 1942 (there was even a typed transcript, too), together with his SAS berets, one maroon, one sand-coloured, the former most probably worn by him in the Malaya operations in the 1950s. Other treasures included first-edition copies of the hardback and paperback versions of his daughter's book, signed by author and subject.

No words can fully do justice to this brave soldier, talented engineer, devoted family man and born survivor. Yet Alan Hoe came close to it in his book *David Stirling: The Authorised Biography of the Creator of the SAS*. Hoe wrote:

> Sergeant 'Gentleman Jim' Almonds, one of the 'Tobruk Four', was in many ways to the desert born. In this environment he was totally at home. He excelled in the velvet darkness and revelled in the vast emptiness of North Africa. His nickname was apt; six feet and four inches tall, his gentle, quiet and considerate manner hid enormous self-discipline and control which left him cool, efficient and deadly when the situation demanded it.

CORPORAL WILLIAM EDWARD SPARKS
Royal Marines
AWARD: DISTINGUISHED SERVICE MEDAL (DSM)
DATE OF BRAVERY: NOT SPECIFIC
GAZETTED: 29 JUNE 1943

It was a chilly evening in November 1955. The world première of the film *The Cockleshell Heroes* had attracted a long list of dignitaries, including HRH the Duke of Edinburgh, cabinet ministers, ambassadors and service chiefs. The actor Douglas Fairbanks and his wife were there, and so too was Earl Mountbatten of Burma who, as Head of Combined Operations, had approved the medal recommendations for one of the most daring raids of the war, which was now being brought to the big screen for the first time. Most important of all, perhaps, the two surviving 'Cockleshell Heroes' took star billing at the première.

The remarkable, real-life events highlighted in the film had taken place more than thirteen years earlier. Operation Frankton has long been recognised as one of the legendary exploits of the war. In his book *The Marines Were There*, Bruce Lockhart claimed that 'in boldness of conception, in skill of execution, and in prolonged intensity of danger' the raid was 'perhaps the most thrilling of all minor episodes in the war'.

Major 'Blondie' Hasler had come up with the idea as part of his role in the Royal Marine Boom Patrol Detachment (RMBPD), a unit set up in July 1942. Initially, the RMBPD had two sections – one for canoe operations, the other for explosive boat operations. Later in the war it was employed in the Middle East and after the war it eventually became a branch of the SBS.

Hasler was in no doubt about the difficulty and danger of the task he had in mind – a daring, undercover raid on an enemy target – and he knew he required a formidable, well-trained unit to carry it out. He warned that the successful candidates would have to be, in order of priority, 'eager to engage the enemy; indifferent to their personal safety; intelligent; nimble; free from family ties or dependents; able to swim; and of good physique and eyesight'. The men, all recruited from Plymouth, spent the late summer of 1942 lodged in boarding houses in the city, their mission shrouded in total secrecy, even from the participants themselves. Indeed, the landladies believed their lodgers were involved in improving local boom defences.

There were many teething problems with canoe design and other equipment but Hasler, who was to lead the raid, was impressed with the dedication of some of his men. One of those to show early promise was Corporal Bill Sparks, known as Ned to his friends. Sparks, the son of a serving seaman, was born in the east end of London on 5 September 1922. A slightly built Cockney with an infectious laugh, he had left school at fourteen and worked as a shoe repairer until the outbreak of war. His father had wanted young Bill to follow him into the Royal Navy, but he opted instead for the Royal Marines. Sparks complemented Hasler, who could get anxious when problems arose. When things were going badly, Sparks was cheerful and cracked jokes to boost morale. When things were going well, he made disparaging remarks in an audible undertone to ensure that nobody got overconfident. Early on, it seems, Hasler chose Sparks as his likely number two for the mission.

The canoes had been designed for loading into a submarine down the forward torpedo hatch, and Hasler also designed a special sling to enable the canoe to be launched fully loaded. However, perhaps the hardest task for the men – particularly in rough seas – was to attach limpet mines to the targeted ship. This was done with the help of six-feet long steel placing rods to which the magnetic mine was attached. The idea was that as the canoe came alongside the enemy ship, one of the crew would make it fast by attaching a magnetic holdfast device held level with his shoulder. His colleague in the canoe was tasked with carefully lowering the limpet – which had been fused before the approach – to a depth of six feet and clamping it to the hull. After doing this, he unhooked the rod thereby enabling the canoe to drift away from the hull. Even in calm waters in daylight, this was a tricky manoeuvre. In choppy water and in darkness, it required great courage, skill and stealth.

There were no written orders, but the military hierarchy decided that Bordeaux in German-occupied France would be the target. The port, located some ten miles up the Garonne and reached via the Gironde estuary, was harbouring blockade-running Axis vessels, which were preparing to carry vital equipment to Japan. It was calculated that an assault landing would require 20,000 men, while bombing the target risked heavy civilian casualties. Instead, Hasler and Sparks would carry out the mission with ten other men in one of the most daring clandestine operations of the war. Initially, Hasler had wanted just six men in three canoes but he was persuaded by Lord Mountbatten, the Head of Combined Operations, that he needed double the number of men and canoes in case of accidents along the way.

The aim was to transport eight limpet mines in each of the lockers of their Cockle Mark II canoes – which had been chosen as the most suitable vessels for the planned three-day trip up the Gironde – plant their charges below the waterline of some twelve merchant ships, scuttle their canoes and then escape. In his book *British Special Forces*, William Seymour writes: 'There was nothing new in hit and run raids from submarines, but what was new in Operation Frankton was the deep penetration that the canoeists were to make – some 75 miles upriver – and the fact that it was considered impossible to arrange any means of picking the men up after they had completed the task.'

The men and their equipment were packed into HM Submarine *Tuna*, which left the Clyde on 30 November 1942. Sparks later wrote of the send-off:

> Then, to our surprise, the submarine fleet commander came on board and addressed us. 'The day that you have all been training for has come. I don't know where you are bound or what the job is to be. What I can say is that people of the highest authority are awaiting the results. Good luck to you all.' He then returned to the depot ship. We stood still and silent in single files as the submarine pulled away from the depot ship and her long black hull slid out towards the North Sea. The still was sounded; we were being saluted. We knew then it had to be something big.

Even as they travelled towards France, Hasler kept up the secrecy of the mission and declined to tell his men exactly what they were doing. People were told only on a need-to-know basis, but eventually he had to unveil the plan. 'Right, lads. This is it. The real thing,' Hasler told his attentive audience, and, in a slow and methodical manner, explained what was to happen and that the mission was codenamed Operation Frankton. The target came as a surprise to most of the men. Sparks and others had become convinced they were going after the German battleship *Tirpitz*. 'How are we going to get back?' asked Sergeant Samuel 'Mick' Wallace, one of the men. Hasler explained why it was impossible for the submarine to pick them up after they had completed their mission. Instead, he told them their escape route – paddling back down the estuary on the ebb tide, landing at low water, scuttling the canoes and travelling overland through France to reach Spain. On hearing this news, the party looked at each other and grinned nervously.

Nobody was in any doubt about the difficulty of their mission and the dangers they faced, but Hasler spelt it out further – the success of the mission was their primary consideration and the men's personal safety could only be of secondary importance. Anyone who ran into trouble was to handle it as they saw fit, but in all probability the men knew they would get no outside assistance. 'I realise that this is a bit more than I originally asked of you, so if any man thinks that he is not quite up to it, let him speak now. I assure you that no one will think any the less of him for it.'

There was silence until Sergeant Wallace piped up, 'If I get captured, I'm going to declare myself neutral – because I'm Irish!'

Shortly before 8 p.m. on 7 December – and after a twenty-four-hour postponement because of bad weather – the submarine surfaced and the six Cockles were lowered into the Bay of Biscay. However, in getting the Cockles on deck in the darkness, one was damaged. Reluctantly, Hasler told its crew that they would have to stay behind, leaving one of the men in tears. The twelve-man mission was now a ten-man operation with five Cockles – Hasler and Sparks in *Catfish*, and the remaining eight men in *Crayfish*, *Conger*, *Cuttlefish* and *Coalfish*. At 8.22 p.m., beneath a star-filled sky, the captain of *Tuna* bade farewell and good luck to 'a magnificent bunch of black-faced villains'.

The strong shore defences and searchlights meant that the submarine had to leave the five Cockles in open seas fully three miles from the mouth of the estuary. Even in relatively flat conditions, the men faced a long haul to paddle ashore and find a suitable place to hide before daybreak. Unfortunately, the

Atlantic swell increased alarmingly until, after three hours of paddling, the five Cockles were hurled into a tide race, in which angry waters surge over rocks and sandbanks. Sparks later recalled, 'We were in swirling waters, and being thrown around like a cork. I dug deep using every ounce of strength, conscious of the need to keep the canoe balanced, and struck ahead.' In the subsequent confusion, *Coalfish* disappeared and, although the other four Cockles waited for her, she never turned up. The operation was now down to just eight men – two-thirds of the original force – in four Cockles. Shortly after one tide race ended, there was an ominous roar of breaking water and the men found themselves in a second, this time with five-foot high waves and, in Sparks's later words, 'We were tossed around like a toy boat.'

Conger was damaged and Hasler ordered the craft to be scuttled. Her crew, Marines Sheard and Moffat, clung desperately to the sterns of *Catfish* and *Cuttlefish*. With no chance of clambering aboard either Cockle, they were given a tow towards land, close to the lighthouse at Pointe de Grave. Hasler spoke to the two men. 'I'm afraid this is as far as we can take you . . . God bless you both.' 'That's all right, sir. It was good of you to take us this far,' replied Corporal Sheard. Both men, already frozen from the December waters, failed to reach land. There were now only six men and three Cockles – half the party that had set out – left to continue the mission.

Hasler's immediate aim was to pass the Verdon jetty and get into the river proper. However, with four German ships at anchor just off the jetty, they had to slip through a narrow, dangerous corridor with sentries on both sides. It was decided the Cockles would go through one by one, with the two men in each craft paddling fast but crouching low to avoid being seen. Hasler and Sparks, who went first, were startled by a lamp from one of the enemy ships, but they were not spotted. Next came *Crayfish*, carrying Marines Laver and Mills, who passed through without incident. Then came a long wait and no sign of *Cuttlefish*. Eventually, Hasler was forced to press on (it was later established that *Cuttlefish* had been temporarily delayed and later tried to go it alone towards Bordeaux). Hasler now found himself in charge of a raiding party that was down to just four men and two Cockles. Sparks later wrote: 'During that first night we had lost two-thirds of our strike force. It began to look as though the operation was doomed to failure.'

Eleven hours and some twenty-five miles from their starting point, *Catfish* and *Crayfish* were hauled up and the men started their search for a hide-out. 'I had never felt so mentally and physically exhausted,' Sparks later wrote. It took nearly two hours to locate a suitable spot near Pointe aux Oiseaux, and there the camouflage nets were spread. As they prepared to get some rest, they looked on the map and realised how dangerous the next stage of their journey would be. Long stretches of bank were marked where German patrols were known to operate. Furthermore, the men had to avoid numerous look-out towers and anti-aircraft batteries.

The next day began badly when their hide was spotted by some French fishermen and their families. Hasler chose to reveal their identity and rely on the fishermen's discretion, but he later regretted his actions. Much worse, however – and unknown to Hasler and his three men – the Germans had picked up *Tuna* on their radar just hours after the submarine had dropped off the men. German suspicions that something was up were confirmed when they captured the two Marines from the first Cockle – *Coalfish* – that had lost its bearings in the tide race. The whole area was now on full alert and swarming with Germans on the look-out for the remaining men of the raiding party.

That evening, Tuesday, the men set off too late to catch the flood tide and had to carry their two craft and their equipment through an area of deep, exposed mud. This left them with only six hours of fair tide and they knew they had to make swift progress all through the night to reach their next stop-off. Keeping up a good pace, the Cockles progressed another twenty-five miles before the men landed again. Their day had been successful but not uneventful. When crossing the shipping channel they were nearly run down by a convoy of six or seven large vessels that had not seen them. One boat had been so close that the Marines had seen the reflection of her stern light on their gunwales. 'More targets for us, sir,' Sparks told Hasler cheerfully as the vessels slid by in the night.

The hide for the second night was better than the first and situated between two hedges in a dry ditch. By now, the four men were cold and exhausted but their brief sleep was broken when they were woken by a low-flying German search plane. Indeed, the plane was so low that the men could easily see the pilot in his cockpit but, fortunately, he was unable to see them. However, unsure they had not been seen, they spent the next twenty-four hours on full alert.

In the twilight of the next evening, the men paddled further up the Gironde, finding themselves silhouetted against a golden sunset but unable to do anything about it. As they slowed at one point, Hasler saw a French farmer approach them and he again gambled on revealing their identity. The farmer was so welcoming that he insisted the men return to his home for a drink. 'Perhaps after the war,' Hasler said, determined to press on. The farmer reassured the men, 'I will say nothing, you may be sure.'

They made good progress that evening, despite a close brush with a German patrol boat, eventually hauling up to a deserted island for a five-hour rest. Just before 3 a.m., they set off in time to catch the flood tide, but had to wade through waist-high mud, which made such a noise that they were convinced they would be heard from far away. For now, however, their good fortune prevailed.

As daylight approached, they needed to land again but this proved difficult. When Hasler carried out a quick recce of the surrounding area, he found only an anti-aircraft post. There was nothing for it but to stop off in a marshy field on the Ile de Cazeau. The four men spent the next day lying in their Cockles beneath a camouflage net. At one point, they found themselves surrounded by a herd of curious cattle, while during another hairy moment they were buzzed by a German reconnaissance plane.

They were, however, making daily progress – though not at the rate they had planned – and had not lost any more men. By now, the Gironde was behind them and they were in the Garonne. Their target lay just twelve miles ahead. All being well they would reach it that night but, after discussing their location, Hasler decided to postpone the attack until the following night in order to ensure they had a suitable hide in the harbour area.

After experiencing more difficulty with the river mud, they set off at 6.45 p.m. Some three hours later, they came around a bend and at last set eyes on some targets – two big ships moored at the quayside of Bassens South. They were hopeful that even larger vessels would be situated in the main docks. They were now in a built-up area, with lights blazing from all angles. After passing under a floating pontoon pier, they spotted a bank of tall rushes. Hidden by plants of up to nine feet tall, they settled down, side by side, for the night. The following day they heard the sound of cars, lorries and cranes only yards away, but as they dozed off they could not help feeling a tinge of satisfaction at having reached their destination. They also knew that an interesting night's work lay ahead.

Hasler decided that the two crews should split up. He and Sparks would take *Catfish* up the western side of the main Bordeaux docks and Laver and Mills would paddle *Crayfish* to the East Docks. If the second crew could find no suitable targets, they were to attach limpets to the two ships at Bassens South. Sparks felt a rush of excitement as the moment they had been waiting for finally arrived. Hasler ordered that the limpets should be armed and at 9 p.m. they started the time fuses. At 9.15 p.m., the four men shook hands and the two Cockles slipped silently into the harbour. 'Now nothing would stop these mines going off in about nine hours' time,' Sparks later recalled. 'It's an odd feeling sitting with explosives between your legs. What if something went wrong with the ampoule? I didn't suppose we would know much about it, so why worry! I put it out of my mind.'

Sparks was struck by how bright it was, 'like Oxford Street at Christmas' he later wrote. Whereas British ports kept lighting to a minimum, Bordeaux was an electrical extravaganza. To avoid detection, they manoeuvred *Catfish* slowly. Some ninety minutes into their mission, Sparks drifted *Catfish* in halfway down a line of vessels. This enabled Hasler to fit the first limpet to his placing rod. Sparks steadied the craft and Hasler was able to fit the charge to the first target, the steamer *Tannenfels*. As they moved further along the ship, the two men exchanged roles and so Sparks placed the second and third limpets on to the ship's hull.

The two Marines then moved on to their next target, the auxiliary minesweeper *Sperrbrecher 5*. Their biggest problem so far had been avoiding the vessels' sewage outlets and the water that poured from the condensing outlets. As they started to grow in confidence, they had a shock. Moments after they had placed the first charge alongside the minesweeper's engineroom, a torch snapped on and a sentry appeared to have spotted them. Refusing to panic, the two men brought *Catfish* right in to the side of the ship. The sentry was only fifteen feet above them and his torchlight appeared to follow the Cockle as it drifted along the minesweeper's waterline. As the two men edged along the ship, they were convinced the sentry would raise the alarm. However, after what seemed like an eternity, they finally reached the end of the minesweeper and swung *Catfish* gently under her stern. They could hear the sentry's heavy boots but were unable to see him – or be seen – as Sparks calmly rolled another limpet on to the ship's stern. Their camouflage had done the trick and the sound of the sentry's footsteps trailed into the night. The two men let go and drifted away from the ship.

Next they moved between a tanker and a cargo ship, *Dresden*. They were lucky not to be capsized or crushed as the two ships slammed close together, yawing in the tide. Eventually, however, they attached two limpets to *Dresden* and their final charge to the tanker. Their part in Operation Frankton was now over other than the less-than-easy task of making good their escape. 'Hasler turned around and grabbed me warmly by the hand. For the first time in ages, we had a smile on our faces,' Sparks later wrote. They paddled *Catfish* into the middle of the river and shot off downstream. They were keen to get as far down the estuary as possible before daybreak, so switched to double paddles. They swept past the two ships at Bassens South and had nearly reached the unsatisfactory hide at Ile de Cazeau when they paused for a short rest. Then they burst out laughing as they first heard, and then saw, *Crayfish* come racing into view 'like a Mississippi stern-wheeler at full speed'. The men's reunion was short but spirited as Laver and Mills recounted their own adventure. The two men had been unable to find a suitable target in the East Docks and had therefore returned to the two ships at Bassens South. There they had attached five limpets to one ship and three to the other. Hasler praised his two comrades and the two Cockles set off down the Gironde for the final time.

At about 6 a.m., they rafted up just north of Blaye. Hasler ordered Laver and Mills to scuttle *Crayfish* and embark on their overland escape. Hasler said that he and Sparks would do the same slightly further on, but they would travel in pairs not as a four to reduce their chances of being detected. The men shook hands for the last time and Hasler and Sparks paddled away. 'See you in Granada. We will keep a couple of pints for you,' Sparks shouted to his two comrades, before his thoughts turned to what had happened to the rest of the lads.

Back in Britain, Combined Operations had intercepted a German High Command report. It read: 'A small British sabotage squad was engaged at the mouth of the River Gironde and finished off in combat.' If the report was accurate and no men had made it to Bordeaux, it was sad but not surprising. Earl Mountbatten retained a sneaking suspicion, however, that one or more of the Cockles had made it through. Shortly afterwards, an aerial photograph of Bordeaux docks confirmed he was right – several ships had been sunk or were badly damaged. Britain's military leaders, however, had received no news of the ten Marines and, indeed, as late as January 1943 all were still posted as missing.

Hasler and Sparks pulled their canoe on to soft mud. 'It was ecstasy to be out of the boat after nine hours of restricted movement. Every bone in my body cracked like a rifle shot,' Sparks later recalled. The men felt sad when they had to slash their canvas canoes so as to leave no trace that they had landed.

'Now I know how a cowboy feels when he has to shoot his horse because it's broken its leg. That canoe had been a faithful friend, but here I was, hacking and slicing at it like a butcher cleaving though a side of beef,' Sparks wrote. As they began their escape across the French countryside, they initially made slow progress. In the darkness, they became snared up in the wires of a vineyard and made just two miles before they were forced to lay up as daybreak approached. At around 9.30 a.m., they listened for the distant sounds of explosions but were unable to detect anything.

By now the two men were soaked to the skin, filthy, bedraggled and exhausted, admitting later that they would have 'frightened many women out of their wits' if they had been spotted on the run. Worst of all, they were still in their military uniforms and their attempts to beg, steal or borrow civilian clothes ended in failure. They decided to lie low during the day and travel at night. That night's journey took them to Reignac, where a friendly farmer's wife did provide them with some scruffy jackets and trousers so that they now resembled a couple of French peasants. Hasler told Sparks, 'Bill, now that we are in civilian clothes, we will have to discard our weapons. If we are captured in civvies, and armed, we will be shot.' Sparks was reluctant to relinquish his pistol and fighting knife but he followed his orders.

They moved on, in short hops, to Ruffec. They had found food hard to come by and, after another night in the open, they set off for Touzac. Here they tried to get some food but were told to 'clear off' by an unwelcoming French woman. They pushed on for another eighteen miles and had the good fortune to come across a woodman who, despite his early suspicions of them, took the two men under his wing. As a committed communist, the French workman wanted to 'kill any German in sight' but his new British friends were keener on sleep and food than more heroics against the enemy.

With the two Britons speaking little French and the woodman speaking no English, progress was slow but Sparks could not conceal his delight when the Frenchman uttered the word *'manger'*. This made their host understand where their priorities lay. In patchy French, Hasler even managed to make their new friend realise that he was prepared to 'eat a horse' to ease his hunger pangs. That night the two servicemen were treated to a feast, washed down by ample quantities of rough red wine. Sparks so enjoyed his hospitality that he asked the woodman, in jest, if he could stay for the rest of the war. That night the Frenchman gave the two men his large double bed so they could catch up on their sleep.

On the next stage of their journey, they brushed past a Nazi soldier who was in a hurry and Hasler joked he must be late for parade. The next morning, they started early and, after only a few miles, arrived at the village of Beaune. They were refused food but found a shelter for the night – only to be turned out when someone reported their presence to the police. 'Friendly little place,' was Sparks's assessment of the village. They knew before they left for their mission that – according to British Intelligence – the town of Ruffec harboured some resistance sympathisers. It was now 18 December and their discreet inquiries led them to a small bistro where, as they settled their bill for their potato soup, Hasler revealed their identities in a short note to the waitress: 'We are escaping English soldiers. Do you know anyone who can help?' They were in luck – they had come to the right place. But they had an agonising wait as they stayed at the hotel that night and were woken by a loud knock on the door the next morning. Hasler told Sparks, 'Go and see who it is.' 'Why me?' came the nervous reply. 'Because I am a major,' said Hasler, with a cheeky grin. Fortunately, an elderly lady – rather than German soldiers – was at their door, offering them chocolate.

Later that day, after a grilling from the resistance members, the men were bundled into the back of a baker's van and driven some twelve miles to an isolated farmhouse. The owner told them they would be collected by a representative from the 'Marie-Claire Escape Line'. After a three-week wait, they were taken, on 6 January 1943, to Roumazières railway station and then on to Lyons. They were greeted by 'Marie-Claire' herself, who was, in fact, a courageous English woman. They were transported from one safe house to another before, with new, fake identification cards, they travelled on to Marseilles.

Their guide to Marseilles was a mischievous young French-man who deliberately put them in a crowded train compartment with two German soldiers and then started speaking to them in English. Their new safe house in Marseilles had been a regular stop-off for RAF men, and their hosts spoke fluent English. They remained in Marseilles for a month and, to pass the time, Sparks spent many hours helping a young French woman improve her English before she was sent to join the Free French forces elsewhere in her occupied country. Hasler, however, expressed concern at some of the choice words and phrases that Sparks had taught her.

Next the two men were put on a train to Perpignan where, soon afterwards, they embarked on a twenty-four-hour trek across the Pyrenees to France. The Spanish were generally unwelcoming to escaping British military personnel and this meant the road journey on to the British Consulate in Barcelona had to be spent hidden under a pile of lavatory fitments. Initially, they were greeted by staff they later described as 'cynical young Englishmen'. However, once Combined

Operations in London confirmed their identity and their story, they were given a warmer welcome. The orders from London were for Hasler to be sent back to Britain as a matter of 'utmost priority', while Sparks was told he could follow later. Sparks spent several days as a guest of the Naval Attaché in Madrid and finally crossed to British-owned Gibraltar on 1 April 1943. His four-month adventure was over – he and Hasler were the only survivors from the twelve men who had been lowered into the water from their submarine on 7 December.

It later emerged that Field Marshal Keitel had been so angry that Hasler and Sparks had escaped that he sent a strongly worded letter to the Spanish Government. General Franco replied that if the Germans thought they could run his frontiers better than the Spanish, he looked forward to hearing their suggestions on how to do it. The *London Gazette* announced on 29 June 1943 that Sparks had been awarded the Distinguished Service Medal (DSM) and Hasler had been awarded the Distinguished Service Order (DSO). Unwilling to give away war secrets to the enemy, there was simply a general citation, which acknowledged the men's 'courage and enterprise'. Sparks had, however, received the news earlier in a letter from Earl Mountbatten of Burma: 'Dear Sparks, I am delighted to see you have been awarded the Distinguished Service Medal and I am writing to offer you my most sincere congratulations. This is a fitting tribute to the courage and resourcefulness that you showed on your hazardous operation.' Sparks later went to Buckingham Palace to collect his medal from George VI. Accompanied by his parents, he described the investiture as 'the proudest moment of my life'.

It was only after the war had ended that the British authorities found out what had happened to the rest of the raiding party. The facts that emerged shamed the German and

French authorities. It became clear as part of a war crimes trial in 1948 that Wallace and Ewart, who had been in *Coalfish* and who had disappeared during the first tide race, were eventually captured by French police at Pointe de Grave. They ended up in the hands of the Gestapo – the much-feared German secret police – and were brutally tortured. After refusing to give any information, they were taken to a wood and shot. The Germans were eventually forced to admit the men had been in uniform and that their actions were indefensible under the Geneva Convention. No less excusable was the treatment meted out to Mackinnon and Conway from *Cuttlefish* and Laver and Mills from *Crayfish*. The latter pair are understood to have been captured by the Vichy police shortly after leaving Hasler and Sparks. Their fate is not certain but it is believed that, along with Mackinnon and Conway, they were taken to Paris and murdered on, or about, 23 March 1943.

Sparks went on to serve with distinction for the remainder of the war in Burma, Africa and Italy. After leaving the Army, he did various jobs including working as a bus driver, in a plastics factory and for the Malay police. It was while he was working in the plastics factory that he got a call at home from Cubby Broccoli, the famous film director, saying he wanted to make a film about the Cockleshell Heroes calling the movie by the same name. Sparks thought someone was pulling his leg and put down the receiver. He eventually, however, became a consultant for the film, along with Hasler. At the film's première in Leicester Square, Sparks had 'quite a chat' with Prince Philip. He later attended premières in France and the US.

After the war, Sparks became increasingly incensed, however, that those on the mission who had given their lives were not decorated. Marines Laver and Mills had been 'mentioned in despatches', but that was the sole official recognition of the bravery of eight men who had died for their country. Sparks was told that only the Victoria Cross (VC) could be awarded posthumously, and even that required the act of bravery to be witnessed by a senior officer. His petitions, lobbying of MPs and even an appeal to the Queen for the other Cockleshell Heroes to be decorated came to nothing.

Eventually, at the suggestion of Sparks's local MP, Sir Bernard Braine, an appeal was launched to build a monument for the Cockleshell Heroes. The *Daily Telegraph* arranged a fund and soon there was enough money to build a memorial. It was erected in the barracks of the Royal Marines Special Boat Squadron and was unveiled in 1983 by Sir Steuart Pringle, Commandant General, Royal Marines. At the unveiling, Sparks told Sir Bernard that he was horrified to see his own name on the memorial – because he was not dead. The MP replied, 'Well, you're not going to live forever and when you are gone, nobody's going to come down and add your name to the list. So I had it put on.' Sparks stood at the ceremony and remembered 'the incredible courage and unbreakable spirit of all my companions who had come to be known as the Cockleshell Heroes'.

Sparks eventually wrote two books about his exploits, *The Last of the Cockleshell Heroes: A World War Two Memoir*, published in 1992, and *Cockleshell Commando: The Memoirs of Bill Sparks*, published in 2002. He ended the latter book with the words: 'I continue to do my best to keep alive the memory of those who paid the supreme sacrifice during those black days in December 1942. *They* are the "Cockleshell Heroes". I am merely the proud spokesman for these exceptionally brave men.' Sparks had three sons and a daughter by his first wife, Violet, who died in 1982. His second wife, Irene, survived him when he died on 1 December 2002, aged eighty.

MAJOR ANTHONY GREVILLE-BELL

Army

AWARD: DISTINGUISHED SERVICE ORDER (DSO)
DATE OF BRAVERY: NOT SPECIFIC
GAZETTED: 21 SEPTEMBER 1944

'The great thing about Major Tony,' said one SAS corporal, 'is that he doesn't get you killed unless he absolutely has to.' This was the tribute to Major Anthony Greville-Bell from one of his men after the officer – despite being injured parachuting into northern Italy – had led a highly successful SAS sabotage team for seventy-three days behind enemy lines before a 250-mile trek back to the Allied forces. The idea for the operation, which took place from September to November 1943, had been devised by Captain P.H. Pinckney and was codenamed Operation Speedwell. The aim had been to target the main troop-carrying railway lines – Prato–Bologna, Florence–Bologna and Bologna–Geno–La Spetzia. Greville-Bell was to be in one of the 'sticks' – small groups of men parachuted into different areas. In his stick, there were seven men and he was second-in-command, but he had to take command when his commanding officer went missing.

Anthony Greville-Bell was born in Sydney, the son of Captain W.E.G. Bell, and educated at Blundell's School, Tiverton. After he enlisted he was commissioned into the Royal Engineers. Perhaps the best tribute to the courage and commitment of Greville-Bell during his military career was written by Lieutenant Colonel William Stirling, who formed 2 SAS:

> Tony Greville-Bell joined G Squadron, 1st SAS towards the end
> of 1942, as an eighteen year old [he was in fact twenty-one by
> then] Gunner subaltern, who had already made a name for
> himself as a dashing officer in the 6th Armoured Brigade. G

Squadron became the nucleus on which 2nd SAS was formed. He thus had the unique distinction of serving in all four of the regiments – 1st, 2nd, 21st and 22nd – as well as having been attached to the 3rd and 4th French regiments.

Tony took part in operations in Africa, various enemy-occupied islands, and Sicily, but distinguished himself most noticeably on a classic SAS operation against the railways in northern Italy, which was a true strategic operation in that it probably did, as was intended, alter or at least affect the course of the war. The Germans were holding their Armoured Reserve, consisting of four divisions, well to the north while they waited to see where the Allies would make their expected amphibious landings. Owing to a shortage of petrol and spare tank tracks they were relying on the excellent Italian railway system to get them quickly south to wherever the landings took place. Between Bologna and Florence there are only three north–south railway lines, one on each coast and the third in the centre. SAS parties were dropped in all three areas to attack these lines and deny their use to the enemy, which they did very successfully, during the weeks following the landings at Salerno. As a result, by the time that the enemy Armoured Reserve began to arrive on the battlefield by road, the Allied forces were already well established and were able to defeat them in detail. General Alexander has since remarked that, had the enemy armour arrived punctually and in force, the outcome of the Salerno landings must have been in the gravest doubt. Tony commanded the party on the central sector. He was badly injured on the drop, but continued to lead his party and destroyed three trains, completely putting the railway out of action for nineteen days. After pausing for a few weeks in the Tuscan mountains to raise and train an army of Italian partisans – 'The guerillas,' he wrote later in his report, 'were not all that good, but the Chianti was excellent' – he continued south, and had the satisfaction of seeing 'while trying to cross the road south of Florence, an apparently endless column of tanks heading for the battle, mostly on their tracks. It must have been depressing for their commander to know that with an effective track mileage of only 250 miles, they had a journey of more than 300 miles in front of them.' Suffering badly from near starvation and very severe weather conditions in the Appenine mountains, Tony finally led his party safely through the enemy lines and rejoined his unit, a journey of some three hundred miles.

After recovering from the ordeal of the Italian operations, Tony was promoted to command a squadron and was posted back to the UK with his squadron to train the newly formed French SAS Regiments. He subsequently served on two operations in France immediately prior to, and after the invasion. As a result of two serious wounds and various injuries he was down-graded medically and transferred to Airborne Forces HQ where he served as Liaison Officer. In August he was seconded to the Political Intelligence Department of the Foreign Office where he remained for some years.

In 1949 he formed a squadron of SAS for service in Korea, but they were diverted to Malaya where they formed the nucleus of the now regular regiment of the SAS, 22nd SAS [in fact, at this point, the regiment was called SAS (Malayan Scouts)]. After completing his service in Malaya, he was posted to the Canal Zone of Egypt as Staff Officer SAS to the C-in-C Middle East Forces. His final job before leaving the army was as CO of the Regimental HQ of the SAS Regiment . . .

It can be said that Tony Greville-Bell was the best type of SAS officer. He was serious about his job, he enjoyed life and wanted everyone else to enjoy life as much as he did, and above all he took care of his soldiers for whom he had the greatest regard . . .

Tony gave up a promising future in the army in 1956 when his wife, Diana, was tragically killed in a motor accident leaving him to bring up his two little daughters. [By this time he was also disillusioned by Army life – see page 118.] There have been quite a few SAS officers as gallant and distinguished as Tony Greville-Bell, but he always seemed to me to epitomise the ideal SAS leader, gay [not homosexual in this context] yet serious, dashing yet careful, and above all, dedicated to the well-being of his men for whom he had an unbounded admiration and respect.

The mission to Italy was not without its casualties. The fate of Greville-Bell's senior officer, Captain Pinckney, who disappeared on the night that they parachuted into the country, has never been fully established, and it is not inconceivable that he was captured and shot as per Hitler's *Nacht und Nebel* decree – the 'night and fog' order, issued in December 1941, which led to the kidnapping and disappearance of political activists and other German 'enemies' found in the occupied territories. It is estimated that around a hundred SAS personnel who fell into enemy hands during the Second World War were shot – in breach of all conventions – even though they were attired in official regimental uniform. Greville-Bell would have known that if he was caught during his two-months-plus undercover he faced being tortured and killed.

An extract from Anthony Kemp's history, *The S.A.S. at War 1941–45*, throws further light on the degree of hardship endured by Greville-Bell and his team behind enemy lines:

Tony Greville-Bell, meanwhile, had badly damaged his back, as well as breaking two ribs. He and his men laid up during the first day sorting out their kit, which consisted of 160lbs of plastic explosive, 4½ lbs of cheese, two tins of sardines, tea and some biscuits per party. Robinson [a comrade] and his men left that evening, and Greville-Bell, unsure whether he could carry on or not, handed over to his Sergeant, 'Bebe' Daniels.

The following extracts are from the official 'after-action report' compiled by Greville-Bell. They indicate an example of sheer courage and absolute determination to see the job through, no matter what physical hardships had to be suffered:

Day 3: Walked again, but was in great pain, and was finished after two miles. Decided to have one more night's rest and if not able to keep up would send Daniels and Tomasso on without me.

Day 4: Felt better and ribs beginning to knit, so decided to carry on, though every time I fell there was an unpleasant grating noise.

Day 5: Head now normal, took over again from Daniels . . . Moved south parallel with road and railway, and went on railway to recce point of demolition. Chose tunnel which was unguarded.

Day 6: Fixed charge 150 yards inside tunnel and retreated up mountain side. At 2205 we heard a fairly fast train approaching from north. It entered the tunnel and set off charge causing the power lines to short circuit. We were unable to see the results, but judging by the noise, I believe the train to have crashed. No traffic on this line observed during the day. Beginning to get very hungry.

Day 7: Moved off towards the next line . . . Ribs merely hurt now, but not impossibly.

Day 8: Found some potatoes and tomatoes to eke out our rations. Getting very weak through hunger.

Day 10: Getting worse through lack of food. Could only make five miles this night.

Day 12: Failed on this operation. Placed charge on the right-hand lines for southbound train. We were told quite definitely before we left that railway traffic keeps to the right. Train came down on the left line and we blew charge (pull switch) before we could see what happened. One line put out of action temporarily at least.

Day 13: Found grapes and tomatoes . . . Repeated charge about one mile south of previous night with fog signal. Train of twelve mixed goods carriages blew charge.

Day 14: Started south.

Day 15: Rations finished, very weak. Went down to house and acquired a little bread and apples.

Day 18: Reached villa of Marquese Roberti at Fiesole who fed us royally, as her sister happened to be a family friend of mine.

Day 21: Rain worse, wet through now for 48 hours.

Day 23: . . . Put in touch with some partisans.

Day 24: Decided to spend a little time trying to organise these partisans. They had a great deal of armament and much ammunition.

Day 26: Italians a little reluctant to do anything in the way of operations.

Day 28: Bought civilian clothes and went to Florence . . . Had an ice at the Loggia bar in Piazza Michel Angelo. Full of German officers and ORs [Other Ranks], mostly drunk . . . The beer in this bar is very bad.

Day 29: Took Daniels and two Jugoslavs off on an operation against railway north of Incisa.

Day 30: Placed charge which was blown by heavy southbound train.

Day 31: . . . Decided partisans were worthless and were not going to be of any use, so decided to move on.

Day 40: While marching along near village of Foursa, were caught on the road by a German truck. Unterfeldwebel [German soldier of Sergeant rank] got out and opened fire with an automatic. We opened fire with carbines and two Germans surrendered.

These above extracts were taken from his diary as Greville-Bell and his men moved steadily south. By the sixty-first day they were high in the mountains and got lost in a blizzard. Greville-Bell and Daniels suffered from snow blindness. Greville-Bell suffered from frostbite because there was a hole in his boot. A week later, Daniels was severely ill with dysentery.

They reached the German front line on the seventy-third day and passed through safely. Their evasion was a great feat of endurance and just the first of many such epic journeys carried out in Italy by members of the 2nd SAS Regiment. On 21 September 1944, Tony Greville-Bell was awarded the DSO for his outstanding leadership and, in the words of the citation, 'unfailing judgment in most difficult circumstances and inspiration to those under his command'.

Greville-Bell's post-war career in the Army, however, ended on a sour note. David Rooney, the biographer of Brigadier Michael Calvert, DSO, the Chindit commander, gave this insight into Greville-Bell's time in Malaya:

Greville-Bell, a distinguished SAS officer who had won the DSO in the war and who brought B Squadron out to Malaya, became increasingly concerned about the whole set-up of the Malayan Scouts and did not wish to see his fine unit besmirched. He agonized over what he should do, because Calvert appeared to pooh-pooh any criticism. The NCOs of B Squadron had an increasingly difficult time trying to uphold normal discipline in the face of drunken disorder which they often came across in the other Squadron. Tension mounted dangerously when the men who had committed court-martial offences – for example the soldier who assaulted the MO [Medical Officer], or when drunken men put out of the canteen assaulted the Orderly Officer with a loaded rifle – were merely ticked off by Calvert. The anger and the tension can easily be imagined and, in the face of this growing crisis, Greville-Bell, for very proper reasons, complained to General Harding. Harding came to Kuala Lumpur and, following the time-honoured army tradition, interviewed Greville-Bell who received, as he said, 'the biggest bollocking I have ever had in my life.' He felt he was treated as a criminal. In complaining over the head of his CO he had committed what the army considered the unforgivable sin, and in doing so he wrecked what had been a very promising military career. After the interview he was taken away and held incommunicado until he was posted to another area. After this he had a few remote staff postings, but by the mid-1950s he realised that he had no future in the regular SAS or the army and he resigned his commission.

His civilian life, like his military life, was full and varied and he spent some time in Sri Lanka where his father had worked as a tea planter before the war. Greville-Bell wrote several screenplays, three of which were made into films – *Perfect Friday* in 1970, starring Ursula Andress; *Theatre of Blood* in 1973, starring Vincent Price and Diana Rigg; and *The God King*, starring Leigh Lawson and Oliver Tobias, in 1975.

Sculpture had been an interest since his schooldays, and by the late 1980s he was working as a commercial sculptor. His work featured nude female torsos, children's heads and birds. His bronze of a wounded soldier being helped to safety by a comrade, mounted on Portland stone, stands in the SAS Garden of Remembrance.

His musical interests, which began with the flute, led to him eventually forming his own amateur orchestra so that he could play with others. Known as the Learning Orchestra and often performing in St Cyprian's in London's NW1, this began with ten instrumentalists but had reached almost sixty at the time of his death on 4 March 2008, aged eighty-seven. He is survived by his fourth wife, Lauriance Rogier, whom he married in 1996. He had two daughters by his first marriage and one from an earlier relationship.

SERGEANT BRUCE OGDEN-SMITH
Army
AWARDS: MILITARY MEDAL (MM) AND
DISTINGUISHED CONDUCT MEDAL (DCM)
DATE OF BRAVERY: 31 DECEMBER 1943 – 1 JANUARY
1944 AND 18/19 JANUARY 1944
GAZETTED: 2 MARCH 1944 AND 15 JUNE 1944

By the end of 1943, the Allies were actively planning how to invade German-occupied France and thereby create a Second Front. By now, America had entered the war and the Allies were able to plan from a position of strength. Operation Overlord was the codename given to the long-awaited Allied invasion of France. Operation Neptune was, in turn, the codename given to the naval assault phase of Operation Overlord. Its aim was to gain a foothold on the Continent. Once Normandy was secured, the campaign in western Europe and the downfall of Nazi Germany could begin. However, before the details of the invasion could be contemplated, intelligence was needed about the nature of the beaches that the Allies intended to land upon. Enter Sergeant Bruce Ogden-Smith, one of the most courageous and colourful characters of the Second World War.

Ogden-Smith had initially been drawn into the world of clandestine operations by his brother, Colin, who was a Special Forces officer. Bruce Ogden-Smith was a member of the Small Scale Raiding Force (SSRF). On the night of 3/4 October 1942, he was one of seven men from SSRF and five from No. 12 Commando to take part in a daring intelligence-gathering raid to German-occupied Sark in the Channel Islands. Operation Baslat, which used *MTB* (motor torpedo boat) *344*, was a complete success. Local islanders passed on invaluable information to the twelve men and an 'informative' German prisoner was captured and brought back to Britain. One German sentry was killed by Second Lieutenant Anders Lassen – later the posthumous winner of a VC and three MCs – while others were bound and gagged. The German High Command, when they learnt of the operation, took a dim view of events and retaliated by ordering that some recently captured Dieppe raiders should be placed in chains. Ogden-Smith later said, 'We never thought about the significance of what we had done until the press took it up.'

However, it was for another activity that Ogden-Smith became best known and that was secretly swimming to French beaches in the dead of night to gather intelligence – what became known as 'beach reconnaissance'. By this point, Ogden-Smith had joined the Commandos' fledgling Special Boat Section – now better known, under the auspices of the Royal Marines, as the Special Boat Squadron (SBS). He was transferred to the SBS in January 1943 and was actively employed in the Middle East during this year. By the end of 1943, he was back in Europe where he won his DCM and MM in the space of three weeks. He received his MM for Operation KJH, a similar reconnaissance of La Riviere on the night of 31 December 1943 to 1 January 1944. His partner – as when he was later awarded the DCM – was Major Logan Scott-Bowden, who was awarded the Distinguished Service Order (DSO) and Military Cross (MC).

The success – or failure – of the Normandy landings depended on accurate and detailed topographical information about the beaches and coastal towns along the French coast. Aerial photographs helped identify locations but, to get further information, the British Government even appealed to the British public to hand in their holiday photographs and postcards from the relevant parts of coastal France. However, despite cooperation on this matter, much more detailed information on the target beaches and their approaches was still required. The Allies needed to ascertain such things as the composition of the beaches, the depths of certain channels, hidden underwater banks and German defensive operations. In conjunction with details on the tide and weather, these could then be taken into account when planning the landings. The stakes were high – bad intelligence would jeopardise the project and cost lives.

The best account of the heroic activities of Ogden-Smith and Scott-Bowden can be found in *Dawn of D-Day* by David Howarth. The author writes:

> Probably everyone who fought his way ashore on Gold beach believed that they were the first Britons to set foot on it in the past four years, but they were not. Two soldiers had been there, on New Year's Eve. They went ashore . . . and made a survey of the beach in the dark; and although this escapade happened five months before D-Day, it had an influence on what happened that day and so it deserves to be mentioned. The men were two

Commandos called Logan Scott-Bowden and Bruce Ogden-Smith; the first was a major and the second a sergeant, and they were the chief exponents of the curious art of swimming ashore by night and crawling out of the water unobserved.

A small unit for the reconnaissance of beaches had existed for years. Like many odd little fighting units, it owed its existence to the passionate belief of one man. That man was a naval navigator, Lt Cdr Nigel Willmott; and his belief was that it was stupid to land an army anywhere on a hostile shore using only charts and photographs, because there were so many things which neither charts nor photographs could show. One of these things was the hardness of the sand; a matter of obvious interest in landing tanks and trucks . . .

After years of half-hearted support, Willmott found his ideas received with enthusiasm in the highest quarters. Although it was mid-winter, he was told to go ahead and get samples of the material of certain French beaches as quickly as possible. Now that his chance had come, he himself was ill and not fit for winter swimming; but he had trained other swimmers. Scott-Bowden and Ogden-Smith were two of them.

Sergeant Ogden-Smith was the son of a family which had made fishing tackle for nearly 200 years and sold it in a formidably dignified shop among the hatters and bootmakers in the neighbourhood of St. James's Palace. He had had the kind of education which makes it easy, in the British Army, to become an officer. When people asked him why he was not one, he explained that he was quite happy as a sergeant. This was an attitude that had been fashionable in the first year of the war, among the intelligentsia of the Territorial Army, of which he had been a member; but few men stuck to it as a principle, as he did, and resisted the comfort and prestige of being an officer right through the war. Once, he had given in to temptation and started an officers' training course, but he had only been half-hearted and had been returned to his unit when he wrote rude words on an intelligence test which he thought was a waste of time.

When he asked why he made a practice of swimming ashore on hostile beaches, he simply said that he liked it – it was not too bloodthirsty, and yet was quite exciting. In short, Ogden-Smith was one of those brave but eccentric soldiers who can be a great asset to an army if it does not have too many of them: a square peg who had luckily found a square hole.

Through most of the winter and spring before the invasion, whenever there were moonless nights, Scott-Bowden and Ogden-Smith were taken across the Channel to within a few hundred yards of the shore of France by small landing craft or midget submarines . . . The equipment they took was simple: a lot of thought had been needed to make it simple. They wore loose-fitting waterproof suits, and each of them carried a torch, compass and watch, an underwater writing tablet, an auger with which to bore holes in the beach and bring up cores of the material it was made of, receptacles for carrying the cores, some meat skewers, and a reel of fine sand-coloured fishing line with a bead on it at every ten yards. The fishing line and the reel, of course, had been made in Ogden-Smith's father's workshops. They also took a fighting knife and a .45 Colt, which they had found to be one of the few firearms which still work when they are full of salt water and sand; but they relied more for their safety on the hypothesis that only an exceptionally wakeful sentry would see a man swimming in surf or crawling on a beach at night.

When the shore was in sight on these expeditions . . . they slipped over the side of the boat and struck out for the breakers together. It was always extremely cold. When they felt [the] bottom, they waded to the edge of the surf and lay there to get their bearings and study the skyline till they were sure of the movements of the sentries; and then, if everything was reasonably quiet, they stuck a skewer in the sand with the end of the fishing line tied to it, and started to crawl on their stomachs up the beach, probing for mines and unwinding the line as they went. At each bead on the line, they bored a hole and took a sample, and skewered the line again and crawled on, on a compass bearing.

In this way they made passably accurate surveys of a great many beaches. They found it difficult, after several months to remember which beach was which; but they did remember their landing at La Riviere because it was there that Ogden-Smith had suddenly remembered the date, and noticed that it was midnight, and had taken into his head to crawl to where the Major was lying listening to the conversation of two sentries on the sea wall, and in a stage whisper had wished him a happy and prosperous New Year.

Sometimes they did other work beside looking for mud and clay. They measured the gradients of beaches, and charted sandbars offshore where landing craft might have stranded; and here and there they went inland to measure and investigate obstacles beyond the beaches . . . In the middle of January they were on top of the fatal shingle bank at Omaha. They made an entirely uneventful tour of Utah; but on a second visit to Omaha, a sentry came along the beach between them and the sea and tripped over their fishing line. It was through this accident, exciting at the time, that the American Army was able to land with the assurance that the beach was not mined; because if it had [been], the sentry would not have been there. The two men bore a charmed life. They were not only never seen, but every time, when they finished their probing, they waded out through the waves again and swam three hundred yards to sea and flashed their torches away from the land and waited, and every time, before cold and cramp and exhaustion crippled them, their boat came in and picked them up again. In the quest for mud, they swam ashore on thirty beaches.

The result of this unique performance was to be seen in the plans of specialised armour . . . General [Omar] Bradley had been worried by a suspicious patch on the photographs of Omaha. He had never heard of beach reconnaissance, but he asked British Intelligence whether anything was known about the texture of the beach. The inquiry was passed to Willmott. Without telling the General, he sailed across and landed Scott-Bowden and Ogden-Smith and the next day he attended an American conference and produced a small sample of the sand from his pocket, explaining that his unit had fetched it the night before, and that the beach was firm and would carry tanks all right. This achievement amazed General Bradley, and he generously said so . . .

As for Ogden-Smith, his wife received an invitation to an investiture at Buckingham Palace, where he was to receive the Military Medal, although nobody told her what he had done to earn it. The date of the investiture was 6 June 1944 [the date of the D-Day landings]. On June 5th, she had already put on her best hat and was on her way to the railway station in Wales when she received a telephone message to say that her husband was unavoidably detained and would not be turning up to meet the King. Nothing surprised her by then. She went home, and sadly put away the hat again, hoping she would need it to go to the Palace one day.

It would have been quite in character for this curious soldier to have been late for his own investiture, but in fact it was hardly his fault. He and Scott-Bowden were on Omaha Beach again:

this time not alone. The American Army had taken them there as guides. They were the only people in England, so far as anyone knew, who had ever been there before.

Ogden-Smith's MM had been announced in the *London Gazette* of 2 March 1944. Owing to the clandestine nature of the mission and the fact that the war was still on, it was announced, along with awards to four others, under a general heading 'in recognition of gallant and distinguished services in the field'. His DCM was gazetted on 15 June 1944 and was announced, along with three others, for the same 'gallant and distinguished services in the field'. However, the original recommendation for this award was made for services with the Combined Operations Pilotage Party at Normandy and states:

> In spite of feeling in bad physical condition, Sergeant Ogden-Smith showed courage, coolness and ability in assisting Major Scott-Bowden to carry out the first experimental beach reconnaissance from 'X Craft', which entailed amongst other things swimming on to vigilantly defended enemy beaches and moving about there 'under the nose' of sentries on two consecutive nights, the 18th and 19th January 1944.

At the end of the war, Ogden-Smith is believed to have returned to his home in Wales, where his wife had been working in a factory during the war. He died in December 1986.

This wonderful man was, fortunately, a hoarder so when, in September 2006, his medals came up for auction at Dix Noonan Webb, the auctioneers who specialise in coins and medals, they were accompanied by some interesting artefacts. These included several small pieces of fabric taken from a kayak used by Ogden-Smith and Scott-Bowden off Normandy; his original

Commando fighting knife used as a silent weapon and for probing mines; and his specially adapted fishing reel and line as made at his father's workshops and taken to Normandy to assist in beach contours. It was the same reel and line that had once been stood on by that enemy sentry on Omaha beach.

4

OMAN, MOGADISHU AND
THE IRANIAN EMBASSY SIEGE

Oman

In the three decades after the Second World War, Oman was a major trouble spot. Sultan Said bin Taimur ruled Oman in 1950 and he saw Britain as his country's natural and staunch ally. Britain had signed a treaty with the Sultan of Muscat as long ago as 1789, giving the East India Company certain commercial rights in return for Britain guaranteeing the Royal Navy's protection. In 1950, oil was discovered in Oman – a turning point that would eventually make the desert peninsula one of the richest areas in the world. However, in the 1950s, it made it one of the most unstable areas on earth.

By 1957, a Saudi Arabia-backed uprising had developed into open revolt. The Imam of Oman, Ghalib bin Ali, and his brother, Talib, sought to overthrow the Sultan. The rebels were entrenched in the mountainous plateau of Jebel Akhdar and, although they had few direct followers, they had formed a powerful alliance with Sheikh Suleiman bin Himyar and his tribe. It was the Sheikh and his men who effectively controlled the area. As the situation became more desperate, the Sultan appealed to Britain for help and the government responded by switching SAS units from Malaya to Oman in 1958 for what was to become the two-year Jebel Akhdar campaign. In 1959, after heavy fighting and clever diversionary tactics, the SAS seized the 'impregnable' Jebel Akhdar, known as the Green Mountain. Victory, however, came at a price – the lives of three of its soldiers. Colonel Tony Deane-Drummond, the Commanding Officer of 22 SAS Regiment, was awarded the Distinguished Service Order (DSO) for planning the operation and there were four Military Crosses (MC), including one for a then young and upcoming officer called Peter de la Billière, who would later command the British forces in the first Gulf War.

A decade or so later, trouble flared in Oman once again, and from 1970 to 1976 the conflict was looked upon by many as a classic SAS operation. In his book The Complete History of the SAS: The Story of the World's Most Feared Special Forces, *Nigel McCrery writes: 'Both militarily and politically the war had far reaching effects on the whole of the Middle East. Moreover, the success of the SAS and the Sultan of Oman's forces helped stabilise the attitude of many neighbouring countries, pushing back the tide of communism which had threatened to engulf the rich oilfields on which the West depends. It offered a challenge which the Regiment eagerly accepted, and turned out to be a classic counter-insurgency campaign of modern times.'*

On 23 July 1970, the Sultan of Oman's son Qaboos – a product of the Royal Military Academy, Sandhurst – ousted his father in a bloodless coup. Within weeks the SAS was sent to Oman to provide the new ruler with advice and assistance. At the time, the country was in turmoil and a huge mountain range in the province of Dhofar was a particular trouble spot, with heavy 'adoo' (Arabic for enemy forces). The enemy forces were led by the People's Front for the Liberation of the Occupied Arabian Gulf (PFLOAG). The SAS fought alongside the 'firqats', Dhofari irregulars from mountain and coastal villages and towns, such as Taqa and Mirbat, which were often attacked by rebel forces.

Much of the fighting was ferocious, including the battle that launched Operation Jaguar in October 1971 – a successful attempt to establish a base on the Jebel Dhofar, which the SAS nicknamed 'Porkchop Hill'. They were soon attacked by a substantial force of adoo *and the battle raged for four days, but after the SAS called in the Sultan of Oman's Air Force for support, the enemy were eventually forced to withdraw. Over the next year, and with more fierce fighting, the SAS consolidated its position, established further outposts and set out to sever the enemy's lines of communications and resupply, and to win the 'hearts and minds' of the Jebel people. On 19 July 1972, a 250-strong rebel force attacked the port of Mirbat on the southern coast of Oman, which was protected by an old fort. A small SAS unit stationed in the town operated the fort and the main gun, eventually winning the day. This incident turned the tide of the conflict. At the end of 1974 and early in 1975, the SAS fought another great engagement in Dhofar, which became known as the Shirshitti Caves operation, and by 1976, the war was over. Nigel McCrery writes: 'It cannot be said that the SAS won this war on its own, for much of the fighting was done by the Sultan of Oman's own forces. However one thing the SAS did undeniably was to bond together the* firqats, *the Dhofari irregulars. These* firqats *and the SAS went on to become the lead elements in most battles in the early days. It was the trust between the Dhofaris and the SAS which won the Dhofar war.' During the six years the SAS were engaged in Oman, the Regiment lost twelve men.*

LANCE CORPORAL JOHN HAWKINS
Army (SAS)
AWARD: DISTINGUISHED CONDUCT MEDAL (DCM)
DATE OF BRAVERY: 30 NOVEMBER 1958 AND 27/28
DECEMBER 1958
GAZETTED: 25 AUGUST 1959

John Hawkins's DCM was announced on the same day as Lieutenant Peter de la Billière's MC. The *London Gazette* of 25 August 1959 revealed that de la Billière was awarded his Military Cross 'For his leadership, courage and determination as a troop commander, in action against a tough enemy in very difficult country. He found and raided a cave used by a large rebel party inflicting heavy losses upon them.'

The same issue acknowledged the bravery of Hawkins thus: 'For courageous and determined leadership in the face of rebel fire. By skilfully withholding the fire of his men he decisively defeated an attack by well armed rebels. On another occasion he bravely exposed himself to throw grenades and thereby succeeded in subduing the enemy's fire. His conduct was an inspiration to his men.'

Hawkins displayed this inspired leadership when he and his men were caught up in a fierce 'contact' on an 8,000ft peak in Aqbat. Hawkins was known to his friends as 'Herbie' and his actions in battle were considered so memorable that the peak was renamed 'Herbie's Hump' and the firefight became known as the 'Battle of Herbie's Hump'. Hawkins's bravery came at a time when he and his comrades from D Squadron had just returned from jungle operations in Malaya, where they had also seen action and where Hawkins had received a commendation from his Commander-in-Chief. Such was the urgency with which D Squadron was required in Oman to fight the rebels that it was forced to retrain and be on the ground in just fifteen days. The decision to move D Squadron to Oman was taken by Lieutenant Colonel Anthony Deane-Drummond, the commanding officer of 22 SAS. Not only was Deane-Drummond a veteran of Arnhem, but he had eluded captivity after that operation by hiding for three days in the cupboard of a German-occupied house.

It was on the peak at Aqbat – part of the Jebal Akhdar area – that Hawkins's qualities of courage and nerve became apparent. He managed to repulse a determined attack by a forty-strong enemy force, even though he had just five men (some accounts say nine) at his disposal. He held the fire of his men until the enemy was just over 100 metres away. After the shooting started, the enemy was quickly dispersed by the accuracy of the fire. In his book *Who Dares Wins: The Special Air Service, 1950 to the Gulf War*, Tony Geraghty wrote: 'The sergeant ordered the men to hold their fire. When the enemy was 120 yards away, they let loose a barrage of Bren [gun] and rifle fire, killing five men and injuring another four. The attack disintegrated.'

The once-confidential internal recommendation relating to Hawkins's DCM gives more details of his conduct than the shorter announcement in the *London Gazette*. It said of his conduct: 'The personal example and coolness displayed by the NCO contributed greatly to the moral ascendance of the SAS troops over the rebels in this area.' It also provided more details of Hawkins's bravery nearly a month later at Sabrina:

> On the night of 27/28 Dec., Sgt Hawkins was again a member of a raiding party which penetrated the main rebel position 3,000 yards in front of our own FDLs {forward defensive lines}. When the patrol was discovered, rebel picquets commenced accurate fire from above at very close range. This NCO with little regard for his own safety stood up and threw grenades into the rebel positions causing the fire to slacken at once and finally cease. Sgt Hawkins continually exposed himself to great danger and his leadership and determination has been an inspiration to all under his command.

Hawkins died on 14 April 2007 at his home in Crawley, West Sussex.

STAFF SERGEANT (LATER MAJOR) ARTHUR WRIGHT*

Army (SAS)

AWARDS: BRITISH EMPIRE MEDAL (BEM) AND MEMBER OF THE ORDER OF THE BRITISH EMPIRE (MBE)
DATE OF BRAVERY: NOT SPECIFIC
GAZETTED: 1969 AND 1971

Few members of the SAS write their memoirs. Still fewer sit down in front of a typewriter long after their career has ended to

---

* name changed at the request of the medals' recipient.

record their thoughts solely for their own family. However, Arthur Wright is one of them – eventually writing his unpublished and incomplete memoirs for his wife, sons, daughters-in-law and grandchildren. Wright wrote that as his memory was never great and unlikely to improve, he would record as much as he could so that his grandchildren would know where their father's stupidity was inherited from.

In fact, Wright's memory of his career proved to be astonishingly good. His honest, vivid and, at times, very humorous, memoirs began:

> On the 9th of June 1935 I made my world entrance. This happy event took place at 92, Maclellan Street in the district of Kinning Park in Glasgow, although much later if asked, I would always give Ibrox as the answer if questioned where I was from. Ibrox adjoined us and, apart from the name having a better tone to it, most people knew where Glasgow Rangers played. This saved me giving long winded explanations as to where Kinning Park was exactly. Maclellan Street's only claim to fame besides me being born there is that it was the longest street in Glasgow without a break. This useless fact, we Maclellan Street dwellers were fond of relating to any one else in Glasgow who was unlucky enough to have been born in a shorter street.

The son of a ships' painter and one of five children, Wright was evacuated from Glasgow during the Second World War. It was at this time that he remembers watching a dogfight off the Scottish coast between three Spitfires and a lone German aircraft, which ended with the latter being hit and its pilot parachuting into the sea – and to a new life as a PoW. Just days later, however, he was 'capturing a brace of enemy myself' when an enemy bomber narrowly missed a row of houses and crashed into a field. He was the only one of a group of children to approach them – both friendly – before the Home Guard turned up to take them away. Wright left school at 15 and started 'soul destroying' work in a factory three days later. He then worked as an apprentice engineer before enlisting into the Army in the summer of 1953, shortly after his eighteenth birthday. He wrote: 'My medical examination had gone all right and I had to give three choices with whom I would like to serve for my two years. I answered "Cameronians, Cameronians, Cameronians" and so it was no great surprise to receive a letter later telling me that I would serve with the REME, REME, REME.' REME stands for Royal Electrical and Mechanical Engineers.

It was on a whim, after being flown to serve in Egypt, that Wright applied to join the SAS at a time when it was a little-known unit. Later, he recalls, he received good and bad news: the former was that his SAS posting order had come through, the latter was that he should have arrived with the Regiment long ago and had now been officially declared a deserter. Wright was told to take a troop ship from Port Said pier on 16 September 1954 and disembark in Singapore, then make his way to Kuala Lumpur, Malaya, and report to 22 SAS Regiment. It was only on arrival that he learnt he had to pass a tough selection course, which others had failed on their first day. Wright, however, passed the course and then embarked on SAS training in the jungle.

On 9 January 1959 – four years to the day since he had boarded a plane for the first time – Wright landed in a hot desert landscape that looked like Egypt, which had been the first foreign country he had ever visited. He was met by Major Johnny Watts, the commander of D Squadron, who, with a broad grin, welcomed him to Azaiba airfield, Sultanate of Oman. Positioned along the airfield was a line of trucks, the floors of which were covered in sandbags. Wright and his comrades realised these were intended as anti-mine protection – and that they had effectively entered a war zone. Soon the men, after some desert training, learnt they were moving from Muscat, the capital, to the Jebel Akhdar.

Here they had a number of contacts with the enemy, during their night patrols when they attacked the Aqabat (known to the SAS as 'Sabrina', a well-known starlet of the day, because in Wright's words, the mountain had 'two big tits on it'). Their task was to probe the enemy's defences until they came under fire and then to retire.

One night, after a mission, the men were returning in pitch dark when, unable to see, Wright fell some ten feet into a sandy *wadi* bottom. He was just about to climb back up when the enemy opened fire from about twenty feet away. A fierce fire fight took place with Wright left stranded in the middle. He called out for his troop to cease fire, which they must have heard because the troop quickly became silent. Wright wrote: 'I called out that I was coming up, turned and emptied my magazine at the flashes on the other side of the bank. This must have surprised them so much that their firing abruptly stopped and I shot up our bank like a man possessed and rolled over amongst the troop. I remember Soldier A [name removed – his comrade] asking in mock surprise: "Where have you been, Arthur? We thought you had gone to join them!"'

This incident was followed by a more major contact which, although the SAS did not know it at the time, was to prove the turning point in their conflict with the rebel fighters. Wright and his comrades headed for 'Sabrina' as usual one night. However, instead of withdrawing as usual, as soon as they came under fire, the plan was to press home the attack. Setting off at midnight, later than usual, Wright's troop led the way and the other troops followed. When they were halfway to their destination, they dropped off the Officer Commanding (OC) and mortar rounds. Then as silently as possible, they climbed the slope leading up to the 'two tits', expecting the usual burst of fire. But nothing happened: as the ground levelled off, everyone realised they were now on top of the main ridge.

Suddenly, there was a hail of bullets and grenades from in front of the advancing party. Almost immediately, Wright heard the call for a medic and, looking to his right, saw a comrade stand up holding his wounded shoulder. Wright ran to the man, who had been hit by a grenade, and told him to go to the rear of the troop where a medic would tend to his injuries.

Wright knew that his injured comrade had been the number two on the Bren gun and so he immediately took his place. Wright could also see where the main enemy fire was coming from: some twenty yards ahead was a large rock and, coming from all around it was a steady stream of flashes. When some enemy fire put the Bren gun out of action, Wright ordered his comrades to stop firing, indicating he was going to take matters into his own hands.

Wright wrote: 'I casually walked forward knowing the rounds that were being fired at me would all miss. All firing stopped as I got to within a few feet of the rock. I raised my FN rifle to shoulder high firing position and raised my head to the level of the top of the rock and waited. I only waited for a few seconds and I saw the silhouette of a rifle barrel rising vertically above the top of the rock, followed by a face appearing. I said "good morning", stuck the muzzle of my rifle in his left eye and pulled the trigger twice. He had just started to smile as I saw the *shemag* wrapped around his head jump as my bullets tore their way through.'

Wright's blood was up and he scrambled on to the top of the rock and opened fire at more of the enemy. Eventually, he walked calmly back to his troop and shouted to them not to fire at him by mistake. Wright informed the troop commander that the party could now advance because he had just killed the enemy's leader and seen off the rest of the dead man's comrades. However, as the British force continued to advance, the enemy opened fire on them again, but it appeared to be coming from a rocky outcrop ahead of and about fifteen feet above the SAS men. Wright wrote: 'In the flashing illumination of one of the enemy's grenades going off nearby, I saw an enemy [fighter] frozen in the act of climbing up the side. I ran forward and pumped three rounds into the centre of his back.' When everything eventually went quiet, the British party concluded accurately that the enemy had fled: Sabrina was in the hands of the SAS for the first time.

Within days, the war was over, although not before one more incident that Wright recalled with relish. On one occasion a shot rang out forcing all the SAS men to dive for cover behind the nearest rocks. However, the OC refused to share his rock with Wright and instead pushed him out into the open. Wright scrambled to shelter behind a much smaller rock as everyone peered ahead to see where the enemy was firing from. Wright recalls being asked by the OC to 'Stand up and draw their fire!' Wright was less than thrilled by the request so responded: 'Go and shag your granny.' However, it then emerged that a young SAF [Sultan's Armed Forces] officer had fired the shots to stop the party walking into a minefield. As he had laid the minefield, he was able to lead the SAS men through it safely.

Wright was awarded the BEM in 1969 for repeated acts

of gallantry, most noticeably his bravery in Oman. His recommendation, which was originally secret, read:

SSgt [Staff Sergeant] Wright transferred from REME to the Special Air Service Regiment thirteen years ago. During his service with 22 Special Air Service Regiment he has been almost constantly on operations and has seen much action in Borneo, South Arabia, Muscat and Oman and against the terrorists in deep jungle operations in Malaya. In one instant in the Oman operations of 1959, he personally killed a terrorist who was, with great bravery, holding up the final SAS assault to control a vital part of the Jebel Akhdar.

SSgt Wright has given such a splendid and outstanding continuous active service to the Regiment that a few highlights should be mentioned. After attending an Arabic course at London University he made it his business to fully understand Arab affairs and problems and during 1962 served alone among the Arab tribes and Federal Guards Unit of South Arabia taking part in their local operations. He was frequently the only white man in the area. After one tour of highly classified operations in Borneo, SSgt Wright returned to the Middle East where he operated well inside dissident territory during periods of 1964 leading a small SAS group, mostly in the Radfan area, during the height of the troubles.

SSgt Wright returned again to South Arabia in 1966 and because of his particular skills, SAS aptitudes and outstanding qualities of leadership he was employed on purely intelligence missions within South Arabia on hazardous tasks of a high political nature and acting entirely alone. The information he gained was of particular value to the high command and other agencies and his standard of reporting, even under the most trying conditions, was of an exceptionally high order. SSgt

Wright worked under particularly dangerous conditions affecting his own personal security. He was under suspicion by certain elements and was watched and shadowed. He was undoubtedly in danger of assassination whilst living alone with the Arabs at this time. Nevertheless, he carried out his tasks quite unperturbed, and continued to transmit his information and whereabouts in a calm and professional manner. His whole security and personal position was aggravated at this period by the critical phase of the British withdrawal from up country in South Arabia, together with the racial feelings and tensions that were running high. His methods of dealing with the local population and armed forces, his diplomatic but firm approach, and his quick reaction to difficult and potentially explosive situations saved him on a number of occasions.

Since then, with very little respite, SSgt Wright has just returned from a further mission abroad to another country where he has carried out, as part of a very small specialist training team, certain covert instruction to a friendly country. This was a mission which was very highly politically charged and once more [with] his conduct, powers of diplomacy and leadership and his extremely high instructional ability he proved [to have] outstanding qualities and devotion to duty.

His service in the Army, and the Special Air Service in particular, during the last thirteen years has been of an outstanding and exemplary nature. He has been on almost constant operations in varied theatres often working alone or in small groups and has shown courage, initiative and patriotism well beyond the normal call of duty. His patience and understanding of difficult political and military problems has been outstanding for a person of his rank and seniority.

Just over a decade later, Wright found himself being flown once again to Oman, this time as the bodyguard and advisor to the Sultan of Oman, Qaboos bin Said, who had overthrown his father in the bloodless coup of 1970. It was a hazardous mission and, amid the turmoil of the time, the new Sultan and Wright were constantly in danger of being assassinated. However, Wright completed his six-month task, from July 1970 to January 1971, which was top secret and classified as a 'deniable' operation. On Wright's return, Edward Heath, the Conservative prime minister of the day, personally instructed that he should be awarded the MBE.

Wright rose to the rank of major and was discharged in May 1988 after nearly thirty-five years' service, thirty-four with the SAS. In February 1983, Wright was one of the serving SAS soldiers invited by the then Brigadier (later General Sir) Peter de la Billière to meet Margaret Thatcher at a private dinner. The black tie event was described, in the letter of invitation, as 'a unique, private, and I am sure, delightful and formal evening'. Wright is now retired and living in Spain.

TROOPER (LATER STAFF SERGEANT) SEKONAIA TAKAVESI
Army (SAS)
AWARD: DISTINGUISHED CONDUCT MEDAL (DCM)
DATE OF BRAVERY: 19 JULY 1972
GAZETTED: 9 APRIL 1974

Soldiers do not come any tougher, or more fearless and loyal, than Sekonaia Takavesi. Known as 'Sek' or 'Tak' to his friends, he became – in the words of his Army superiors – 'a legend in his own time within the SAS'. Takavesi was born in Fiji in 1943. Brought up on the Pacific island, he enlisted in the British Army on 13 November 1961, joining the King's Own Border

Regiment. Two years later, he successfully sought selection to the SAS.

Takavesi had undertaken invaluable and dangerous undercover surveillance in Aden during the mid-1960s. At one time, he and fellow Fijian, Trooper Talaiasi Labalaba, had confronted and shot dead two terrorist gunmen. However, it was in Oman in July 1972 that the same two men were given the opportunity to display their immense courage and determination. By this time, the *adoo* rebels were looking for a major military victory after a series of setbacks in their conflict with the Sultan's troops and their SAS allies. On the morning of 19 July 1972, the *adoo* launched a carefully planned attack with the aim of using 250 of their most élite fighters to capture the small town of Mirbat on the Arabian Sea. They were heavily armed with a powerful Carl Gustav gun, mortars, RPG-7s (rocket-propelled grenades), Kalashnikov assault rifles, heavy machine-guns and hand grenades. Their aim was to overrun the town and slaughter everyone in their path.

The enemy's attack on the garrison began at dawn and their intelligence sources had indicated correctly that it was not heavily defended. In fact, the garrison was equipped with one 25-pounder gun from the Second World War, one mortar, a .50mm calibre machine-gun and a few general purpose machine-guns. There were just nine SAS soldiers in the town, who were staying in the British Army training team (BATT) house. The property was within a compound and some 400 metres from the small fort built to defend the town and some 500 metres from the gun-pit containing the 25-pounder.

The *adoo* attack came during the monsoon season on a day when it was raining lightly and with low cloud cover. Their first target was a small detachment of Dhofar Gendamerie (DG) occupying a picquet, or watch point, about 1,000 metres north of the fort. The rebels had hoped to kill the eight DG members quickly and quietly by slitting their throats, but things had not gone to plan and an exchange of fire was heard by the SAS in the garrison. Captain Mike Kealy, their commander, was able to see waves of *adoo* advancing towards the BATT, and was soon barking orders, including to Takavesi to ensure the .81mm mortar was used to support the DG outpost. A signaller was told to communicate with SAS headquarters at Um al Quarif (also spelt Um Al Gwarif). Meanwhile, Labalaba ran the fifty metres to the gun-pit in order to man the 25-pounder. Other SAS, armed with machine-guns, began firing on the enemy from the roof of the fort. Within a short time, a heavy firefight was raging in several areas of the town and ten-man squads of *adoo* were ready to advance from one target to the next. A detailed and vivid account of Takavesi and Labalaba's actions is provided by Pete Scholey in his book *SAS Heroes: Remarkable Soldiers, Extraordinary Men*. Scholey is a former SAS soldier who served alongside, and was friendly with, both men.

Scholey describes how Labalaba was in the gun-pit aiming, loading and firing the 25-pounder single-handedly, even though, for maximum effect, it would usually be manned by a team of five men. He did not underestimate the importance of his role or his position. If the gun was captured, the *adoo* would be left to sweep through the town. As Labalaba kept up a relentless fire, his shirt was soon drenched in sweat and blackened with powder. The gun was capable of firing high-explosive rounds more than three miles. Labalaba, however, was sighting the gun down the barrel and firing into the advancing men at near point-blank range from behind an armoured shield.

Almost inevitably, Labalaba was eventually seriously wounded by a 7.62mm round from a Kalashnikov rifle. 'I've been chinned but I am okay,' he said over the walkie-talkie.

Knowing his friend would not bother to report a minor injury, Takavesi was determined to go to his aid. He grabbed his self-loading rifle (SLR) and a few magazines and ran from the BATT house to the gun-pit. His comrades gave him covering fire but he nevertheless ran into a hail of bullets. Takavesi was, however, formerly a top-class rugby player and he dodged and weaved his way to his destination before leaping into the gun-pit. Labalaba was in bad shape. He had used a shell dressing, now blood soaked, to tie around his face but the bullet had smashed his jaw. Yet still he continued to fire the gun. Takavesi decided the two men needed more manpower so he leapt from the gun-pit and dashed to the fort. There he persuaded Walid Khamis, an Omani gunner, to race back with him to the gun-pit. There were now three men holding off the *adoo* – Labalaba and Khamis were operating the 25-pounder, while Takavesi used his SLR.

As enemy fire pounded the gun-pit, Walid slumped backwards. He had been shot in the stomach and was writhing in agony. The two Fijians were on their own again, with Takavesi now helping his friend, time and again, to remove the hot shell case, ram in a new one, close the breech and fire. Soon it was Takavesi's turn to take a bullet, which threw him backwards on to the sandbags. He was in great pain and losing a lot of blood, but he remained conscious. Labalaba propped him up and handed him his SLR. Labalaba, who was peering down his rifle-sights picking off the advancing enemy, realised he was almost out of ammunition for the 25-pounder. As he tried to reach a 60mm mortar positioned nearby, he was shot fatally in the neck.

Back in the BATT house, Kealy heard the 25-pounder fall silent and became worried the position had been taken. With a volunteer, Tommy Tobin, a trained medic, the commanding officer dodged bullets and ran to the gun-pit where they witnessed a gruesome scene. The dead body of Labalaba lay face down on the ground, Khamis was lying on his back, bleeding profusely. The only one still able to fire was Takavesi, who, still propped on the sandbags, was also seriously wounded. Every time he fired his SLR, he grimaced with pain as the rifle kicked back into his body. As Tobin turned to get his medical pack, he was shot in the face, receiving serious injuries from which he later died.

Scholey, who was provided with eyewitness accounts of the events at Mirbat, wrote:

> Tak called to Captain Kealy for more ammunition and the two men began a desperate battle for their lives. An *adoo* popped up at the edge of the gun emplacement, ready to shoot Tak, and Kealy blasted him with his SLR. Another appeared from a ditch close to their position and Kealy cut him down, too. Kealy took out *adoo* gunmen as they slunk round the walls of the fort and Tak concentrated on those coming from the direction of the perimeter wire. Although the 25pdr was no longer firing, it was clearly a primary target for the *adoo* as rounds clanged into its metalwork like hammer blows. The *adoo* were now close enough to sling grenades, which were bouncing and exploding close to the walls of the gun-pit. Kealy froze for an instant as a grenade landed inside the bunker right in front of him. Mercifully, it failed to explode.

Just as the situation appeared hopeless – and the enemy were just twenty metres from the gun-pit – the two men and their comrades had two strokes of luck. The first was that the cloud had lifted slightly, high enough to enable two jets from the Sultan of Oman's Air Force to fly low over the scene, strafing the *adoo* with cannon fire. The pilots had to fly their aircraft with great precision – the cloud base was at just 150 feet, so they had to hug the ground, fire and then peel off into the cloud before coming around again. Kealy was able to relay instructions on the enemy's positions – and therefore where the jets should fire – via a walkie-talkie to the BATT house, from where the instructions could be radioed to the pilots. Slowly but surely, the *adoo* were forced to retreat. Many took refuge in a *wadi*, which was then hit directly with a 500lb bomb dropped by one of the jets. Kealy and his men knew, however, that the BAC Strikemaster jets would not be able to stay around forever. One was eventually hit by machine-gun fire from the *adoo* and, trailing smoke, was forced to limp back to its airbase and crash land. It was followed, shortly afterwards, by the second jet, which was low on fuel and out of ammunition.

Kealy was unaware of the second stroke of luck, which resulted from his early radio message to SAS headquarters in Um al Quarif that Mirbat was under attack. The men of B Squadron in Mirbat had been due to go home on the very day of the attack. This meant their replacements from G Squadron were already at Um al Quarif, on the outskirts of Salalah, the southern regional capital, which is some sixty-five kilometres west of Mirbat. G Squadron was ordered into action. Twenty-two men were taken, along with their equipment, by trucks to the airstrip at Salalah. Once the mist had lifted, they were airlifted in helicopters to the beach on the edge of Mirbat. As Kealy used a lull in the fighting to tend to his wounded men, it still looked as though it would be just a matter of time before the *adoo* swept in and slaughtered all the SAS men. In fact, by now, G Squadron, led by Captain Alastair Morrison, had fought its way through the town and the *adoo* were in full retreat, leaving behind forty dead and ten wounded.

In an article for *Medal News* magazine published in 2006, Ron Gittings writes: 'It had been a close run thing, had the *adoo* chosen a different day, or a different location to attack, the outcome may have been very different. They say that fortune favours the brave; it was certainly on the right side this day . . .'

The once-confidential recommendation for Takavesi's gallantry award did justice to the courage – and led to him being awarded the DCM. The recommendation also made clear just how important victory had been that day and also revealed just how brave Takavesi had been to the very end:

> At 0530 hours on the morning of the 19th July mortars started to rain in on the Mirbat Garrison. The garrison was stood to and under Captain Kealy's direction commenced the battle for the town. For over four hours the Communists pressed home their attack; they infiltrated the town; they destroyed the stone defences with RCL [recoilless weapons systems], rocket launcher and mortar fire; they concentrated a major effort against the SAS personnel in the town; they closed to grenade range and fought with a ferocity, tenacity and blind dedication that is the mark of all Communist shock troops. They launched this attack with an estimated 250 men against a small garrison town whose defence was designed to repel attacks from no more than a dozen men acting without determination. It was only after four hours of continuous and ferocious fighting that they finally admitted defeat, leaving behind some 40 wounded and killed. A subsequent radio intercept indicates that they suffered at least 86 casualties and subsequent intelligence reports indicate that this figure may be as high as 100 or more.
>
> On the morning of the 19th July the enemy opened a highly effective and concentrated fire from mortar and RCL pieces onto the town of Mirbat. Tpr Takavesi, together with Cpl Labalaba, had the responsibility for manning the 25pdr. It should be pointed out that none of these two soldiers had any previous

artillery training other than a two-day course on the mechanics of handling this particular gun. Under heavy and accurate mortar fire Takavesi, together with Labalaba, covered the 500 yards of the main SAS position to the Dhofar Gendamerie fort, where the 25pdr was sited. Quickly and effectively they brought it into action.

It soon became clear that the enemy considered the 25pdr to be a key objective in the initial stages of the attack and they demonstrated this by concentrating an effective and accurate fire at the crew with all their available weapons. Subsequent debriefing of captured enemy personnel confirmed this impression and made it clear that the enemy intended to capture the gun, man it with their trained crews and turn it on the town. They had not bargained with Takavesi and Labalaba.

The battle continued to rage around the 25pdr position while Takavesi, quite undaunted, continued with his task of firing the weapon over open sights and at point blank range. Inevitably, he was wounded, the bullet entering his right shoulder and passing through both lungs and finally lodging in his left shoulder, while a second bullet gave him a nasty wound in the back of the head. He continued to assist as far as his wounds permitted him. Eventually when they had been dressed he wedged himself between the gun and some sandbags in a half-lying, half-sitting position from which he could cover a vital enemy approach around the corner of the fort some thirty metres from the position. For over two hours he prevented the enemy from rushing the position by firing his SLR at anyone who was foolish enough to come within his sights.

Eventually Cpl Labalaba was killed and the only able-bodied British soldier remaining in the position was Captain Kealy – Tobin, the Medical Orderly having been severely wounded and rendered unconscious. Thus Takavesi's continued resistance was essential for the maintenance of the position and it was only by his determined, continuous and resolute defence on this particular flank that the position was not lost. For over two hours he prevented the enemy from rushing the position by effective use of his SLR and thus supported his Troop Officer to his right. Takavesi displayed, throughout this period, the greatest calmness and bravery, for not only was he severely wounded, but was under intensive enemy fire including grenade attack. His gallant action prevented the enemy from capturing the gun position and this in turn denied them the prize of Mirbat itself.

In the end he refused to be casevaced [evacuated] until all the other wounded had been taken out by helicopter. When he finally staggered to the aircraft he refused any form of support from other people. The seriousness of his injuries may be judged by the fact that he remained on the VSI [very seriously injured] list for some two weeks after the incident.

Takavesi eventually talked about his own role when Jack Ramsay interviewed him for his book *SAS: The Soldiers' Story*. Takavesi told how he felt compelled to support Labalaba, when his friend radioed to say that he had been 'chinned'.

That was enough for me. I had to join him, so I picked up my SLR and started to run. I ran up the hill, dodging as much as I could, taking cover when I had to. They were advancing and the firing was getting heavier all the time, but I had to get there because Laba was on his own with the Omani artillery and I didn't know how many of them were with him at the time. I got to the top and crawled in to where Laba was and he was alone. Normally it takes three men to fire the gun and he was doing it all by himself. When he said he had been chinned he meant he'd been grazed by a bullet, either a ricochet or a direct hit.

Takavesi told how he went to get help and Walid Khamis returned with him, but once his comrade was wounded, it was just the two Fijians on their own.

When Laba and I were firing, we were really under heavy attack. As soon as you put your head up you could hear the bullets whistling by. It was so close. We literally had to crawl to be able to do anything. We'd crawl and load the gun, fire it and then crawl down and do it again. It was ridiculous. They were almost on top of us, shooting from all directions. At least we could hear on the radio that our comrades back in the house were still okay. It was getting very, very fierce, and Laba and I were joking in Fijian. All the fear seemed to go away. We knew the gun was their main target and we were still firing at point-blank range. We had no time to aim. All we could do was pick up a round, load it in and fire as quickly as we could. But the guerrillas were coming closer and closer towards us, and at the end we had to abandon it. You can't fire a 25-pounder at 50 metres. You'd just get metal fragments in your face. And we had to cover ourselves.

I heard the crack of a gun. Something hit my shoulder and the shock knocked me over for a few seconds. I really didn't know where I was. I totally curled up. The clearest way of describing it is like an elephant charging at you at 120 miles an hour, with a sharp, pointed trunk.

Laba, still bleeding from the graze on his chin, crawled across to give me a shell dressing to cover the wound, which was on my left side. After that I had to fire my rifle single-handed with my right hand. I still wasn't frightened. It was us or them. I always had a feeling we would survive in the end. So we just fought on.

We were pretty short of ammunition by now, and the battle was getting fiercer. They were still advancing towards the fort.

They were close. Maybe 100 yards at the most and moving slowly from all directions. Laba and I knew we were almost surrounded. Then he told me there was a 66-millimetre mortar outside the gate of the fort.

Again we were joking in Fijian and I said: 'Laba, keep your head down.' And Laba did the same to me. He crawled away from the gun-pit towards the mortar. I was covering him. I looked at him, and he looked at me as though he knew something was about to happen. Then I heard a crack. I turned. All I could see was blood. A bullet had hit Laba's neck and blood was pouring out. He died instantly, within seconds. I was very sad when it happened and very alone.

Takavesi estimates that he spent fifteen minutes alone, with his dead friend nearby, fighting off the *adoo*.

I'd propped myself up against the *sangar* wall and was potting [shooting] away at the enemy with my SLR. There was no time to grieve for Laba. I had to think of how to survive. There was hardly any ammunition. I could hear the radio going but I was too far away to call for help. Then I saw Mike Kealy and Tommy Tobin coming towards me, dodging bullets. As they approached, the *adoo* were getting nearer the fort, advancing. They were so close you could almost reach out and touch them.

Tommy was the first to reach the *sangar* and as he climbed over he got shot in the jaw. I heard machine-gun fire and all I could see was his face being totally torn apart. He fell, and Mike Kealy dragged him to a safe area. Then Mike spoke to me. He decided that we'd be better off if he got himself in an ammunition pit a few metres away. It was four feet deep. He ran to it and jumped in and landed on the body of a DG soldier, a 'powder monkey', one of those who had been detailed to carry the ammo to the gun-pit. There was another soldier cowering in the corner. Kealy told him to move the body and checked out our situation.

Mike and I were now about three or four metres away from each other. We couldn't see each other but we could talk. I was shouting at him to tell him that I was running out of ammunition. Luckily, he was with one of the local Omani artillery who still had loaded magazines, so he started throwing them to me. At last I could reload my magazine and keep on firing. The battle was really getting heavy. Mike and I could see two or three people on the corner of the fort throwing grenades only about four or five metres away from us. Mike said, 'Look, we'll take one each on each corner.' While he was firing I was covering, likewise when I was firing he was covering me. We managed to kill a few. All I could hear was Mike trying to get across on the radio, trying to get some support, although our guys were giving all they could with mortars, firing to the side and on top of the fort itself to protect us.

He said that the arrival of the Sultan of Oman's air force was a huge relief. 'In the gun-pit, I thought the screaming of the jets was the best sound I had ever heard,' said Takavesi. After the battle was over, he found his friend's body, lying on a stretcher.

The jaw line had been shot away but I could tell it was Laba by his eyes. They were still open. It was like a sledgehammer blow to morale. I was still hyped up after the battle but all feelings of exhilaration disappeared in a flash. Here was a man I'd drunk with, fought with, laughed with . . . and here he was laid out on a stretcher, stiff as a board. It was just too much. I was engulfed with sorrow at the loss of a comrade.

Takavesi made light of his own injuries. 'I went out on the last helicopter,' he said. 'They wanted me on a stretcher but I could walk, slightly off-balance but I was okay. It was just a bit of pride, but I walked down to the helipad which was about twenty yards from the fort.'

Takavesi summed up the importance of the battle and the fact that the bravery of so few men was recognised:

> I believe we achieved quite a lot denying the coastal town to the guerrillas, although we were outnumbered. I think everyone did very well: us – the British Army Training Team – and the local force, the Omani forces and also the local *firqas* and the Askaris. The enemy did not achieve their aims. They were totally destroyed, morally, physically and psychologically, as a result of being defeated at Mirbat. I believe one of their aims was to capture the main gun, kill all the British Army Training Team and then use the victory as propaganda to warn the Omani forces who were calling the shots.
>
> I don't think it was heroism. We were given a task and we did it. There was nothing special to it. I'm sure that any of my comrades would have done the same. But it was very sad to see Laba and Tobin die. I do feel let down that all the men who were involved in the battle were not recognised. I think all the people involved should have been given a medal. But it didn't happen. Blokes who served in places like Northern Ireland or the Falklands got medals for nothing compared to what my lot went through.

The Battle of Mirbat had, unquestionably, been a turning point in the conflict. Trouble continued in Oman for four more years but the *adoo* never really recovered from the setback it received at Mirbat and, eventually, the rebel force was defeated.

Takavesi's wounds were so serious that most people would have died from them. Yet he not only survived but he went on to serve with distinction in the SAS for thirteen more years. He was discharged from the Army in January 1986 with his military conduct described as 'exemplary' and a glowing testimonial from his commanding officer. It read:

> SSgt Takavesi has just completed 22 years service with the British Army and SAS. He was awarded the DCM for extreme gallantry at the Battle of Mirbat in July 1972. He has seen action in Aden, Borneo, Dhofar, N. Ireland and the Falklands. SSgt Takavesi has become a legend in his own time within the SAS due to his outstanding operational exploits. His loyalty to Queen and country is absolute and his dedication and service to the Regiment is both an example and inspiration to those still serving in the SAS. SSgt Takavesi is both versatile and intelligent. He also possesses a native wit which allows him to turn his hand to most jobs. These qualities, combined with his honesty, integrity and complete trustworthiness, will ensure him suitable employment in civilian life.

After leaving the SAS, Takavesi shunned the quiet life and continued to visit trouble spots in his role working for private security firms. Pete Scholey tells in his book how Takavesi, by now sixty years old, narrowly escaped death after the Second Gulf War. He and another former SAS colleague were driving separately in a two-car convoy near Basra when they went to overtake a truck. The first car passed successfully but the truck, which contained four armed Arabs, then swung out in front of Takavesi's vehicle to block him. Three times he tried to pass it but each time the vehicle swerved to prevent him from overtaking. When Takavesi went off-road on to the desert scrub in an attempt to outmanoeuvre the truck, the Arabs – believed to be Iraqis – opened fire across his path. Takavesi was forced to brake and as he slowed down his car became bogged down in the soft sand. The truck also stopped and the four gunmen, each with a Kalashnikov AK-47, approached the car. Takavesi did not move until the men levelled their weapons at his car. Then he grabbed a machine pistol from beside him and sprayed fire at the men through the windscreen. Takavesi's partner, who by now was on the scene having stopped his car, gave him covering fire as he dived from the vehicle, wrestled with one of the gunmen and clubbed him to the ground, being shot in the thigh in the process. His partner helped him to his car and they sped off leaving one gunman dead and another injured. Takavesi's partner was shot in the hand. After initial treatment at the British Military Hospital in Basra, Takavesi was flown home to a private hospital in the UK. For the second time in his life, Takavesi made a good recovery from serious wounds.

Scholey writes: 'Both Laba and Tak have become legends within the Regiment and are hailed as heroes in their homeland of Fiji. They are, without doubt, two of the bravest men I have known and I am proud to consider myself as having been their friend.' Takavesi lives in Britain and continues to work in the security industry.

There are a few important footnotes to the Battle of Mirbat. Just a handful of bravery medals were awarded for the heroic events of 19 July 1972, including a Distinguished Service Order (DSO) for Kealy, the commanding officer. This was largely because, at the time, the SAS was engaged in such a secret war that nobody – not even the families of those in Oman – was meant to know their whereabouts and Britain was not officially at war. However, to this day, it still rankles with SAS servicemen, past and present, that the only official recognition for Labalaba's bravery was that he was mentioned in despatches. Many of his colleagues thought his bravery was worthy of a posthumous Victoria Cross. Kealy later left the SAS, only to return as a squadron commander. Tragically, he died, quite needlessly, from exposure on the Brecon Beacons in February 1979. Nobody should be in any doubt just how hard it is to train and survive in the SAS.

One of those to be singled out for his bravery at the Battle of Mirbat was Trooper Peter Winner (see page 171; his name has been changed for security reasons) who was one of fifteen men praised in a confidential Army report. 'Winner showed coolness and bravery throughout the action, giving covering fire to the fort with his .50 Browning machine-gun from the BATT house. He engaged numerous enemy targets most accurately.'

A fuller account of Winner's courage at Mirbat is provided by Pete Scholey:

> During the action, Peter had two responsibilities: he had to establish and maintain radio contact with B Squadron HQ at Um Al Gwarif, and also operate a .50 calibre Browning heavy machine-gun (HMG) on the roof of the BATT House, firing at the waves of enemy fighters whose objective was to take the 25pdr. Peter sent a quick radio message stating 'situation desperate – send reinforcements', then ran back to the HMG to engage the enemy, who by this time had closed to within grenade-throwing range of the field gun. Pete kept firing, helping to hold the attackers at bay until an air strike drove them back and reinforcements eventually arrived. The battle of Mirbat raged for almost seven hours and was witness to many acts of individual heroism. The rebels had saturated the defenders' positions with rifle fire from their AK-47s, mortars and rockets. As the source of some of the heaviest defensive fire,

Lieutenant John Bythesea and a comrade slipped unnoticed into enemy territory during the Crimean War to ambush a party delivering despatches containing Russian secrets. This sketch of the scene from 1855 appeared in the *Illustrated London News*.

There was a great sense of anticipation when Lieutenant John Bythesea's Victoria Cross came up for auction at Spink in London in 2007. His VC, for an SAS-style operation, has guaranteed its place in history as only the second to be won.

Commander John Commerell was awarded his VC for a daring commando raid in 1855. A series of promotions culminated in him becoming Admiral of the Fleet in 1892. This portrait of him is from the 'Men of Mark' gallery.

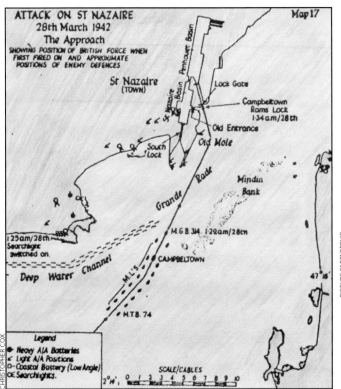

ATTACK ON ST NAZAIRE
28th March 1942
The Approach
SHOWING POSITION OF BRITISH FORCE WHEN
FIRST FIRED ON AND APPROXIMATE
POSITIONS OF ENEMY DEFENCES

Map 17

St Nazaire
(TOWN)

Lock Gate

Campbeltown
Rams Lock
1·34 a.m/28th

Old Entrance

Old Mole

South
Lock

Grande Rade

Mindin
Bank

1·25am/28th
Searchlight
switched on.

M.G.B. 314 1·29 a.m/28th

Deep Water Channel

M.L's

CAMPBELTOWN

47°15'

M.T.B. 74

Legend
● Heavy A/A Batteries
✕ Light A/A Positions
□ Coastal Battery (Low Angle)
Œ Searchlights.

SCALE/CABLES
2°W' 0 1 2 3 4 5 6 7 8 9 10

CHRISTOPHER COX

Coastguard's son Petty Officer
Ernest Pitcher (below) was
awarded his VC for bravery at se
during the First World War. Hi
award was for courage on board
a Q-ship, a gunship disguised to
look like a merchant ship that w
used to decoy German submarin

Corporal Bill Sparks (below) was
one of only two survivors from
the ten 'Cockleshell Heroes'. In
December 1942, Royal Marines
in canoes paddled up the Giron
estuary in order to destroy Germ
ships. Sparks and a comrade
escaped across land to Spain.

This map, showing the daring attack by British forces on the French
port of St Nazaire in March 1942, was in the possession of Troop
Sergeant Major George Haines. He was awarded the DCM for leading
a fourteen-strong commando assault group.

After the Second World War, Corporal Bill Sparks – and fellow
survivor Major 'Blondie' Hasler – achieved near celebrity status for
their bravery. Sparks, who was awarded the DSM, is photographed here
back on the water long after the war ended.

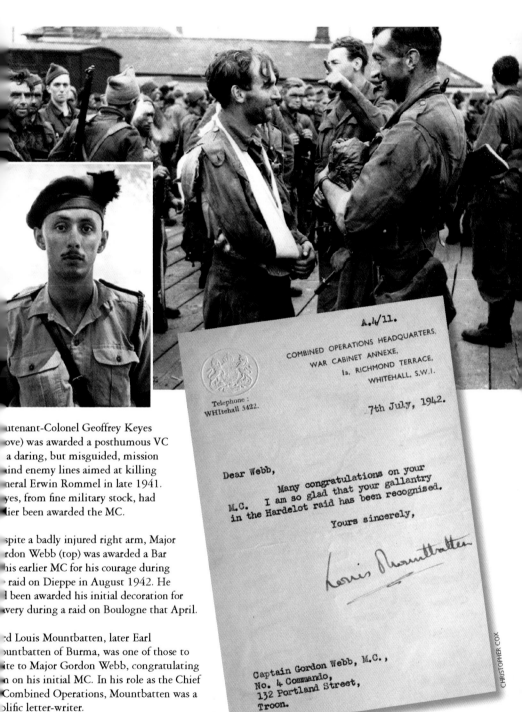

...utenant-Colonel Geoffrey Keyes
...ove) was awarded a posthumous VC
...a daring, but misguided, mission
...ind enemy lines aimed at killing
...neral Erwin Rommel in late 1941.
...yes, from fine military stock, had
...lier been awarded the MC.

...spite a badly injured right arm, Major
...rdon Webb (top) was awarded a Bar
...his earlier MC for his courage during
... raid on Dieppe in August 1942. He
...l been awarded his initial decoration for
...very during a raid on Boulogne that April.

...d Louis Mountbatten, later Earl
...untbatten of Burma, was one of those to
...te to Major Gordon Webb, congratulating
...m on his initial MC. In his role as the Chief
...Combined Operations, Mountbatten was a
...olific letter-writer.

...geant Bruce Ogden-Smith
...s awarded the MM and DCM
... valour in late 1943 and early
...44, in recognition of his brave
...ims to German-occupied French
...aches to get vital information
...them for the D-Day landings.
...is drawing shows how he did it.

Letter

A.4/11.

COMBINED OPERATIONS HEADQUARTERS,
WAR CABINET ANNEXE,
1a, RICHMOND TERRACE,
WHITEHALL, S.W.I.

Telephone :
WHItehall 5422.

7th July, 1942.

Dear Webb,

Many congratulations on your
M.C. I am so glad that your gallantry
in the Hardelot raid has been recognised.

Yours sincerely,

Louis Mountbatten

Captain Gordon Webb, M.C.,
No. 4 Commando,
132 Portland Street,
Troon.

CHRISTOPHER COX

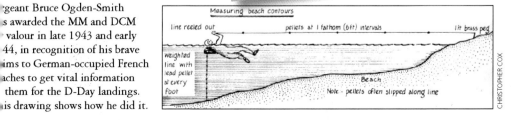

Measuring beach contours

line reeled out   pellets at 1 fathom (6ft) intervals   1ft brass peg

weighted
line with
lead pellet
at every
foot

Beach

Note - pellets often slipped along line

CHRISTOPHER COX

A group shot of 3 Troop, 22 SAS Regiment, from 1955–6. Corporal John 'Herbie' Hawkins (front row, second on the left) was awarded the DCM for his courage in a battle in Oman in late 1958.

The wounded from the Battle of Mirbat in Oman in 1972 are casevaced by helicopter after one of the fiercest battles in SAS history. Badly wounded men, including Trooper Sekonaia Takavesi, were brought to safety and to receive hospital treatment.

The gallantry and service medals of Trooper Sekonaia Takavesi, including his DCM for the Battle of Mirbat. Few DCMs can ever have been won in such difficult and dangerous circumstances. His friend and fellow Fijian, Trooper Talaiasi Labalaba, died during the fierce attack by elite rebel forces.

...ptain Jürgen Schumann sits
...the open door of the hijacked
...ufthansa jet at Dubai airport
...October 1977. The next day
...e terrorists forced him to fly to
...ogadishu, where they killed the
...erman pilot and dumped his
...dy from the plane.

...he gallantry and service
...edals of Sergeant Barry
...avies, including his unique
...EM awarded for his courage
... Mogadishu in 1977. The
...AS man played a key role in
...e mission to overpower the
...rrorists and free the plane's
...ssengers and crew.

...he SAS begin to storm the
...anian Embassy in central
...ondon at the end of a dramatic
...x-day siege on 5 May 1980. In
...e successful raid, the terrorists
...ere shot dead or overpowered
...d most hostages were safely
...eed. These images flashed
...ound the world and confirmed
...e SAS's reputation as one of the
...orld's most elite fighting forces.

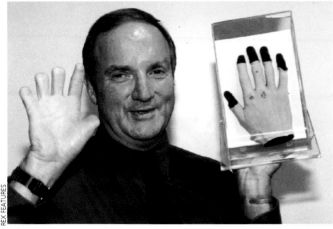

SAS legend 'Bronco' Lane (above) donates the preserved ends of his frostbitten fingers and toes to the National Army Museum in 2000. He lost them climbing Mount Everest in 1976, but was later awarded the MM for his courage in Northern Ireland.

Warrant Officer Kevin James (below) was awarded the QGM after taking the law into his own hands and storming a hospital to save the life of a wounded colleague in Northern Ireland in 1978. He later served in the SBS and was Mentioned in Despatches for the Falklands War.

Frank Collins was the first man through the roof at the Iranian Embassy siege and was also a sniper in Northern Ireland. Yet, while serving in the SAS, he found God and was ordained as a minister. He is pictured left meeting the Queen some time before sadly taking his own life in 1998.

Warrant Officer John McAleese, a SAS hardman known as 'Mac' to his friends, was awarded the MM for courage in Northern Ireland in the late 1980s, nearly a decade after taking part in the storming of the Iranian Embassy siege.

The gallantry and service medals of Warrant Officer Class 2 Peter Jones. He was one of just two men to receive the combination of the QGM and GM for his undercover intelligence work in Northern Ireland.

CHRISTOPHER COX

geant Thomas Harley (second n left) meets the Prince of les, the Commander-in-Chief he Parachute Regiment. rley, who served with the Paras, awarded the MM for bravery ing the Falklands War.

This sword, which had belonged to Argentinian officer Lieutenant Roberto Estevez, was claimed by Sergeant Thomas Harley after fierce fighting at Goose Green. Estevez, as well as Colonel H. Jones, lost their lives at the battle.

The gallantry and service medals of Sergeant Thomas Harley, including his MM awarded for courage at Goose Green, one of the key battles of the Falklands War.

CHRISTOPHER COX

Regimental Sergeant Major Peter Ratcliffe was awarded the DCM for courage behind enemy lines during the Gulf War in early 1991. Later, as Major Ratcliffe, he received his decoration from the Queen at Buckingham Palace.

Major John Potter appeared on the front page of a tabloid newspaper after he was photographed with a captured Iraqi during the Gulf War. Potter was awarded the MC for his courage in battle during February 1991.

The gallantry and service medals of Major John Potter, including his MC awarded for bravery during the Gulf War. Potter is now living and working in Canada.

MIKE MOORE

Peter had been the focus for a great deal of the enemy's ordnance. When he checked his machine-gun when it was all over, he found that it had scrapes and dents where it had been repeatedly hit by enemy fire, although he had come through it all without a scratch.

Winner remains furious that Labalaba did not receive more recognition for his bravery. 'Nobody ever tackled Laba,' he told the author Jack Ramsay.

He was a bear of a man. Just to see him walk down the street was enough for most people, but when he was fully tooled up he was the original Rambo. He would never surrender. He just didn't know the word surrender. He would give his life for his comrades. Same with Sek [Takavesi]. They wanted to give Laba the VC for his actions at Mirbat but because the war was a secret in 1972 they said a VC awarded to a Fijian would be headlines in every newspaper in the UK. So to keep the war secret, all they gave him was MID [mentioned in despatches]. You can get that for walking up the Falls Road. The guy deserved a VC for what he did.

Eight years after the Battle of Mirbat, Winner and Takavesi would stand shoulder to shoulder again before storming the Iranian Embassy in London and ending a six-day siege. But that's another story (see page 172).

Mogadishu

On 12 October 1977, a Boeing 737 carrying five crew and eighty-six passengers, mostly holidaymakers, was hijacked by four Palestinian terrorists.

Lufthansa Flight LH181 had been due to fly from Palma, Majorca, to Frankfurt, West Germany. The story was to dominate world news for six days as the terrorists and their hostages moved to six different airports in Europe and the Middle East. Behind the scenes, Chancellor Helmut Schmidt had requested the help of the SAS from Jim Callaghan, the British prime minister, on the second day of the crisis. Two SAS members were soon involved in one of the most dramatic incidents in the history of the Regiment.

SERGEANT BARRY DAVIES

Army (SAS)

AWARD: BRITISH EMPIRE MEDAL (BEM)
DATE OF BRAVERY: NOT SPECIFIC
GAZETTED: NOT AVAILABLE

Sergeant Barry Davies had spent the second week of October 1977 on routine duties – routine, that is, if you are in the SAS. By Friday, 14 October, he was on his fifth day of a visit to Heathrow by a ten-man SAS anti-terrorist team, which had been invited to familiarise itself with the international airport and the aircraft using it. By the end of the day, however, Davies was being rushed to 10 Downing Street for a high-level briefing. James Callaghan, the Labour prime minister of the day, had been telephoned by Chancellor Helmut Schmidt, his West German counterpart, seeking help. Schmidt had been told that Britain's SAS had a specialist knowledge of the Middle East and state-of-the-art weaponry, thereby making them ideal candidates to tackle the crisis on board Lufthansa Flight LH181 from Palma to Frankfurt. The Boeing 737 had been hijacked and there were more than ninety passengers and crew on board. Speaking on a secure line and in confidence, Schmidt told Callaghan that Germany was intending to launch an assault on the aircraft – and he wondered if the SAS would help.

Davies spent that evening at a meeting in the Cabinet Office, again refused. This time, however, the authorities failed to switch off the auto-landing equipment and Schumann landed the plane safely with just three minutes' fuel to spare.

As Mahmud demanded fuel, armed soldiers surrounded the aircraft. Fearing an attack, he threatened to shoot the co-pilot unless the soldiers pulled back within five minutes. Realising the seriousness of the threat, Vietor asked for permission to speak to the control tower himself. With the clock ticking, Vietor appealed for his life first to Mahmud – saying he had a wife and children – and then directly to the control tower: 'There is a man next to me with a gun at my head. If you do not withdraw your soldiers immediately, he will shoot me.' Seconds before the deadline ended, the soldiers began pulling back. Soon the refuelled aircraft was back in the sky and heading for Dubai, where it touched down at 6 a.m. on 14 October. Mahmud now issued his first deadline for the release of Baader-Meinhof members – midday GMT on Sunday, 16 October.

The passengers were in for a long and uncomfortable stay on the tarmac in Dubai. When the fuel ran out, there was no power for electricity or the air-conditioning system. It was dark inside the plane as temperatures rose to 120° Fahrenheit. The passengers became restless and some started to faint from the heat and the stress. Schumann told Mahmud that unless the plane had power the passengers would start to die from heat exhaustion. Two men were eventually permitted to bring a power unit to the plane and Vietor, the co-pilot, was allowed outside to attach it. Mahmud now angrily interrogated Schumann, the pilot, in front of the passengers, threatening to shoot out first his left eye and then his right if he did not tell the truth. Schumann admitted he had given a message to the authorities that there were four hijackers armed with two pistols, four grenades and explosives. 'This man is the enemy,' Mahmud told the passengers. 'He has betrayed you. He now admits his guilt. No one will speak to this man – no one.' But the air conditioning was soon working once again.

At 6.30 a.m. on Saturday, 15 October, Major Morrison and Sergeant Davies were landing at Bonn, where they were greeted by the two GSG9 members they had met in London. They were taken to the barrack headquarters in St Augustin and given a briefing on the situation in Dubai. Finding a basement corridor similar in size to the interior of an aircraft, Davies gave some GSG9 members a demonstration of how a stun grenade operated. Moments later several shocked, but impressed, members of the German Special Forces staggered from the cellar and shortly afterwards the two SAS men were *en route* for Dubai – via Kuwait – with their secret weapon – seven stun grenades in a box.

They arrived in Dubai at 2 a.m. on 16 October, exactly ten hours before the deadline that day set by the hijackers. The hijacked aircraft was on an old runway a mile from the main airport buildings of the oil-rich sheikhdom. Soldiers of the Dubai Defence Force lay hidden in the low sand dunes that surrounded the aircraft on three sides. The two SAS men were introduced to Sheikh Mohammed bin Rachid, the Defence Minister, who was in overall charge of the hijack. The Sheikh had been in negotiations with Mahmud, but the hijacker refused his request to let the children go free. The SAS and GSG9 men devised a plan to attack the plane in the event of the hijackers starting to shoot hostages. The aim was to use eight men including – at the insistence of Sheikh Mohammed – two Arabs from the Palace Guard. It was decided to do nothing until daylight and, at 5 a.m., the two SAS men grabbed two hours' sleep. The SAS men had requested a 737 plane so they could practise an attack; by daybreak, it was waiting for them. At 8 a.m. on 16 October, sixty-five hours after LH181 had left Palma, the training and practice operations were in full swing. The deadline was 3 p.m. local time.

Davies later wrote:

> Both Alastair and I firmly believed that, under cover of darkness, we could approach the hijacked aircraft and establish ourselves undetected. Once in our assigned starting positions, and given that we could put two four-men assault teams inside LH181, using the APU [auxiliary power unit] lights plus the stun grenades as cover, there was a 99 per cent chance that we could close with the terrorists and eliminate them.

They were confident, too, that they could kill the terrorists and minimise the loss of life and injuries to passengers by entering through the emergency exits rather than the main front and rear doors.

> For myself, I had no fear of the terrorists on LH181 – that is not conceit, it's just that I knew my own capabilities and I had total confidence in the training I had undertaken. Added to this, I had just spent several years fighting in far more dangerous conditions during the Oman War. It is a misconception that when a hijacked aircraft is assaulted the terrorists start shooting their hostages . . . Fear makes terrorists' survival instinct come to the fore, and shooting hostages does not help the situation. A terrorist's instinctive first action is to stop the invading beast bearing down on him. It takes only micro-seconds to choose between resistance or surrender, but he will be dead before he ever makes that choice.

As the deadline loomed, Mahmud resumed his negotiations with Sheikh Mohammed. When the terrorist threatened to shoot hostages, the Defence Minister eventually agreed that the plane should be given a small amount of fuel, which was intended for the air-conditioning system. Shortly after 2 p.m., Mahmud screamed down the radio to the control tower, 'We are taking off! We are taking off!' Sure enough, Flight LH181 started to taxi down the runway before gathering speed and lifting off. Soon, the SAS and GSG9 men were taking off, too, on board a 707 tasked with following the hijacked aircraft. It was while they were in the air that they learnt the hijackers had landed the plane in Aden. But the following plane was told it could not land – and diverted instead to Jeddah, Saudi Arabia. A small executive jet was acquired to take the Special Forces teams closer to Aden but, in mid-flight, they heard the news that the pilot of the hijacked plane, Jürgen Schumann, had been shot dead while it was on the ground. German officials now had a new plan – to release the hostages before more people were killed. Soon, however, there was more news from Aden. The hijacked plane had taken off bound for Mogadishu, Somalia. It was only in Mogadishu that Schumann's body was removed from the aircraft by ambulance men. He had been shot dead by Mahmud after a hasty 'tribunal'. A pistol was put in his face and the hijacker pulled the trigger, then he took Schumann's hat, placed it on his own head and sat in the pilot's seat. By now, the situation was so desperate that even the Pope offered to take the place of the hostages.

The SAS and GSG9 men were soon on their way to Mogadishu in their plane and, as they approached the runway, they were told to fasten their seat-belts and brace themselves. Davies later wrote:

Our pilot was about to approach the single runway with the intention of landing a short distance behind the hijacked aircraft. If he was successful, the terrorists would not realise that another German aircraft had landed. As the pilot levelled the 707 for its final approach, we were only a few feet above the ground. The flat roofs of the airport buildings flashed beneath us as, with fantastic skill that bordered on genius, the pilot managed to touch the aircraft down on the very edge of the runway. Weird screeching noises and smoke came from the undercarriage as the brakes were applied, bringing the giant aircraft rapidly to a halt. In the final seconds the pilot managed to turn our plane around and head back away from the hijacked aircraft. On board the 707 we all clapped.

The Somali government – including President Said Barre in person – soon gave the Special Forces team a warm welcome. The Germans continued to negotiate with the self-styled 'Martyr Mahmud', who was threatening to blow up the plane – with the hostages in it – if his demands were not met. Meanwhile, President Barre had concluded the hijack should be brought to an end by the West's anti-terror team. General Abdullah, the Somali Chief of Police, was also negotiating with Mahmud. The General's promise to Mahmud that he would have safe conduct from Mogadishu if the hostages were released was, however, rejected.

The Special Forces team ran through their assault plan but, with more troops now available to them, they decided also to attack the front and rear main doors. The plan was to approach the aircraft from the rear, taking advantage of a blind spot. The men would approach the aircraft in a pre-arranged order and go to their assigned positions. The negotiators were instructed to tell Mahmud that the Baader-Meinhof terrorists had been released and that the two Popular Front for the Liberation of Palestine men were being flown from Germany to Turkey.

The plan was then to light a diversionary fire at the end of the runway, some 300 metres from the nose of the hijacked aircraft. Seconds later the 'go' would be given and the assault would begin. The GSG9 men were to open the doors, allowing Morrison and Davies to throw stun grenades close to – but not into – the aircraft, one over the wings and another over the cockpit. Good concealment sites were found for GSG9 snipers. Plans were also made for the collection of the hostages after they were freed. Initially, it was decided to guide them to the rear of the aircraft and, provided the assault on the plane was a success, the snipers would step forward to take charge of them until ambulances arrived. On board, the hostages were by now close to despair. Most of the men had been tied up and the interior was doused with inflammable spirits.

When Mahmud was assured that his demands were in the process of being met and the imprisoned terrorists were being freed, he told the plane's co-pilot that he had done his job and was free to leave. 'I think I will stay, if that's okay with you?' came Jürgen Vietor's courageous reply. Mahmud's new deadline for all his demands to be met in full was now 0130 European Standard time the next day. At 8 p.m. that evening, a Lufthansa 707 with another twenty-eight members of the GSG9 landed at Mogadishu airport – the necessary reinforcements had finally arrived.

As the preparations for the assault of the aircraft began, the German assault team put on their British-made body armour and fitted up their Heckler and Koch MP5 machine-guns – just as the SAS would have done. However, it was decided to use pistols as they entered the plane. By 23.30, the whole assault group had assembled on the edge of the runway, with the two

SAS men wearing spare GSG9 shirts. They approached the aircraft from the rear and, once they reached the plane, started to assemble the assault ladders, keeping tight in to the plane so they could not be seen.

Mahmud was in discussions with the control tower by radio when the planned huge fireball was ignited by Somali soldiers 300 metres in front of the aircraft and the assault team was given the instruction to 'go'. Davies takes up the story:

Instinctively I stepped away from the aircraft, having already pulled two pins from the two stun grenades which I was clutching. I tossed the first one casually in an arc over the starboard wing. It exploded about three feet above the two GSG9 soldiers standing there, causing them great surprise! Just as it exploded, they punched in the panel which released the small hatchway into the aircraft. Taking a better swing, I threw the second grenade high over the cockpit. It actually exploded about two feet above the flight deck, to dramatic effect.

After throwing the second grenade, I whipped round to see the GSG9 soldier on my left turn the handle of the rear starboard door and with a kick throw his body clear of the ladder, still hanging on to the handle and pulling the door open on its hydraulics. The moment he did this the internal lights of the aircraft revealed one of the female terrorists standing there in a Che Guevara tee-shirt, wearing an expression of utter astonishment. At that instant the [man on the] right rung of the ladder fired a burst and stitched her with at least six rounds. She fell to the door, dead, and the soldier disappeared into the aircraft.

Returning my attention to the starboard wing, I ran forward and scaled the small ladders, positioning myself by the open hatchway where the two GSG9 [men] had already entered. As I looked into the aircraft I saw that the hatchway had fallen on the laps of the two passengers sitting there. They sat frozen, their eyes closed tightly. Continuous gunfire rattled up and down the aircraft for what seemed like a lifetime. I can remember saying to myself, 'Come on, do it, do it – get it done!' Then came a couple of low thuds as two of the terrorists' grenades exploded.

After our stun grenades had gone off Abbasi [the second male terrorist] was the first to move, trying hard to shake off the ringing effect in his ears. He almost made the first-class compartment but Soraya [one of the women terrorists] was blocking his way. At first Abbasi could not understand it – Soraya seemed to be running into the toilet, someone was chasing her down the aisle. Then the door to his right opened. Abbasi never knew what hit him as he got caught in the cross-fire. Mahmud watched as his colleague crumpled to the floor with over twenty bullets in him, then he too felt bullets ripping and burning through his body. He could not remember having pulled the pins from the grenades, but they now rolled out of his hands, forwards into the first-class section.

Vietor heard the first explosion. 'This is it,' he thought. 'I am going to die.'

Gaby Dillmann [one of the air stewardesses on the hijacked flight] sat in the aisle seat, her legs in the gangway. As the grenade exploded, a fragment of white-hot metal ripped into her calf muscle. She thought, 'It's only my leg – it doesn't hurt.' Then men were rushing past her, shooting towards the flight deck and shouting: 'Get down! Get down!'

In the chaos no-one saw Soraya dive into the toilet, from where she now started to shoot. But instantly the fire was returned, and the door burst open and her body hit the floor.

The firefight had now lasted some four or five minutes and

was confined to the cockpit part of the aircraft, where sudden sharp bursts interspersed with single shots could still be heard. It was quite clear that the passengers had been strapped into their seats in the economy section, and would therefore be clear of any immediate danger. Cries of 'Get down! Get down!' from the GSG9 [men] continued to echo around the aircraft as they fought the remaining terrorists. Then, out of the rear starboard door, I saw figures start to appear and descend the assault ladders. One of the GSG9 soldiers pulled the hatchway off the laps of the people who had been trapped and at last they opened their eyes; I reached in to help them out of the aircraft. The exodus continued smoothly as more and more people disembarked. Once on the tarmac they were guided towards the rear of the aircraft where they assembled, waiting for the stream of ambulances and buses now making their way across from the main terminal buildings.

I climbed down and went round the port side, where I found Alastair Morrison. He was helping a young lady climb down the wing, catching her in his cradled arms. She looked like one of the eleven beauty queens. 'You'll have to give her back!' I warned him. Alastair insisted on carrying her to safety at the rear of the aircraft.

Suddenly, shouting broke out on the port wing and I looked up to see a man crouched in the emergency hatchway over the wing, with the GSG9 shouting: 'Come down! Come down!' He refused and, reaching back into the aircraft, he dragged out a small boy who turned out to be his son. Of all the incidents that night, this was one of the few things I remember clearly. It was a simple action but when you consider the situation – fear that the aircraft might explode at any moment – people around you screaming, soldiers shouting commands – an action like that takes great courage.

Leaving Alastair to his beauty queen, I went round to the starboard side to check on progress. Suddenly the GSG9 sergeant major stood up in the rear doorway and shouted: 'They're all out, they're all free!'

Climbing back on to the wing, I re-entered the aircraft via the emergency hatch. Strangely, as if this Boeing 737 was a living thing, it seemed tired, like a hunted fox. Exhausted and hurt, it now sat quietly resting.

The assault had been an overwhelming success. Two terrorists were dead and two were injured. Mahmud was seriously wounded and died later in hospital. He was eventually identified as Zohair Youssif Akache, a renowned international terrorist. The second woman terrorist was on a stretcher shouting defiantly that she was not dead. 'Kill me! Kill me!' she yelled, before raising her right hand to give the V for victory sign. 'Free Palestine!' she then screamed several times. One member of the GSG9 had been hit but was not seriously wounded. Gaby Dillmann, the air stewardess, had shrapnel in her leg, but once again her injury was not serious. Minutes later, in the crowded airport lounge, the passengers – unkempt and exhausted – were milling around unable to believe they were free. Chancellor Schmidt and Prime Minister Callaghan were soon given the news they had been hoping for – and the SAS had more than done its bit again on foreign soil.

The next year Davies was awarded the BEM. In November 1984, after eighteen years with the SAS, Davies left the Regiment. He set up a military survival manufacturing company, has acted as a consultant on television series and has written more than a dozen books. *Fire Magic*, on the hijacking and raid in Mogadishu, was published in 1994. Movingly, he opened his book with the words: 'This book is dedicated to the airline pilots of the world. But in particular, to those who endured the terrors of hijacking. Especially Lufthansa pilot Jürgen Schumann who was murdered in Aden in 1977.'

Davies continues to work in the security industry and as an advisor on books and films.

The Iranian Embassy Siege

The climax of the Iranian Embassy siege came at a difficult time for the SAS. A run of bad luck had culminated in the death of Captain Richard Westmacott during an operation to seize IRA weapons. In a bungled security operation, he was machine-gunned to death on 2 May 1980 in the Antrim Road, Belfast. He was the first SAS soldier to die in Northern Ireland.

Yet, just three days later, the SAS was handed an opportunity to restore its reputation. Not only did the incident take place on British soil but it was filmed on national television – and the images were soon being beamed across the world. The SAS's 'fifteen minutes of fame' – in fact the whole rescue operation took seventeen minutes – came in response to a group of armed Arab terrorists seizing the Iranian Embassy in central London and taking more than twenty hostages.

SERGEANT PETER WINNER*
Army (SAS)
AWARD: NON SPECIFIC
DATE OF BRAVERY: NOT RELEVANT
GAZETTED: NOT RELEVANT

Peter Winner – 'Snapper' to his friends – is one of just three servicemen written about in this book who has not been awarded a specific gallantry medal. However, like his SAS

---

* name changed at the request of the former servicemen.

comrade Frank Collins (see page 263), Winner had a remarkable, action-packed career in the SAS and is, without question, worthy of his place – not just for his role in the Iranian Embassy siege but for his bravery during eighteen years of service in the Regiment. Similarly, Winner is one of a handful of servicemen in the book who have asked not to be identified.

The Iranian Embassy at 16 Prince's Gate, in the heart of London's diplomatic quarter, was taken over by six heavily armed terrorists at 11.32 a.m. on Wednesday, 30 April 1980. PC Trevor Lock, a diplomatic protection squad officer, was bundled into the elegant, terraced Georgian building as he was sipping his mid-morning cup of coffee on the pavement. Although some Embassy staff managed to escape, twenty-six people, including Lock, were taken hostage by the group, who purported to represent the Democratic Revolutionary Front for the Liberation of Arabistan. The Iraqi-based terrorists were opposed to the rule of Ayatollah Khomeini and were seeking the liberation of the oil-rich province of Khuzestan – which they called Arabistan – from Iran. The whole group had been living in a property in Earls Court, west London, which they had left early on the morning of the terror attack. During the next few hours, they had somehow collected an abundance of weapons, including two Polish-made sub-machine-guns, three Browning self-loading pistols, five Russian hand grenades and plenty of ammunition. By 11.20 a.m., they were grouped outside the Embassy and ready to strike.

However, after grabbing the uniformed British police officer and pouring inside the building, all did not go to plan and the sound of a burst of machine-gun fire alerted those nearby to the fact that something was wrong. The police were soon on the scene, including armed officers from Scotland Yard's D11 unit. Some staff in the building managed to escape – two men through a back window and another through a fourth-floor window. Dr Ali Afouz, the chargé d'affaires, jumped from a first-floor window but injured himself in the fall and was dragged back inside. By the time the doors of the building were slammed shut, twenty-six hostages were trapped inside. They were mostly Iranian, but they also included four Britons. In less than an hour, the Metropolitan Police had cleared a two-kilometre square area around the building.

One of the first to learn about the crisis was 'Dusty' Grey, an ex-SAS man from D Squadron, who was at the time working for the Metropolitan Police. By 11.47 a.m., he had phoned Major Clive Fairweather, then second in command of 22 SAS and who was in the 'Kremlin', the operation room at Bradbury Lines, the Regiment's Hereford headquarters. This meant the SAS had been put on stand-by from early on in the crisis – although only the Home Secretary can ask the Ministry of Defence to order them into action. The SAS had formed an anti-terrorist team more than five years previously and it soon looked as though the siege was going to become their first major challenge.

The police had quickly assembled a huge team at the scene. Number 16 Prince's Gate was soon surrounded by anti-terrorist officers, police marksmen and others. The police moved into the Montessori nursery school at 24 Prince's Gate and established a link with the terrorists. No stone was left unturned. A Farsi interpreter was brought in, along with a psychiatrist with experience of sieges. At around 3 p.m., Willie Whitelaw, the home secretary, chaired a meeting of COBRA (Cabinet Office Briefing Room A), which was attended by several senior Ministry of Defence staff, members of the security and intelligence services and Brigadier Peter de la Billière, the director SAS and SAS Group.

Normal phone lines to the Embassy were cut but an Army

field telephone was given to the terrorists so they could have contact with negotiators outside the building. This had one great advantage for the police and security services – it could not be switched off so they could hear exactly what was going on in the room where the phone was placed. On the first day, at 2.35 p.m., the terrorists' leader, Oan, issued his demands – autonomy and recognition for the people of Arabistan and the release of ninety-one Arabistani prisoners. He said that unless the demands were met by noon the next day – 1 May – the group would kill all twenty-six hostages and blow up the Embassy.

Scotland Yard had set up a negotiating team to deal with the terrorists and on the first day of the siege they were relieved when the terrorists agreed to release one of the hostages, an Iranian woman who had fallen ill. On the second day, it was the turn of Chris Cramer, a BBC journalist and one of the hostages, to fall sick with acute stomach pains. Sim Harris, a sound recordist, persuaded the terrorists to call a doctor for his colleague but, when the medic arrived, the police would not allow him into the building. Eventually, Cramer was released, stumbling out of the main door of the building to a waiting ambulance. He had suffered a recurrence of dysentery he had caught in Ethiopia, but he had exaggerated the extent of his illness in order to get out of the Embassy. He was soon well enough to brief people on how many terrorists were in the building, their descriptions and the sort of guns they had with them.

On the second day, when the noon deadline passed without incident, the negotiators allowed Oan to make a telephone call to Sadegh Ghotzbadeh, Iran's foreign minister. The call did not go well. The politician accused the terrorist leader of being an American agent and said that the hostages held in the Embassy would consider it an honour to die for their country and the Iranian Islamic Revolution.

By the early hours of the second day, the anti-terrorist team was being assembled in Regent's Park Barracks, which had been chosen as a holding area where information could be assembled and assessed. Lieutenant Colonel Michael Rose, the Commanding Officer of 22 SAS for less than a year, had flown by helicopter to London from Hereford the previous day in order to carry out a recce of the scene. Number 16 Prince's Gate was quickly named the 'Stronghold' for the purpose of any operation, a scale model of the building was constructed and an intelligence cell was brought in to gather information that could be used in any possible assault of the building. Everything from the number of terrorists, their descriptions, precise details of their weapons, and where exactly the hostages were being held was useful. Furthermore, the caretaker was able to give a detailed briefing on every part of the building, including the cellar. The SAS men had tackled situations like this countless times in training at their Hereford headquarters. They had spent much time in the 'Killing House', practising abseiling, breaking and entering skills, using explosives to gain access, working with night-vision goggles and wearing gas masks and gloves. It was called the Killing House because that is what they did inside. There was no training in taking prisoners.

The fifty SAS men in the barracks were split into two teams – Red and Blue. The Red Team concentrated on the immediate action (IA) plan, the ultra-violent action of breaking down the doors and storming the building if shooting started inside or the negotiators were certain a hostage, or hostages, were about to be killed. The Blue Team concentrated on the deliberate assault plan (DAP), which was more complicated and involved the SAS

– not any action by the terrorists – deciding on when to enter the building.

The instructions from COBRA remained consistent for five days – there was to be no giving in to the terrorists' demands, the negotiators must strive for a peaceful solution and the SAS were not to be sent in unless a hostage was killed. By Monday, 5 May, the May bank holiday, the SAS had been on stand-by for five days during which a total of five hostages had been released unharmed. Willie Whitelaw now announced that the 'ambassadorial phase' of the siege was over and a firmer line would be taken about the hostages. For the first time, too, the Red Team and Blue Team got together for a morning briefing. At 16 Prince's Gate, the situation inside the building had started to deteriorate. The terrorists were becoming increasingly frustrated by their lack of progress and had spent the morning making numerous threats to execute their hostages. At 1.31 p.m., three shots were heard. At 6.50 p.m. three further shots rang out and, shortly afterwards, the dead body of Abbas Lavasani, the Iranian Embassy press officer, was pushed out of the front door (in fact, he had died during the earlier round of fire). His body was picked up and placed on a stretcher – all this was shown on live television. Oan, who had been codenamed 'Salim' by the SAS, was now making threats to kill a hostage every half hour, or even to kill all the hostages.

By killing one of the hostages, the terrorists had effectively ended all chances of a negotiated settlement. They had also – at a stroke – lost all sympathy from the hostages themselves. Harris, the sound recordist, said later that up until the execution of Lavasani, he would have been happy for the terrorists to walk away, having made their point. His attitude changed significantly after the killing – and he also became convinced that only the SAS could save the lives of the remaining hostages.

Even as he pondered this, three SAS teams were preparing for an assault on the building. COBRA – supported by Prime Minister Margaret Thatcher – had agreed to transfer control of the operation from the Metropolitan Police to the British Army. The SAS had been committed to action at 6.53 p.m. – as soon as there was proof that a hostage had been killed. Mrs Thatcher's words were, 'The time has come to use the final option.' Whitelaw telephoned de la Billière and said, 'You can send them in.'

At 7.07 p.m., Lieutenant Colonel Michael Rose took control of events on the ground. Operation Nimrod was officially under way. The negotiators stalled for time. Oan was told that a coach was coming to take him and his five comrades to Heathrow, from where they would be permitted to fly out of the country. Meanwhile, the SAS's plan was relatively simple – Red Team would deal with the three floors in the top half of the building and Blue Team would go in and clear the basement, ground and first floors. A support group was tasked with pumping CS gas into the building. The first team had to break down the rear garden door, another was to enter the first-floor balcony using frame charges to blast open the windows, which it was believed had been reinforced against terrorists. A third eight-strong team had to abseil forty feet from the roof of the building to gain entry through a second-floor rear window set next to a balcony. Between them, the SAS teams had to search and clear more than fifty rooms on six floors – and they had to reach the hostages before they came to harm. It was feared that even if things went relatively smoothly there could be up to 40 per cent casualties among the hostages.

As Oan became bogged down in negotiations about the precise length of the bus he wanted, he started to become concerned by the sound of 'suspicious movements'. The negotiator insisted, 'There are no suspicious movements.' But at 7.26 p.m. his job was over. An explosion could be heard – the sound of the skylight on the Embassy being blown by Red Team. The assault was under way and the SAS was involved in a race against time to prevent the hostages being killed. All the SAS men wore black kit weighing about fifteen kilos and designed for an anti-terrorist role. Beneath their carbon-lined nuclear-biological-and-chemical (NBC) suits, they wore black overalls fitted with body armour, including trauma plates capable of stopping a high-velocity round. There were not enough trauma plates to go around and so they became, in the words of one SAS man, 'as rare as rocking horse shit'. The men were armed with MP5 German-made machine-guns, 9mm Browning pistols and stun grenades. They also wore hoods, respirators and personal radios with earpieces and throat microphones that were tuned to a communal network so that everyone could hear everyone else talking.

Winner was one of the SAS men who had been patiently waiting for nearly six days to assault the building. By chance, after a short time out of the Regiment (which meant he had been reduced in rank from a sergeant to a trooper), he had rejoined and found himself in Six Troop and detached from many of his old friends with whom he had served in Eight Troop. There were, however, some familiar faces in Six Troop, including Sekonaia Takavesi, the Fijian hero of Mirbat (see page 141) and John McAleese, a tough, no-nonsense Scot known as 'Mac' to his friends (see page 255). Both men had been waiting patiently with Winner as the siege unfolded. Winner described Takavesi as 'being like a cuddly teddy bear' when he played with children in Oman but added he had an 'awesome temper' which made him 'as ferocious as a grizzly bear'.

Winner, who was born in Morecambe, Lancashire, in 1946,

was a tough and popular member of the SAS. Barry Davies, a former SAS soldier (see page 158), tells a story in his book *Heroes of the SAS* that illustrates Winner's toughness. When in Hong Kong early in his SAS career in order to train the police and local servicemen, Winner got caught up in a bar-room fight in which he and his friends were outnumbered. Brandishing a knuckle duster, Winner laid out several men but was then arrested. Davies takes up the story:

A few hours later he was dragged in front of a judge. The sentence was simple: ten days in jail – or ten lashes and go free. Snapper [Winner] was already late reporting back to the barracks. And while he could explain away a few hours' delay, several days in jail were out of the question. Having opted for corporal punishment, Snapper was led downstairs to a windowless cell, the centre of which was taken by a table covered with several straps. There were two guards with Snapper and two more Chinese in white coats stood watching from the side-lines, while in the corner stood the largest Chinese man Snapper had ever seen: he was selecting a whip from a rack. What the hell, thought Snapper, it's only ten lashes, I'll be out of here in a few minutes. With that, he allowed himself to be examined. Then, his trousers around his ankles, he was bent over the table and strapped to it face down. He could only hear the footfalls of the giant as he ran forward with the whip – then he felt the contact. In his own words, 'It felt like someone had stuck an electric wire up my arse.' Snapper held it together for the first few lashes, then he let it all go. As a result of the whipping, he was hospitalised and sent to Cyprus. Once he was better, he was RTU'd [returned to unit] from the Regiment – but not for long.

Winner tells me that this story is absolutely true – except that he had a choice of six months in jail or six lashes, rather than ten of one or the other. He also spent three weeks in detention – not hours – before a court hearing, which, in turn, took a full three days.

In his anonymous autobiography, *Soldier I: SAS* – written with Michael Paul Kennedy – Winner tells how he became convinced the SAS would storm 16 Prince's Gate as soon as one of the hostages was murdered. 'There could be no going back now . . . Direct action would have to be taken,' he wrote. He also told of the thoughts that had been going through his mind as he and other SAS men waited, often bored by the many hours of inactivity.

> I let my mind wander through the problems of attacking a building with over fifty rooms. We would need speed, we would need surprise, we would need aggression. I thought of the words of advice from Paddy Mayne, one of the founders of the SAS: 'When you enter a room full of armed men, shoot the first person who makes a move, hostile or otherwise. He has started to think and is therefore dangerous.'

Winner gives a vivid description of the moment when the SAS went in, and I will not try to improve on it:

> Boooooom! 7.23 p.m. The deafening explosion of the diversion charge was like a thousand wind-slammed doors. It rocked the Iranian Embassy and shattered the eerie silence. Two call signs from Zero Delta located behind the high wall at the front of the building began pumping CS gas through the broken windows. Orange-yellow flames burst through the windows and licked into the mellowing gold of the early evening sun which layered

the Roman columns and ornate balustrades with a soft coat of creamy light.

My troop was waiting, counting the microseconds, in the Royal College of Physicians next door to the Embassy. I stared in disbelief as Mac [McAleese], ex Royal Engineers and as tough a Jock as they come, his MP-5 [German-made 9mm machine-gun] on a loose sling around his neck, held up a novelty cardboard frog suspended on two pieces of string. As he pulled on the ends of the string, the frog's green-coloured legs made a ridiculous leaping motion. This act of pure pantomime cut through the tension like a hot knife.

Seconds later, the voice in my earpiece screamed, 'Go. Go. Go.' There was no turning back now. We were on our way. I was number one in the crocodile. The rest of the call signs were strung out behind me. Hell, I thought, what am I doing at number one? The new boys should be at number one. I have done my time under fire. I should be at the rear with Sek [Takavesi], my Mirbat mate with whom I have a sixth-sense intuitive understanding in the operational field. Damn the RTU! Damn the demotion! I was pushing out the French windows at the rear of number 14. As I led the crocodile out of number 14 towards the rear of number 16, I glanced up at a block of flats to our left. It was bristling with snipers.

We took up our position behind a low wall as the demolition call sign ran forward and placed the explosive charge on the Embassy French windows. It was then that we saw the abseiler swinging in the flames on the first floor. It was all noise, confusion, bursts of sub-machine-gun fire. I could hear women screaming. Christ! It's all going wrong, I thought. There's no way we can blow that charge without injuring the abseiler. Instant change of plans. The sledge-man ran forward and lifted the sledgehammer. One blow, just above lock, was sufficient to open the door. They say luck shines on the brave. We were certainly lucky. If that door had been bolted or barricaded, we would have had big problems.

'Go. Go. Go. Get in at the rear.' The voice was screaming in my ear. The eight call signs rose to their feet as one and then we were sweeping in through the splintered door. All feelings of doubt and fear had now disappeared. I was blasted. The adrenalin was bursting through my bloodstream. Fearsome! I got a fearsome rush, the best one of my life. I had the heavy body armour on, with high-velocity plates front and back. During training it weighs a ton. Now it felt like a T-shirt. Search and destroy! We were in the library. There were thousands of books. As I adjusted my eyes to the half-light – made worse by the condensation on my respirator eyepieces – the thought occurred to me that if we had blown that explosive charge we might have set fire to the books. Then we would really have had big problems: the whole Embassy would have been ablaze in seconds.

The adrenalin was making me feel confident, elated. My mind was crystal clear as we swept on through the library and headed for our first objective. I reached the head of the cellar stairs first, and was quickly joined by Sek and two of the call signs. The entry to the stairs was blocked by two sets of step-ladders. I searched desperately with my eyes for any signs of booby-traps. There wasn't time for a thorough check. We had to risk it. We braced ourselves and wrenched the ladders out of the way.

Mercifully there was no explosion. The stairs were now cleared and we disappeared into the gloom of the basement. I fished a stun grenade out of my waistcoat and pulled the pin. Audio Armageddon, I thought as I tossed the grenade down into the darkness. We descended the stairs, squinting into the blinding flashes for any unexpected movement, any sign of the enemy, and then we were into the corridor at the bottom. We had no sledge, no Remington with us. So we had to drill the locks with 9-milly, booting the doors in, clearing the rooms methodically as we went along. Minutes turned into seconds; it was the fastest room clearance I have ever done.

It was when I entered the last room that I saw the dark shape crouched in the corner. Christ! This is it, I thought. We've hit the jackpot. We've found a terrorist. I jabbed my MP-5 into the fire position and let off a burst of twenty rounds. There was a clang as the crouched figure crumpled and rolled over. It was a dustbin!

Nothing, not a thing. The cellars were clear. I was now conscious of the sweat. It was stinging my eyes, and the rubber on the inside of the respirator was slimy. My mouth was dry and I could feel the blood pulsing through my temples. And then we were off again, no time to stop now, up the cellar stairs and into the Embassy reception area. As we advanced across the hallway, there was smoke, confusion, a tremendous clamour of noise coming from above us. The rest of the lads, having stormed over the balcony at the front and blasted their way into the first floor of the building with a well-placed explosive charge, were now systematically clearing the upper rooms, assisted by a winning combination of the stunning effect of the initial explosion, the choking fumes of CS gas, the chilling execution of well-practised manoeuvres and the sheer terror induced by their sinister, black-hooded appearance. We were intoxicated by the situation. Nothing could stop us now.

Through the gloom, I could see the masked figures of the other team members forming into a line on the main staircase. My radio earpiece crackled into life. 'The hostages are coming. Feed them out through the back. I repeat, out through the back.'

I joined a line with Sek. We were six or seven steps up from the hallway. There were more explosions. The hysterical voices of the women swept over us. Then the first hostages were passed down the line. I had my MP-5 on a sling around my neck. My pistol was in its holster. My hands were free to help the hostages, to steady them, to reassure them, to point them in the right direction. They looked shocked and disorientated. Their eyes were streaming with CS gas. They stumbled down the stairs looking frightened and dishevelled. One woman had her blouse ripped and her breasts exposed. I lost count at fifteen and still they were coming, stumbling, confused, heading towards the library and freedom.

'This one's a terrorist!' The high-pitched yell cut through the atmosphere on the stairs like a screaming jet, adding to the confusion of the moment. A dark face ringed by an Afro-style haircut came into view; then the body, clothed in a green combat jacket, bent double, crouched in an unnatural pose, running the gauntlet of black-hooded figures. He was punched and kicked as he made the descent of the stairs. He was running afraid. He knew he was close to death.

He drew level with me. Then I saw it – a Russian fragmentation grenade. I could see the detonator cap protruding from his hand. I moved my hands to the MP-5 and slipped the safety-catch to 'automatic'. Through the smoke and the gloom, I could see call signs at the bottom of the stairs in the hallway. Shit! I can't fire. They are in my line of sight, the bullets will go straight through the terrorist and into my mates. I've got to immobilise the bastard. I've got to do something. Instinctively, I raised the MP-5 above my head and in one swift, sharp movement brought the stock of the weapon down on the back of his neck. I hit him as hard as I could. His head snapped backwards and for one fleeting second I caught sight of his tortured, hate-filled face. He collapsed forward and rolled down the remaining two stairs, hitting the carpet in the hallway, a sagging, crumpled heap. The sound of two magazines being emptied into him was deafening. As he twitched and vomited his life away, his hand opened and the grenade rolled out. In that split second my mind was so crystal clear with adrenalin it zoomed straight in on the grenade pin and lever. I stared at the mechanism for what looked like an eternity, and what I saw flooded the very core of me with relief and elation. The pin was still located in the lever. It was all over, everything was going to be OK.

But this was no time to rest, this was one of the most vulnerable periods of the operation, the closing stages. This is where inexperienced troops would drop their guard. The radio crackled into life: 'You must abandon the building. The other floors are ablaze. Make your way out through the library entrance at the rear. The Embassy is clear. I repeat, the Embassy is clear.'

I joined Sek and we filed out through the library, through the smoke and the debris. We turned left and headed back for number 14, past the hostages, who were laid out and trussed up on the lawn ready for documentation, past the unexploded explosive charge, past the discarded sledgehammer and other pieces of assault equipment – all the trappings of battle in the middle of South Kensington. It was 8.07 p.m.

Another dramatic account of the events that day – seen from another perspective – is provided by Frank Collins (see page 263), who was part of the SAS team that stormed the building from the roof. Collins also told of his thoughts as he waited to go into action: 'We are to storm the building from a number of different points simultaneously. My team is going down through the roof. My heart is still thumping. I'm not scared, just scared I'll make a mistake. We've trained for this and we're good, the best. The dry spot in my throat is self-doubt.'

Collins and his colleague moved on to the roof of 16 Prince's Gate from the adjacent building. He wrote:

> Our ball of plastic explosive is in place, so is the detonator. We're waiting for the go, knowing there should be a delay of a few minutes while everyone else gets into position. When the word comes, I'm to be first in. A ladder will be lowered for me and I'll go down into the building. I'd like to use these few minutes to prepare myself but, before we expect it, things are happening. We're waiting for 'Stand by, stand by . . . go!' but instead we get a voice over our headphones yelling, 'Go, go, go!' This is it. Bang. We hit our explosives device. There's a woomph of smoke and dust.
>
> I feel misgivings. Everyone can't be in position by now, something must have gone wrong. My heart's hammering. I hear the words 'Go, go, go' again inside my head.
>
> Alpha-three is hooking the caving ladder onto the roof rails for me to climb down but there's a problem: it won't hook. I tell him to hurry but he fumbles some more. It's essential to take everyone in the building by surprise by attacking simultaneously so I decide to go down with the ladder only half-stabilized. Alpha-three stands aside for a moment. I lower myself into the dark hole at the heart of the building. I have never felt so alone.
>
> I'm twenty-four and have smelled my own fear on occasions, but this isn't one of them. Once the action starts and I am climbing down the rope ladder, hand under hand because it's so unstable, I am no longer aware of my heart beat, my breathing. I am working now.
>
> I am waiting for my feet to touch the ground. When they do,

I am in half-darkness. There is smoke and dust and the smell of explosives. Silence, for a split second. Then the bang and shudder of the building arranging itself around our bomb. I can't hear the rest of the team behind me or the other lads storming through the windows at the front. Am I the only one in? Have the terrorists guessed what's happening? I feel vulnerable. I know the others will be inside in a few seconds but I slide a couple of stun grenades out of their holders and chuck them down the stairwell. They're a spectacular light and sound show. Fairly harmless, but guaranteed to terrify the uninformed.

I enter the telex room. The windows have been blown out. I cover the hall, down on one knee. By now the team has sorted out the rope ladder and my partner, alpha-three, is there behind me. The building is smoking. Perhaps my stun grenades have caused a fire.

When alpha-three taps me on the back, I go. We know the layout on the fourth floor. Our job is to comb this area for people, terrorists or hostages. I burst out, sweeping my gun ahead of me. I stop at each door until my partner taps me on my back. I open it, my gun goes in first, then me, then my mate, and it all happens in a split second. I decide on the instant whether to go right or left and he covers me while I search behind the curtains, and I cover him while he searches the cupboards and under the desks on his side of the room. We've done this back in Hereford a thousand times. It's like clockwork. He yells, 'Clear, clear, out, out, out!' We've shut the door behind us.

Below us is the sound of gunfire, screams, a cloud of CS gas. In my earpiece voices are shouting. Sixty men, one radio channel. What's happening? a voice is saying. The politicians and top brass are anxious for news but they're blocking the channel with their questions. Shut up, someone tells him, we're trying to carry out an operation here.

My mate and I find no one. One door is locked and alpha-three tells me to shoot the lock. I use my MP-5. You'd expect a sub-machine-gun to deal with a lock. Guys in a detective movie are always shooting them off with 38s, but I feel splinters of brass bouncing off into my legs and the lock hasn't budged. I use my axe and in a few swings it's off. We open the door. It's empty. It's a loo. I've shot the lock off the ambassador's toilet.

'Congratulations alpha-three-bravo,' says alpha three.

We've cleared the floor now, our team. The boys upstairs have cleared the fifth. We all go down to the third.

This floor is chaotic. There's a lot of screaming, more gunfire, a strong smell of burning, voices yelling at each other inside my ear.

Someone, I can't tell who, one of the team, runs up to me. My gun is equipped with a streamlight, a powerful torch which is zeroed to my weapon and illuminates the target in the dark. He says: 'You've got a torch, come with me.' I leave my partner as we run downstairs.

He leads me to a door. 'There's a terrorist in here,' he says. 'Not sure if I killed him or not.'

We hit the door. Darkness. Nothing. No noise, no movement. Torches on, I go left, he goes right. I run the beam over the floor and chairs and we advance on the curtains. They are big, heavy velvet curtains and they swish as we rip them down. A yell from the other lad. He's found the terrorist. We both shine our torches on his body. He's dead, fallen back across the sofa, blood on his face, a small sub-machine-gun cradled in his arms, grenades strapped to his body. His eyes and mouth are open. Outside, we tell the team leader about the body. We know the next man who goes into that room will be a scenes of crime officer.

We join the human chain in the stairwell. The boys have already started grabbing the hostages and passing them from man to man down the stairs. I seize each warm, sobbing body and throw it to my left. Some of them are trying to hug me, but I am not gentle. We're trained to handle hostages and I know that any of these grateful, sobbing people could be a terrorist acting as a hostage. And then I pause. I am holding a man by the lapels. He is wearing a green denim jacket. He has bushy hair. Instead of passing him along, something about him stops me. His eyes aren't saying, thank God, I'm rescued. He's afraid. We look at each other but I can't hesitate for longer, the next hostage is being passed to me. I hand him on. A few seconds later a yell comes.

'That's him! That's Salim!' Salim is the leader of the terrorists. I feel sure this is a man with the fight gone from him, a man whose bravado has been replaced by terror. But intelligence tells us that he is carrying grenades and he is thrown up against the wall to be searched.

He is shouting, *'Taslim, taslim.'* No one understands him. The firing begins. His body is rapidly riddled with bullets. A question comes into my head: why so many? But there's no time to ponder it further. The embassy is on fire and we are ushering the hostages out through the back door. [Winner vigorously disputes this account of events.]

The building blazes. There are big flames in the rooms behind us. Outside in the garden we lay all the hostages down, handcuff them and search them. We are all still wearing our gas masks. Anyone who takes off their respirator rapidly puts it back on when they see the TV crews. We climb into the police vans and are driven away from Prince's Gate.

In an interview published in Jack Ramsay's book *The Soldiers' Story*, McAleese said:

I went out on the first-floor balcony with Mal [a comrade] as my cover while Tom and Derek stayed in the room. I carried the frame charge. Once I found my footing on the target balcony I began to place the charge. There was a f***ing zing and a puff of dust at my feet and I realised that I had an incoming shot from somewhere. To this day I don't know whether it was a police marksman who let one go accidentally, or a marksman who thought I was a terrorist appearing. Then there was a clunk beside me and I looked down to see a grenade rolling off the balcony. Then it was gone, so it didn't bother me. The terrorist who dropped it on me had forgotten to take out the pin.

I spotted a white-faced man in the room where we were placing the charge. Miles, one of the team members, waved at him to move away from the window. I didn't know who he was. Tough shit if he got blasted. We had to get in and fast. There were nineteen [in fact there were still twenty] hostages to rescue.

As soon as I had placed the charge, we took off back across on the other balcony, shouting 'Fire!' as we went. This was the signal to the guys inside to detonate the charge. All this happened in seconds. When the charge blew, half the balcony f***ing disappeared. The balustrade was blown clean off. There were clouds of dust from the shattered brickwork.

We stepped through the rubble and smoke into the room and went into our rehearsed routine. Mal went in first and peeled off to the right and I went left. My head kept twitching from side to side because of my gas mask. I had to keep moving in order to be able to see around. I saw this body covered in shit lying on the ground in front of me. Then, still covered in bits of plaster and wood and glass, he began to get up. Later I found out it was Sim Harris, the BBC guy. I sniggered to myself, sort of through relief.

Tom and Derek came in right behind us and went forward down the right-hand side of the corridor. They went into the first room on the right and we took the first on the left. A quick look, flash of the torch, nothing there. Behind us we could hear shooting. It was Derek and Tom killing Salim. We came out of the room and moved on down the corridor. Immediately, Derek and Tom also emerged back into the corridor, pointing to the room we had just cleared, and shouted, 'There's one gone in that room.' We heard scuffling and firing and then Tom yelled: 'I think I hit him,' and we piled into the room. The guy had fired at us and missed, thank f***. He was lying on the couch and he wasn't going anywhere. He was shot up all one side. He wasn't dead yet but I could see he was on his way out. Harris was now up on his feet but we ignored him. We finished off the dodo on the couch. He never said a word.

During the action my mask got knocked and I got a lungful of [CS] gas. As soon as I pulled it back on, I puked up into it. It was only water but it stank. I forced out as much as I could but later had to take it off.

I put Harris out on the windowsill to get him out of the way before going into the right-hand room where PC Lock was. He was very shocked. Tom was talking to him gently, saying, 'Calm down, mate, you're all right. It's all over.' Stuff like that. We instinctively took up guarding positions, one covering the door, one the corridor. The old flames were starting to lick about the room and somebody said, 'I think we better get moving.'

We took Harris back across the balcony into Number 15. He was whimpering and in a right old state of near-total panic. He got slapped a couple of times to bring him down, and apparently complained afterwards, saying he had been handled too rough. But it's the old thing from the training. You know vaguely who the goodies and the baddies are, but you treat every survivor the same way: firmly and roughly to stop them panicking, and to ensure they do exactly what you want them to do. It keeps you personally in control as well. Panic has to be contained.

While this was going on I remember thinking to myself, I wish those bastards in the control room would stop f***ing talking. We were all linked with radio communications and had pressure pads on our kit with which to transmit messages to each other, but the trouble was the bloody people outside kept on asking ridiculous things like 'What's going on? What's happening?' At one point there was so much traffic that several of us lifted our gas masks so that we could shout to each other. The dick-heads on the outside were in a panic because they didn't know what was going on. You couldn't blame them, really. It was easier for us because we knew. You just reacted by instinct.

Mac also described the chaos and confusion in the Embassy as the SAS were unsure who was a hostage and who was a terrorist.

I was at the top of the stairs, and I saw this bloke wearing a green jacket push past me, with hostages in front and behind, and I remembered that we had previously been given a description of most of the terrorists. I realised that he was one of the f***ing baddies. I shouted over the banister, 'There's one coming now!' I pointed him out as I shouted, 'That's f***ing one of them!' Minky had also seen him and shouted as well. Rusty heard me and so did Snapper [Winner], who'd come up from the cellar.

It was another SAS man, Rusty, who shot the terrorist by putting twenty-two rounds into him at point-blank range. Mac continued:

And that was it. No more shooting. Then we found that one of the baddies had got past us and got ready to take him back inside and finish him off. As he was being dragged back in, one of the women hostages put her arms tight around his legs and begged us: 'No, no, no, please don't. He was really good to us.' I guess she had formed some kind of bond with her captor. Other people were now watching and he was kept alive. That's the only reason there was a survivor [a view disputed by others, notably Winner himself].

The boss appeared and checked we had finished the job, then everyone was ordered out of the building, which was now burning fiercely. Some of the guys got souvenirs. I got PC Lock's hat as a memento. Sek noticed the guy with all the bullets in him was wearing a Rolex. There was a bullet clean through it. What a waste.

Amazingly, Lock, unknown to his captors, had remained armed throughout the entire siege but had drawn his gun only when the assault on the Embassy began. He had struggled with Oan during the initial stages of the assault, but had been quickly pulled aside by two SAS men, who pumped fifteen bullets into the terrorist leader to allow him to become the martyr he had seemingly craved to be. There were many other heroics too. In the early moments of the siege a sniper had shot one of the terrorists in the telex room with a single bullet, thereby saving the lives of up to fifteen hostages who were with him.

Operation Nimrod had taken just seventeen minutes but during those seventeen minutes they transformed the reputation of the Regiment because, for the first time, its members had operated in the full glare of the world's media. The rescue had been an overwhelming success. Of the twenty-six hostages taken prisoner, five had been released before the assault and one had already been killed when the SAS went in. Of those still in the building, nineteen had been rescued but one had been killed by the terrorists, bringing the overall death toll to two. Of those who were rescued, two had shotgun wounds. Willie Whitelaw was quickly on the scene and had tears of relief and joy streaming down his face. 'I always knew you would do a good job, but I didn't know it would be this good,' he said. Later he thanked everyone for their role, adding, 'This operation will show that we in Britain will not tolerate terrorists. The world must learn this.' The SAS suffered just one injury – third-degree burns to the man who had got caught up in his abseil, but he later made a good recovery from his injuries. The siege was officially declared to be over by Scotland Yard at 8.15 p.m.

That night, in the Regent's Park Barracks, the SAS men who had taken part in the raid were sipping celebratory beers when Margaret Thatcher and her husband, Denis, unexpectedly joined them. 'Gentlemen, there is nothing sweeter than the taste of success, and you boys have got it,' she told them. At 10 p.m., a television was wheeled in and they watched the day of drama unfold on the news. The prime minister was blocking the view of some of the men, including McAleese, who without thinking shouted, 'F***ing sir down, Maggie, I can't see.' Mrs Thatcher, without flinching and in the knowledge she was the guest in a tough, no-nonsense, male-dominated environment, simply did as she was told and immediately sat cross-legged on the floor.

In his book, *The Regiment: The Real Story of the SAS*, Michael Asher writes:

> It was not only, as de la Billière said, the 'surgical precision' of the operation that impressed the watching millions, but the visual effect, the frisson of menace, of terrible purpose, that exuded from these men in their black hoods, suits and masks. It

was something that touched deep into the collective unconscious. Nothing quite like it had ever been seen before. Operation Nimrod was the single most important event in SAS history. The TV cameras robbed the Regiment of its anonymity and converted it from 'a shady presence' into a national icon. They launched what was to become no less than the great warrior-myth of the late twentieth century . . . In the decade before the Iranian Embassy siege, the SAS was in danger of disbandment for lack of a role. Now its future was assured. In an era when warfare was the domain of smart bombs, multi-billion-dollar defence systems and hierarchies of faceless technocrats, the SAS soldier was a reversion to the idea of individual chivalry. Invulnerable and unstoppable, swinging on ropes, leaping balconies, rescuing the innocent, dolling out death to the villains, SAS-men became instant folk-heroes.

Winner summed up the importance of what had happened at 16 Prince's Gate in his book: 'The day would live for ever in regimental history, of that we were sure.' He was given the name 'Soldier I' nine months later when he gave evidence at the inquest into the deaths that resulted from the storming of the Iranian Embassy. He was one of four SAS men to give their account of the events at Westminster Coroner's Court. The jury ruled that the deaths were the result of justifiable homicide. Five SAS men and Lock were decorated for their courage during the siege. The sixth terrorist, Fowzi Nejad, the only gang member to survive the siege, was sentenced to life imprisonment.

In his book *Special Forces in Action*, Alexander Stilwell writes:

In some respects, at the Iranian Embassy siege a whole country was held hostage. Terrorists had simply walked in and effectively put a gun to the head of the British people and their diplomatic guests . . . Now was the opportunity for the masters [the SAS] to show their hand. They did not fail. They dared and they won. The Iranian Embassy siege may have been a watershed. A certain type of terrorist activity had been proved to be futile against the determination of free societies not to be held hostage and by the professionalism of their armed forces.

In the weeks after the siege, the Regiment received hundreds of cards, telegrams and letters of support from members of the public, as well as numerous gifts. There were also more than 2,000 applications from regular soldiers wanting to join the SAS. Of those just ten were eventually accepted.

Winner retired from the Army on 31 December 1987 after eighteen years' service with the SAS all around the world. During that time – quite apart from taking part in the Battle of Mirbat – he had seen action in numerous danger spots. He had been responsible for undercover surveillance and raids on the IRA in Northern Ireland, he had been involved in dangerous operations in Sudan and he had parachuted into icy seas during the Falklands War. Since leaving the Army, Winner has lived in Herefordshire and worked in the front line of international VIP security. Winner dedicated his autobiography, which was published in 1989, to the anonymous author of the following verse, with which he has easily associated himself since leaving the SAS:

> You served your country for years and years.
> Many laughs through many fears.
> That life ends now, so another can start.
> But a soldier you'll always remain at heart.

5

NORTHERN IRELAND

The Troubles in Northern Ireland lasted broadly three decades from 1968 to the peace process of 1998. During this period of intense violence over the partition of Ireland earlier in the century and its resulting sectarian divisions, some 3,500 people lost their lives. During the early years of the Troubles, the SAS had a highly limited intelligence-gathering role in Northern Ireland. It was left largely to the regular Army to tackle the terrorists, patrol the streets and try to act as a peace-keeping force. However, 1974 proved to be a turning point in the SAS's uneasy relationship with the IRA – first on the mainland and then in the Province itself. A Provisional IRA unit had been active in London for months and had tried to assassinate Edward Heath, the former prime minister, by placing a bomb under his car. When two plain-clothed policemen followed an IRA gang that attacked a central London restaurant, the terrorists abandoned their car, broke into a flat near Marylebone station and took a couple hostage. The Balcombe Street siege – named after the cul-de-sac in which the stand-off took place – lasted six days. It ended when the terrorists surrendered after hearing a BBC radio announcement that the SAS was about to be sent in.

Although the Balcombe Street siege ended peacefully, it prompted a series of terrorist attacks in Northern Ireland. The wave of violence culminated when a band of some twenty Provos stopped a bus carrying Protestant linen workers at Kingsmill Junction. The workers were dragged out, lined up and mown down with sub-machine-guns. In one of the most vicious mass murders of the Troubles, ten died and the eleventh was badly injured. The Kingsmill Massacre was widely condemned – Merlyn Rees, the Northern Ireland Secretary, described it as 'Al Capone gangsterism'. Loyalist politicians demanded action to combat the escalating violence and, within forty-eight hours of the incident, Prime Minister

Harold Wilson announced the SAS would be deployed on patrol and surveillance duties in South Armagh – so-called 'Bandit Country' – because the county was such an IRA stronghold. South Armagh was strategically placed, having a border with the Republic of Ireland. IRA men who carried out terrorist attacks in Northern Ireland could slip back over the border and into the Republic where the Army and security forces were not allowed to pursue them.

The news surprised many, not least the SAS leadership who, at the time, had their depleted reserves operating – as small-group missions – in difficult 'theatres' all around the world. However, the prime minister's announcement had to be followed up and the SAS were given quarters at Bessbrook Mill, which had been a British Army base since the 1970s. Well equipped and set in the rolling countryside of South Armagh, it would be home to many SAS soldiers for some years. As small numbers of SAS men arrived at the former linen mill, the scale of their task quickly became apparent. They were dealing with a highly organised and ruthless terrorist force, which, at the time of their arrival, had taken out forty-nine British soldiers – mainly using radio-controlled bombs. There were other difficulties – the SAS were not allowed to set foot in the Republic of Ireland, which became a safe haven for many a terrorist being pursued by the men from the Regiment. In other locations around the world, the SAS was able to win 'hearts and minds'. However, in Armagh, the Catholic population was overwhelmingly pro-IRA and anti-British. There was jealousy and resentment, too, from the regular Army – the SAS's presence suggested their strategy had failed.

The SAS drew up a list of eleven top Provisional IRA (PIRA) leaders in South Armagh whom they planned to hunt down and arrest. However, they had to follow the same 'rules of engagement' as other British forces in the Province. They were entitled to open fire only if they had reason to believe a person was about to endanger life and they had no other means of stopping him or her. Alternatively – and provided they had issued a warning – they could open fire if a person had just killed or injured someone and there was no other way of making an arrest. The prime minister's initial statement had specified that the SAS would operate 'in uniform' and would carry standard British Army weapons. There was, therefore, lots of scope for errors – deliberate and accidental – as the SAS quickly built up their numbers to squadron strength and set out to thwart the hidden enemy. Some critics of the SAS's presence branded them a 'death squad' that had been brought in to dispose of the IRA units illegally, and early human rights observers pledged to scrutinise their every move. Claud Cockburn, a journalist, wrote in the Irish Times: *'Is South Armagh so short of terrorist gangs . . . that it needs a new one to be imported?'*

During the 1970s and 1980s in particular, the SAS carried out a series of daring and successful operations against the IRA. Sometimes the SAS would wait unnoticed for literally weeks in a field or beside a road in order to target a terrorist or an IRA cell. But there were occasional setbacks and failures, when the SAS were themselves ambushed or their cover was blown. This resulted in death, injury and, occasionally, gruesome torture for those who fell into IRA hands. Perhaps most famously of all, Captain Robert Nairac, an intelligence officer, suffered an horrific death at the hands of the Provos when he was drinking alone in The Three Steps Inn, near Dromintee in May 1977. After his cover was blown, he was brutally tortured and, after he refused to reveal Army secrets, was eventually shot with his own Browning pistol.

Two other secret organisations should be mentioned for their extremely dangerous intelligence and surveillance work during the Troubles – 14 Intelligence Company and the Force Research Unit (FRU). In his book Brits: The War Against the IRA, *Peter Taylor writes:*

> *14 Intelligence Company – known as the Detachment or 'Det' – is the army's most secret undercover surveillance unit in Northern Ireland, so secret that it doesn't exist. Its 'operators' have no names, identities or numbers. They are the eyes and ears of the SAS and the RUC's Special Branch – the men and women trained to gather vital intelligence by breaking into IRA men's houses, bugging or 'jarking' IRA weapons and vehicles, and working undercover at huge personal risk. Regular soldiers call them 'The Muppets' because of their various disguises. Since its formation in 1973, 14 Intelligence Company's role in the 'war' against*

the IRA has been critical, latterly playing a vital – and unacknowledged – part in helping to bring the IRA to the negotiating table.

Members of the 'Det' were chosen from various elements of the armed forces and were usually trained at a number of secret locations on the mainland. Candidates, both male and female, usually volunteered for 'special duties' – leaving their parent unit for, first, training and, then, work in Northern Ireland that initially lasted between eighteen months and three years. Some operatives returned to their parent unit, while others chose to remain for longer with the 'Det'. The organisation was so secretive that even comrades who worked together for years were discouraged from using their real names when speaking to each other. It has to be said, however, that 14 Intelligence Company was at times controversial as well as secretive. There were allegations that it colluded with loyalist paramilitary groups to target IRA terrorists. Today the 'Det' no longer exists, having been absorbed into the Special Reconnaissance Regiment, which was officially formed in April 2005. Some of those men who were given gallantry awards during the Troubles, and were said to be SAS, were in fact serving with 14 Intelligence Company. It was impossible for the authorities to identify them as members of 14 Intelligence Company when, in theory at least, the organisation was 'invisible' and did not officially exist.

No less secretive than 14 Intelligence Company was the Force Research Unit. Its crest was a man with a net and its motto was 'Fishers of Men'. The FRU was set up in 1980 by the Ministry of Defence as a covert intelligence unit. It was intended to replace the Unit Intelligence Offices for Agent Running, which had existed from 1969 to 1978, and the Research Office, which had existed for two years until 1980. The FRU had its headquarters at Thiepval barracks in Lisburn, Northern Ireland, from where its members recruited and ran agents in order to collect intelligence against terrorist activities. However, the FRU had ceased to exist under that name by 1992, following an inquiry led by Sir John Stevens (the one-time Metropolitan Police Commissioner and now Lord Stevens). His inquiry was initiated to investigate allegations of collusion between the security forces (RUC and Army) and loyalist paramilitaries in the aftermath of a number of murders of prominent republicans by loyalist gunmen. The most notable of these killings was that of Pat Finucane, a Belfast solicitor, who represented alleged republican terrorists. Finucane was shot dead in his home by masked men on 12 February 1989. The Ulster Freedom Fighters (UFF), the loyalist paramilitary group, later claimed responsibility for his death. A number of Security Force personnel (although none from the FRU) were convicted of various charges as a result of the Stevens Inquiry.

The two highest-profile 'terrorists' in the pay of the British and handled by the FRU were identified as Brian Nelson, a loyalist leader, and Alberto 'Freddie' Scappaticci, a republican. Nelson, who had previously served in the British Army, is said to have simultaneously worked as the FRU agent codenamed 6137 and as Chief of Intelligence of the loyalist paramilitary group, the Ulster Defence Association (UDA). Nelson is known to have gathered a considerable amount of intelligence on republican suspects, PIRA volunteers and Catholics unconnected with paramilitary activity. When asked by the UDA for an assassination target, Nelson is said to have consulted his index system, selected a target, checked the victim's movements and then passed the information to the assassins. He was also involved in surveillance and intelligence gathering on suspected PIRA members. Nelson was eventually found guilty of terrorist activities and sentenced to ten years in jail. However, he was permitted to serve the bulk of his sentence in England and was released in August 1996 after serving less than four years in prison. Scappaticci, the son of an Italian immigrant, is alleged to have provided the British with detailed information on the IRA's Northern Command, although he denied acting as an agent. The controversy involving the Stevens Inquiry overshadowed much of the brilliant work by FRU intelligence officers.

When I began researching this book, I was in no doubt that the chapter on Northern Ireland would prove infinitely more difficult than all the others. This is because much of the work carried out by the SAS, 14 Intelligence Company and the FRU was so secret. In some cases, the exact circumstances surrounding an incident are not known to me. In other circumstances, I have discovered what *happened but for security reasons have not told the whole story. In still more actions, it would be wrong for me to identify some of the participants because they were working undercover and to do so could still endanger not just their lives and those of named comrades, but also civilians in Northern Ireland who worked with them. In a handful of cases, the individual accounts are all too short both in length and information. However, after working closely with some of the medal recipients themselves, and others, I have come up with a chapter that I hope encapsulates some of the difficult, daring and dangerous work that was undertaken in Northern Ireland. Due to the restrictions on what I can write, I have included some medals that were not awarded for classic Special Forces operations – in fact, there are three incidents in which the British forces were themselves ambushed before fighting back with devastating results. However, presented with the unique set of problems that I have just outlined, I feel anything but apologetic in recounting the bravery of these men in this chapter.*

WARRANT OFFICER LOUIS CLIVE BARNETT

Army

AWARDS: MILITARY MEDAL (MM) AND QUEEN'S GALLANTRY MEDAL (QGM)
DATE OF BRAVERY: 1 AUGUST 1972 – 31 OCTOBER 1972 AND 1 FEBRUARY 1982 – 30 APRIL 1982
GAZETTED: 1 MAY 1973 AND 14 SEPTEMBER 1982

It is certain that Louis Barnett received his two gallantry awards for two exceptional and lengthy periods of bravery that took place a decade apart in Northern Ireland. It is equally certain that the precise details of what he did to deserve them will not – and cannot – ever be made public. Suffice to say the combination of the MM and the QGM is unique for Northern Ireland – and that Barnett was a past master and skilful exponent of undercover work in the Province.

Barnett was born in 1948. He enlisted for the Royal

Regiment of Fusiliers in Birmingham on 2 June 1965. During his Army career, he served in the German Federal Republic, Hong Kong, Brunei, Singapore, Gibraltar, Berlin, Canada, Ascension Island, the Falkland Islands and, of course, Northern Ireland. Initially, at the start of his work in Northern Ireland, Barnett served with Mobile Reconnaissance Force (MRF), an intelligence-gathering forerunner to the Force Research Unit (FRU) and 14 Intelligence Company. He served his first tour of duty in Northern Ireland from July to November 1972 and completed nine further tours in the Province before finally leaving for the last time in March 1983. Altogether he served a total of four years and eleven months in Northern Ireland – far longer than most soldiers.

Barnett was discharged from the Army on 31 July 1988 as a Warrant Officer Class 2, having served for twenty-three years sixty days. His military conduct was described as 'exemplary' and he received the following testimony from a senior officer as part of his Certificate of Discharge:

> WO2 Barnett is a first-class soldier whose loyalty, trust-worthiness, total reliability and devotion to duty have always been in the highest tradition of the service. During his service he has spent many years employed upon duties of a highly classified, extremely sensitive and often very dangerous nature. His courage, the professional manner in which he has carried out these duties and his ever-present good humour have not only set a shining example to his colleagues but have also deservedly won him the respect of all those with whom he had contact.

At the request of the Ministry of Defence, little can be made public about the dangerous nature of his work. According to military sources, he was awarded the QGM for a covert ambush incident at Stranmillis, near Belfast, being accompanied at the time by a serviceman from the Royal Green Jackets. The officer is understood to have been awarded the QGM at the same time. The announcements of his two awards in the *London Gazette* give away little, or nothing, of Barnett's role. On 1 May 1973 it was announced he had been awarded the MM 'In recognition of gallant and distinguished service in Northern Ireland during the period 1st August 1972 to 31st October 1972'. The announcement on 14 September 1982 that he had received the QGM gave away even less: 'In recognition of service in Northern Ireland during the period 1st February to 30th April 1982'.

However, it is understood that Barnett and the officer had been going to meet an informant who, unbeknown to them, had turned double agent and was working with the terrorists. The two men were ambushed but, in the words of one insider: 'Fortunately they gave a good account of themselves which resulted in a number of people [terrorists] being wounded. Later a sweep of the whole area was made which accounted for a number of arrests, seizure of weapons and consequent convictions for terrorist offences.'

Barnett is currently living in the West Country.

CORPORAL GEORGE WILLIAM COURTENAY
Army
AWARD: DISTINGUISHED CONDUCT MEDAL (DCM)
DATE OF BRAVERY: 1 MAY 1973 – 31 JULY 1973
GAZETTED: 18 DECEMBER 1973

George 'Sniffer' Courtenay was born in London in 1946 and was brought up in the capital. He joined the Army on 25 April 1962 direct from an approved school and served in the 1st Battalion, Gloucestershire Regiment. He was wounded during a search operation in the Lower Falls in Belfast, when he was shot in the shoulder from a distance of about 30 metres while he was covering a colleague from beneath an armoured vehicle. Although the injury was serious, he recovered well and was back with his battalion within three months.

His DCM was announced in the *London Gazette* of 18 December 1973: 'For gallant and distinguished services in Northern Ireland during the period 1 May 1973 to 31 July 1973.' During this time, he carried out some work in conjunction with the SAS but he never actually served with the Special Forces. An indication of the type of work he undertook in this period may be gleaned from the following letter from his commanding officer, Lieutenant General Sir Frank King, dated 17 December 1973:

> I am writing to say how delighted I am that you have been awarded a DCM for your bravery and dedication to duty whilst serving with your Battalion in the Lower Falls. I know that last year you were seriously wounded but that you have constantly displayed great leadership, courage and devotion to duty which resulted in large finds of terrorist weapons and explosives particularly during the period 29 April and 20 July this year.

A diary of events for the 1st Battalion, Gloucestershires, in Northern Ireland has revealed evidence of the dangers inherent in searching properties for explosives – on 17 July 1973 two privates were killed and a corporal blinded by an IRA bomb placed on the fifth floor of a building in West Belfast. It tells, too, of the regular 'encounters' of one form or another, whether rocket or mortar attack, or direct gun battles. Courtenay left the Army, with the rank of Acting Colour Sergeant, on 17 May 1986 after more than twenty-two years' service.

Courtenay worked in a newsagent's for some time, but had to retire because of ill health following a brain haemorrhage. Married with two grown-up children, he lives in Worcestershire. 'I suppose I was awarded the DCM because I found some kit [terrorists' weapons] and caught a few people [terrorists],' he told me, with great modesty.

CORPORAL PRIVATE MICHAEL O'CONNELL
Army
AWARD: MILITARY MEDAL (MM)
DATE OF BRAVERY: 16 MARCH 1974
GAZETTED: 8 OCTOBER 1974

Every time an Army patrol went out in South Armagh they knew they were putting their lives on the line. Private Michael O'Connell was part of a four-man patrol that was ambushed by IRA gunmen near Crossmaglen on 16 March 1974.

Unusually, O'Connell, who was born in 1946, had two spells in the Army. He enlisted in the Royal Army Ordnance Corps on 12 September 1961, aged just fifteen, and was discharged on 13 September 1966 on completion of his agreed term of service. However, he re-enlisted on 11 October 1971, this time with the Parachute Regiment, and was twenty-eight when sent to Northern Ireland in 1974.

Two soldiers from the Parachute Regiment – Lance Corporal Philip James and Private Roy Bedford – were killed in the ambush and a third man was seriously wounded. O'Connell fought back ferociously and came to the aid of his badly injured comrade. For his actions, he received the Military Medal. The award was announced in the *London Gazette* of 8 October 1974 but, as with many actions in the Province, scant details were provided in the citation: 'In recognition of gallant and distinguished service in Northern Ireland during the period 1st February to 30th April 1974'.

O'Connell's medal was presented to him by the Queen at Buckingham Palace. He said of the incident: 'I was a member of a four-man patrol which was ambushed by the IRA. The patrol was fired on and two were killed outright. A third member of the patrol was seriously wounded, half his face was shot away [he was later discharged from the Army and received compensation for his wounds]. I dived into a ditch and dragged the wounded soldier in with me, and commenced to return fire. Later, when the scene of the ambush was checked, over 170 spent cases were found in the area where the ambushers had been.'

O'Connell was discharged from the Army for a second and final time on 8 August 1978. His whereabouts today are not known.

MAJOR MICHAEL 'BRONCO' LANE
Army (SAS)
AWARDS: MILITARY MEDAL (MM) AND BRITISH EMPIRE MEDAL (BEM)
DATE OF BRAVERY: NOT SPECIFIC
GAZETTED: 1 JANUARY 1977 AND 9 OCTOBER 1979

It was General Sir Michael Rose, the former commanding officer of the SAS, who perfectly summed up one of the greatest SAS careers of all time. 'Bronco Lane is an exceptional soldier whose spirit of adventure and readiness to take risks has led him to the most extreme and dangerous places on earth – including the summit of Mount Everest. His SAS career spanned more than eighteen years during which he rose from trooper to major, serving for some of that time in the coveted rank of regimental sergeant major. In a deadly fighting force where heroics were not uncommon, Lane was nevertheless a modern-day SAS legend.

Yet he became much more than a soldier – he is also an adventurer, climber and author.

Lane, who was born in Manchester in 1945, enlisted in the Royal Artillery in his home city on 20 September 1961 and he joined the SAS six years later. His award of the MM is unique for Northern Ireland in that it was both gazetted and it named him as a member of the SAS. Even before he became renowned for his courage in the face of the enemy, he had already made a name for himself within the SAS for the circumstances under which he conquered the world's highest mountain. Lane was a keen mountaineer and in 1976, aged thirty, he was part of the Army Mountaineering Association expedition to Mount Everest. Indeed, he was chosen to be one of the 'summit pair', the two sent to the top of the mountain, which stands at more than 29,000 feet. On the way down they encountered a 'white out', which led to conditions described by the expedition leader as 'the worst under which the mountain had ever been climbed'.

It was only when they tried to thread up a new oxygen bottle during an icy blizzard that Lane realised the extent of his frostbite. As he removed his right glove, the ends of his four fingers and thumb remained in the garment. He eventually lost all ten toes to frostbite, too. However, were his mountaineering days and SAS career over – or did he feel sorry for himself? Not a bit of it. He went on to climb Everest twice more, to be awarded the MM for bravery in Northern Ireland, and he even played a role in the Iranian Embassy siege and in the Falklands War.

The recommendation for his BEM, announced in the *London Gazette* on 1 January 1977, detailed the full extent of Lane's courage on Everest. The expedition leader wrote:

As a result of the skill, determination and fitness that he has shown during the early part of the expedition, Sergeant Lane was selected as one of the pair to attempt the summit of Everest. With the help of a support party, he and his companion Sergeant John 'Brummie' Stokes were established at Camp 6, at 27,500 feet, on 14th May 1976. It was planned they should make their bid for the summit on the 15th, but during the night an unexpected and very severe storm developed. This was the worst weather we had experienced so far and made all movement impossible. The summit bid was now in doubt.

The storm abated during the afternoon of the 15th and that evening I discussed on the radio with the summit pair the possibility of them making the attempt the next day. By then they would have been weakened by their prolonged forced stay in the high camp but they assured me that they were fit and well and that, provided the weather was reasonable, they would get to the summit next day. They realised that to delay further would mean all members moving to lower camps to re-stock with essential oxygen and food. This could take many days and we might lose our only chance of reaching the summit.

The early morning of the 16th was fine and they set out to complete their mission. The weather soon deteriorated again and climbing conditions became more difficult but with great determination they pressed on and reached the summit at 15.15 hours. This should have allowed them plenty of time to return safely to Camp 6 and they were right in the decision not to turn back sooner.

However, as they began their descent the weather continued to worsen. They were climbing under 'white out' conditions which became exceedingly dangerous. Their progress was slow. When darkness fell they were still some way from Camp 6 and so were forced to bivouac for the night on the exposed and dangerous knife-edge ridge. They passed the night at this extreme altitude and in intense cold sustaining each other as best they could. Chances of survival under these conditions were slim but they were a very close pair who had worked and climbed together for many years. And so were able to rise to this supreme test of endurance. They displayed extreme heroism in encouraging and helping each other. When morning came, they were exhausted, frost-bitten and barely alive but they forced themselves to continue to climb down. They were met by the rescue party that had moved up to search for them. It was then several days before they were eventually helped down to reach the safety of Base Camp.

From my personal knowledge of high mountains, based on many expeditions to the highest peaks of the Himalayas, I consider the conditions under which they reached the summit of Everest were the worst under which the mountain has ever been climbed. There are few other mountaineers who could have survived such conditions. It was only their extreme valour, determination and sound training that enabled Lane and Stokes to reach the summit of Everest and return to tell the tale.

A letter to Lane dated 18 May 1976 from Peter de la Billière, then based at Staff College in Camberley, Surrey, praised the soldier's 'magnificent achievement on Everest'. The senior officer, who as General Sir Peter de la Billière commanded the British forces in the first Gulf War, added: 'It will be difficult for anyone to beat your record from within the Regiment [SAS].' He ended his letter: 'I am proud to know you and to have served with you. And I know the rest of the Regiment have similar feelings. Magnificent – well done.' It later emerged that Stokes had come desperately close to death overnight. Lane had been forced to feed him oxygen from his own bottle, which revived him when he seemed to be fading away and suffering from snow blindness.

Lane's sympathy was not for himself but for a colleague who died after falling down a crevasse on the ascent. 'Our team had no prima donnas, and unselfishness was displayed to a very high degree. Unfortunately we lost Terry Thompson in a tragic accident, which marred our ascent. Losing a climbing companion is a stark reminder that you do not conquer mountains, but sneak up and down when nature has turned her back.'

With typical modesty, Lane made a short reference to his expedition in his book *Military Mountaineering, 1945–2000* published in 2000. He failed to make any mention of his injuries and devoted just one paragraph to the two men's fight for life on the descent:

> By now the weather had worsened and our only option was to make an emergency bivouac in a small hollow. Taking turns to breathe the life-giving oxygen, we sat out the seemingly endless night, shivering violently and rubbing each other's bodies to stay awake and alive. Occasionally hallucinating, it was a frostbitten, exhausted, dehydrated but extremely grateful pair that witnessed the windless dawn. From the depths of his wind proof suit pocket, Brummie produced some long forgotten pieces of Kendal Mint Cake for breakfast which, despite being covered in weeks of fluff and assorted debris, proved to be delicious.

Lane was once asked if the expedition to Everest had ended his career and he shot back the response, 'Good God, no. A surgeon amputated everything and I was nearly as good as new!'

'But,' continued his questioner, 'you didn't have any toes – and only one hand of fingers?'

'Yes, but they made special boots for me in Hereford and

extended the safety catch on my Armalite rifle and I was fine. You know, fine.'

It was remarkable that Lane continued to serve with distinction in the SAS, with whom much of his most valuable work was carried out in Northern Ireland. He went on countless tours to the Province during which he was awarded the MM for his work in Operation Gingal – an attempt to neutralise part of an IRA Active Service Unit (ASU) in early 1979 – less than three years after he had nearly died on Everest.

Lane and another member of the SAS were in an unmarked car when they were alerted that terrorists had gone to a hidden arms dump to retrieve their weapons for a mission. The arms – waterproofed weapons buried in the ground – had been found days earlier by Special Branch and fitted with transmitters. The transmitters had gone off when they were moved and the SAS was sent into action to try to prevent a bombing mission or an assassination. Lane and his colleague found the car containing four IRA men and there was a shoot-out on the Crewe Road, near Maghera, Co. Derry, at 9 p.m. on 24 January 1979. Details of the incident are sketchy but the IRA is said to have opened fire first, spraying the undercover soldiers' car with automatic fire. Lane was hit in the arm and his colleague took a bullet in the back, but they also succeeded in shooting and wounding one of the terrorists. The IRA car eventually sped off and, once it was a safe distance away, the IRA men abandoned their vehicle and made their getaway, leaving a trail of blood in the snow. There is little doubt that they were on their way to carry out an attack – four rifles and a parcel bomb were found in their car. Lane and his SAS colleague were taken to hospital, but neither was seriously hurt.

Brigadier Colin Shortis wrote to Lane just four days later to congratulate him on his bravery:

I was delighted to hear of your swift recovery. And send my warmest congratulations to you and your troops on the very successful outcome of Operation Gingal . . . I am very satisfied by the overall result; not only have you dented the ASU's confidence very considerably but you have made a very positive contribution to the morale of the more vulnerable civilians, UDR [Ulster Defence Regiment] and reservists in the area. As well as that we have four traced weapons with intelligence potential and one man charged with hopefully more to come. Finally at least one life and possibly more were saved. Whatever way you look at it this adds up to a very considerable success.

Lane continued to serve in the Army long after receiving the MM. He played an active role in the operations room during the Iranian Embassy siege of 1980 and was also present with the SAS during the Falklands War of 1982. Lane was finally discharged from the SAS on 8 February 1987 after more than twenty-five years' service in the Army, eighteen of them with the SAS. He has since sought to play down his own courage and has repeatedly declined to write, or talk, about his bravery in the heat of battle because he refused to compromise what he felt was the code of silence of the SAS – or endanger any future operations. In short, many felt his courage is matched only by his principles. However, as well as his book on Army mountaineering, he wrote an environmental thriller, *Project Alpha*, in 2004. To this day, he retains his black sense of humour. When he was contacted by the National Army Museum about the loan of some memorabilia from his 1976 expedition, he offered his frostbitten toes, which, it emerged, he had preserved and kept in the SAS's regimental mess. The toes have since been returned to Hereford for safe keeping.

Lane, a widower, lives with his new partner in Herefordshire. He is retired but keeps fit by cycling and hill walking.

WARRANT OFFICER KEVIN MICHAEL JAMES
Royal Marines (SBS)
AWARD: QUEEN'S GALLANTRY MEDAL (QGM)
DATE OF BRAVERY: 1 AUGUST 1978 – 31 OCTOBER 1978
GAZETTED: 27 MARCH 1979

Few servicemen are awarded a gallantry medal after being shot at by law-abiding members of the Royal Ulster Constabulary (RUC) and the Scots Guards before holding up hospital staff at gunpoint. But then Warrant Officer Kevin James is no ordinary serviceman and when he was faced with what to do with a dying comrade he took the law into his own hands.

James was born in Westbury-on-Trym, near Bristol, in 1949 and joined the Royal Marines in November 1967, aged eighteen. During a long and distinguished career, he served variously in 3, 41 and 45 Commandos, in addition to the SBS. It was while on a tour of duty in Northern Ireland that an under-cover operation in Dungannon, Co. Tyrone, was compromised and a comrade, who today remains identified only as Noddy, was shot and seriously wounded. When James's QGM was announced in the *London Gazette* on 27 March 1979, it said only: 'In recognition of service in Northern Ireland during the period 1 August 1978 to 31 October 1978'. However, the extra-ordinary story of what happened one night in October 1978 was fully told in Duncan Falconer's book *First Into Action*, published in 1998. The incident happened when James was serving with 14 Intelligence Company, the secretive surveillance organisation, in operations in Northern Ireland. Falconer, who also served in 14

Intelligence Company and who was present on the night of the incident, wrote:

> When several shots rang out, interrupting the cold stillness that had shrouded Dungannon all that week, no one knew where they had come from. A couple of operators reported it, but they were quickly told to leave the net free in case there was an emergency. A radio then opened up and we could hear the sound of gurgling, mixed in with a few inaudible words. The Det commander tried to contact each of the operatives to eliminate them as sources, but whoever was gurgling on the net was holding down the send button preventing all transmission. Luke [a pseudonym for Kevin James] felt certain the shots had come from the Bear Cage area and decided not to wait until the comms [communications] cleared to inform ops [operations]. He leapt out of the car and tore up the hill, gun in hand, towards the car park. The rest of us could do nothing until we found out what was going on. Some operatives suspected it might be one of ours parked up by the lake and quickly drove there, but the operative was fine. We were all unaware of Luke tearing through the town alone and in great personal danger from a number of sources.
>
> If he had encountered an Army or police patrol they would shoot him without hesitation – a man in civvies running with a gun in his hand was a legitimate target, and they would never expect him to be a British undercover operative. Then there were the gunmen themselves – they could still be around and waiting for such a reaction. Luke felt certain it was Noddy who had been hit, but he had no idea from what direction. He saw the car at the far end of the car park in the shadows and sprinted to it. When he got there he found Noddy lying slumped in his seat. The driver's window had been shattered by bullets. Blood seeped from holes in Noddy's face, torso and legs, but he was alive, just.

Luke's only option was to get Noddy to the hospital as soon as possible. He manhandled him over the handbrake and gear lever and into the passenger seat. There was no time to be gentle, he was oozing blood. The threat of gunmen was still at the forefront of Luke's mind. As he sat in the driver's seat to start the car, he could feel the pints of warm blood soaking into the arse of his trousers. He screeched out of the car park, passed the pub where [name removed – an alleged IRA quartermaster] had been standing and sped up the road.

By now the RUC had sent patrol cars to investigate the shooting and the Scots Guards, the local Army unit, were also heading towards the area. As Luke made a sharp turn out of the car park an RUC patrol car appeared in his rear. They flicked on their flashing lights and pursued him. As if matters could not get any worse the RUC assumed Luke was escaping from the shooting and was, therefore, the gunman. Suddenly Luke heard shots. The RUC were trying to shoot out his tyres. A bullet hit the car. Luke was an excellent driver and although he was scared shitless, as he endlessly reminded us afterwards, he never lost control. He was driving for his friend's life. He could not stop to surrender and explain the situation because by the time the RUC had got through their arrest procedure, Noddy would probably have been dead. Luke had no choice but to lose them. We all knew the town like the backs of our hands, and perhaps better than the police. The RUC could not compete with his driving skills, nor did they have the incentive, and in less than a minute he gave them the slip. Other police patrol cars were reacting, but they assumed he was trying to make his way out of town and so coordinated themselves on the outskirts to stop him. That was just fine by Luke because he was headed for the hospital in the centre of town. Noddy rolled around in the passenger seat while Luke continuously talked to reassure him.

Suddenly, Luke's car came under fire again, this time from the Scots Guards, and then, a few streets later, from the UDR. This was becoming ridiculous. Luke eventually screeched into the hospital car park and came to a halt outside the main entrance. He dived out of the car, gun in hand, and ran inside. He was literally covered in blood and the few people in the foyer stopped and stared with gaping mouths. A couple of civilian security guards saw him from the other side of the entrance and made their way towards him. He ignored them, grabbed a wheelchair and pushed it outside to the car. He dragged Noddy out of the passenger side and into the chair. Noddy was still alive but slipping in and out of consciousness. Luke charged up the ramp with the wheelchair and burst in through the entrance doors once again. He was just in time, because now the Scots Guards and UDR were surrounding the hospital and moving in, convinced he was a terrorist. He levelled his gun at the security guards in the foyer, who immediately backed off – they were unarmed.

Luke was filled with adrenaline and shaking. The hospital was not safe ground. The majority of the staff and patients were Catholics and not to be trusted.

'Where's a doctor?' Luke shouted.

A couple of nurses stepped into the foyer, but froze in horror along with everyone else at the sight of these two men covered in blood, one pushing a wheelchair, wild-eyed and pointing a gun. Luke didn't wait for an answer and charged on, pushing Noddy through swing doors and along the corridor as blood dripped from the wheelchair, leaving a trail. He paused outside every door to kick it open, gun levelled, in search of a doctor. He scared the hell out of patients and nurses as he made his way through the hospital.

He finally burst into a room where two doctors were tending

to a patient. Luke could not care less about anyone else. His buddy was dying.

He pointed his shaking gun at them and yelled, 'Fix him. Fix him or I'll f***ing kill you!'

A security guard burst in and Luke aimed at him like lightning. 'Move and I'll f***ing kill you too.'

The guard froze in his tracks and threw his arms up. 'I'll kill all of you!' Luke left Noddy and grabbed one of the doctors and pulled him over to the chair.

'If he dies, you die! I f***ing swear it!'

The doctors were initially frozen with fear themselves, but they pulled themselves together, their professionalism kicked in and they set to work on Noddy. The doors suddenly burst open once again and a tough-looking matron stepped in. Luke levelled the gun at her as she stood beside the security guard with his arms in the air. But this woman seemed fearless. She looked at Luke and said, 'Put the gun down, please.'

'I'm a British soldier!' Luke shouted.

'And this is a hospital. Put the gun down.'

There was something about her calm, assertive manner that Luke latched on to. But he kept his gun aimed as she passed him and started helping the doctors. Noddy was lifted on to a bed and they worked quickly and efficiently. Commands were given for blood: everything was now directed towards saving Noddy's life.

The matron turned to Luke and looked him over. 'Have you been shot too?' she asked.

Luke shook his head.

'Then sit down over there, please. You're in the way now.'

Luke found himself obeying her. He lowered his gun at last as the activity concentrated on saving Noddy.

After a while she came over and looked down on him. She said softly, 'They killed my husband a year ago. He was RUC.'

Noddy had been shot seven times at close range by a .38 special and a 9mm pistol. One bullet had passed through his mouth, shooting a piece of his jaw and tongue away, which is why we could not understand what he had been trying to say over the radio when he was first hit. The other bullets had entered his torso, and one went through his thigh and scrotum. But he survived . . .

James admitted to me that it was an unconventional way for anyone to be awarded a gallantry medal but he said that if he had stopped to explain what was happening his comrade would have died. 'They [the RUC and the Army] thought I was one of the bad guys so they were entitled to take pot shots at me. It was seven minutes of pure bliss. I loved it. The adrenaline was flowing and it was what I had trained all my life to do. I never again met the man whose life I saved and I don't even know his real name. He not only survived but he served his full twenty-three years in the Army.'

This, however, was not the end of James's bravery. After serving in the SBS during the Falklands War, he was mentioned in despatches in the *London Gazette* of 8 October 1982. The original recommendation stated:

Special Boat Service patrols, each comprising four men, were deployed in the Argentinian-held East Falkland Island three weeks before the main landing in order to find suitable beaches and landing areas. The enemy knew the patrols were somewhere on the island and deployed troops, helicopters and EW [Electronic Warfare] means to attempt to detect them, but failed. With the Battle Group 200 miles away and the Task Force still on Ascension Island, the patrols could expect little immediate help if found and probably unsympathetic handling.

However, they were not found. Each patrol remained hidden on a mainly bare island, carried out its task and brought back valuable information which allowed the Commander to decide on the landing area. In every patrol, each man was under considerable strain, not knowing whether he would be found at any moment whilst having to live under physically very demanding conditions. The men engaged in these operations showed a high degree of courage and resourcefulness beyond that normally expected.

Sergeant James was landed in East Falkland Island on 3 May 1982. During his patrol, he came into close contact with the enemy and his patrol became split. He was withdrawn with only half his team on 8 May 1982 but, on 12 May 1982, returned to the same area to find his missing men. His route took him again through the enemy locations he had previously reached and, on 15 May 1982, he went forward to search for the missing men and by chance saw them. During a tense half-hour, he approached and made himself known to them and was nearly shot in the process. He then conducted a skilful withdrawal. Sergeant James therefore successfully conducted two difficult patrols within a short time. He is recommended for the award of a mention in despatches. [See Tom Collins page 270.]

Duncan Falconer said of James, 'For those who really knew him, he was high up on the list of men you would want on your side. He showed a seemingly uncharacteristic coolness and determination under fire. He was very bright, and . . . he could be counted on to do the right thing.'

James retired with the rank of Warrant Officer in late 1989. He joined the police, where he was placed in the Armed Response Unit. Once again Falconer takes up the story:

He was not in the force very long before he joined a section called in to help calm demonstrators who were trying to block the building of a motorway through some woodland. The situation turned nasty and at one point Luke found himself cornered by a dozen anarchists who were responsible for the increased tension between the demonstrators and the police. This group's only objective in life was to travel to demonstrations and incite trouble. By the time other police officers had arrived, the anarchists had beaten Luke to the ground, surrounded him and kicked him unconscious. It was obvious his career was over even before he went to hospital.

For some time James, whose back was badly injured, could walk only with the aid of a cane. He has since suffered from severe pain day and night, as well as with post-traumatic stress disorder.

Today James, who is married with two grown-up sons, lives on the south coast of England.

SERGEANT RICHARD GEORGE GARMORY
Army
AWARD: MILITARY MEDAL (MM)
DATE OF BRAVERY: 21 DECEMBER 1978
GAZETTED: 27 MAY 1979

It was four days before Christmas in December 1978 when Richard Garmory faced his biggest moment of truth since joining the Army – as a Grenadier Guard – nearly ten years earlier, aged just fifteen. Garmory, who was born in 1952 in Washingborough, Lincolnshire, was on his fifth tour of duty in Northern Ireland when all hell broke loose shortly before midday.

This was the confidential 'announcement' – to those in the know on 27 May 1979 – that revealed that Garmory had been awarded the MM:

> At 11.45 hours on 21 December 1978 Sergeant Garmory was in command of an eight-man patrol [Garmory says this detail is incorrect – it was a four-man patrol] operating up the Newry Road in Crossmaglen. He was the leading soldier in the first of two four-man bricks, with the Light Machine-Gun deployed to his rear and two riflemen across the street. When he was fifty metres from what appeared to be a Post Office wagon loaded to the roof with parcels, Sergeant Garmory noticed what seemed to be three unusual gaps/slits in the piles of parcels. He raised his Self Loading Rifle to his shoulder in order to use the Night Sight to gain better definition of the vehicle. At this moment rapid automatic fire was brought to bear on all members of the patrol from the vehicle. Sergeant Garmory immediately issued a contact report, and without any thought for his own life engaged the enemy. Meanwhile, behind him the other members of his patrol were all lying mortally wounded. Realising that his patrol was in desperate danger, Sergeant Garmory then ran back, still under fire, picked up the Light Machine-Gun from the wounded Guardsman behind him and fired the complete magazine at the still stationary vehicle. During this exchange of fire the vehicle began to move away. Sergeant Garmory then ran across the road, picked up the Self Loading Rifle of another wounded Guardsman and fired a further four rounds at the retreating vehicle.
>
> It is not clear at this point in time whether any terrorists were wounded or killed by Sergeant Garmory's actions. Certainly the rear of the enemy vehicle (probably protected from fire by sandbags) was hit a number of times and enemy fire was halted

at one stage as if a man had been hit, but what is beyond a doubt is that in the face of intense and accurate enemy fire at close quarters, and with his patrol in desperate danger, Sergeant Garmory fought like a tiger. He showed a burning courage and fighting spirit beyond praise; his actions were truly heroic. He has set an example as a fighting soldier of single minded purpose and high courage which is an inspiration to us all. For his courage, aggressive resolve and fighting spirit in the face of great danger, Sergeant Garmory deserves high recognition.

The incident had been a telling one because it showed for the first time that even local clergy were unwilling to help wounded and dying British soldiers. Garmory later recounted how he had been with the three others in his brick as they passed St Patrick's Church in Crossmaglen; Guardsman Graham Duggan was behind him carrying a light machine-gun, while Guardsmen Kevin Johnson and Glen Ling were across the road. Garmory had become suspicious because, although it was market day, he noticed that the road was almost deserted. In an interview with Colonel Oliver Lindsay – for a history of the Grenadier Guards – Garmory elaborated on the earlier account of the incident, which had been written after seventy British soldiers had been murdered in South Armagh alone in the previous decade.

Crossmaglen was rather like the Somme that December with duckboards and mud everywhere. We were all living on top of each other; morale was very good – the strange thing with Guardsmen is that the worse the conditions, the better they do. No Army vehicle was about – all movement was on foot or by helicopter. The food was adequate with vast egg sandwiches at all hours. The RUC policemen were very good. They didn't come on to the streets unless they were well protected, and then only to serve a summons for example. Every time we stepped out of the camp we knew we were an available target to an IRA sniper. It was real soldiering and so I enjoyed the danger as did most of the others. All the locals were unfriendly: nothing could be done to break down their hostility.

He said of the ambush:

On coming round the bend near the Rio Bar I saw, forty yards away, what looked like a British Rail parcel delivery van parked partly on the pavement on the left facing away from us. It had an eighteen-inch tail board with a roll shutter that could be pulled down. The van immediately struck me as highly suspicious because I saw what looked like cardboard boxes piled to the top in the back, all flush with the tailboard – so they would fall out if the van moved off fast. I instantaneously put my magnifying sight to my eye and saw four firing slits, two above another two, among the boxes. I immediately opened fire. A lot of things then happened at once.

Garmory went on to say that, from past experience, he knew he was under fire from three Armalites and an AK-47. He thought it likely that two IRA men were firing from a standing position, with two others lying down and firing. His account continued:

I feel I killed the man detailed to take me out. Even so, bullets passed through the sleeves of my smock. I could see them hitting the pavement in front of me and also the wall just to my left. Having fired off my whole magazine I whipped back behind a wall, gave a quick contact report and saw my three Grenadiers had been hit. I ran back to Duggan who was still conscious although an Armalite round had penetrated his liver. I told him to hang on. I was still under fire and the van was still stationary which made me think I'd hit the driver too. I fired off Duggan's LMG [light machine-gun] magazine from the hip in one quick burst which quietened them down a bit. I could see the van's rear must have armoured plating behind the 'boxes' because every third of my rounds was tracer and I could see them ricocheting upwards off the plating. When the magazine was empty I ran across the road to Johnson, moved his body off his rifle and fired more shots at the van as it careered off, partly hitting a telegraph pole just in front of it . . .

He told how staff from a nearby health centre tended to the three guardsmen, but it was too late. Duggan (twenty-two), Johnson (twenty) and Ling (eighteen) were all pronounced dead after being flown by Army helicopter to Musgrave Park Hospital in Belfast. They were later buried with full military honours.

'Looking back on it, as I've done so often since, the terrorists were highly professional,' said Garmory. 'Their supporters' signalling presumably indicated to them that our armoured car [which had been accompanying foot patrols earlier that day] was being refuelled. Months later I heard I'd got the Military Medal. The Queen presented it to me at Buckingham Palace in front of my mother, father and fiancée. It was all very grand.'

A report of the incident from Lieutenant Colonel Michael Hobbs, commanding the Grenadier Guards battalion in South Armagh, highlighted the attitude of the local clergy:

Five minutes after the incident, Guardsman Saunders saw a priest by the church. He went over to him and spoke to him saying that three soldiers were lying badly wounded. The priest made no comment and turned away. Ten minutes after the incident, a second priest walked from the Parochial House to the church. He made no move towards the bodies. On withdrawal, Major Woodrow was going towards the church and saw a priest 20 metres away. He called to him; the priest turned and walked away. Comment: St Luke Chapter 10 Verse 31 would seem appropriate.

The biblical reference comes from the parable of the Good Samaritan and reads: 'Now by chance a priest was going down that road; and when he saw him he passed by on the other side.'

When Garmory was discharged from the Army on his thirtieth birthday in April 1982, he had completed more than fourteen years' service. His military conduct was described as 'exemplary' and his commanding officer wrote: 'Garmory is an intelligent man who can work with minimum supervision. He shows enthusiasm for his job and is generally competent. He is a likeable person and gets on well with most people whether they are his superiors or subordinates.'

After leaving the Army, Garmory joined the Metropolitan Police, working first as a uniformed officer, then a firearms' officer. He left the Met in 1994 and went on to work for the Probation Service and with ex-offenders. Garmory, who is married with two grown-up sons, lives in Derbyshire.

COLOUR SERGEANT ALAN WILFRED HARTLAND

Army (SAS)

AWARDS: BRITISH EMPIRE MEDAL (BEM) AND QUEEN'S GALLANTRY MEDAL (QGM)
DATE OF BRAVERY: 1 MAY – 31 JULY 1979 AND 1 APRIL – 30 SEPTEMBER 1994
GAZETTED: 8 JANUARY 1980 AND 1995

During more than twenty-eight years in the armed forces – most of them in Special Forces – Alan Hartland proved himself time and time again to be a dedicated and courageous soldier. His career achievements were officially recognised on no less than four occasions and he eventually left the Army with a glowing assessment of his military conduct and character. It is frustrating that so little about his work is in the public domain. However, there is no doubt that this is a man who bravely conducted a series of surveillance and undercover operations in Northern Ireland over a period of fourteen years. The quality and quantity of the letters of congratulation that he was sent when he received each decoration bears this out.

Hartland was born in 1947 in the Warwickshire village of Broom and enlisted into the Worcestershire Regiment in 1966, aged nineteen. He joined the Parachute Regiment in September 1971, aged twenty-four, and then served in the SAS from 1983 to his discharge in May 1996. He was awarded the BEM in December 1979. The Queen, unable to attend the ceremony in person, wrote him a signed letter, congratulating him on his achievement.

From May 1980 to July 1994, he served almost continually in Northern Ireland and became one of the most highly decorated soldiers of the campaign. In March 1982, he was awarded the Commander Northern Ireland's Certificate of Commendation

'. . . in formal recognition of your outstanding service in Northern Ireland'. His commanding officer, Lieutenant General Sir Richard Lawson, wrote to him saying, 'Your courage, initiative, skill and determination have been of the highest order.'

He received a certificate for being mentioned in despatches on 6 November 1990 and, finally, his service in Northern Ireland was rewarded with the QGM in May 1995. The Prince of Wales sent him a telegram: 'Having heard the splendid news of your decoration, I wanted to send you my warmest congratulations and very best wishes for your future activities.'

Field Marshal Sir Peter Inge, Chief of the Defence Staff, wrote to Hartland, saying, 'Your exceptional performance during what I know was your fifth tour on operations of this nature was characterised by your excellent planning, skilful coordination and considerable courage. Your wealth of experience together with your fine personal qualities combined to inspire your team. Together you surmounted many complex and dangerous challenges.'

Lieutenant Colonel Peter Telford, from the Joint Intelligence Unit in Northern Ireland, wrote to him thus: 'During your five tours with the unit, covering a period of more than twelve years, you have demonstrated that you are a courageous, dedicated and totally committed special duties soldier. Your very high levels of skill and professional ability enabled you to prevent the loss of life and the destruction of property on many occasions. In recent years your experience also helped many new members to the unit. You will receive only a few letters of congratulations over the coming weeks as your award is not for general release. However, the letters you will receive will come from those who fully appreciate the true significance of this well deserved award.'

When Hartland left the Army on 7 May 1996, the assessment of his military career was given as 'very good'. His testimonial read: 'SSgt Hartland has served twenty-eight years in the Armed Forces, mainly on operational duty. Most of his career was spent with Special Forces. SSgt Hartland is an intelligent and mature individual, with a temperament and character proven in environments of high pressure. He is an experienced manager, administrator and instructor.'

Hartland is married with three children and lives in Herefordshire.

COLOUR SERGEANT (LATER WARRANT OFFICER CLASS 2) PETER CHARLES JONES

Army

AWARDS: QUEEN'S GALLANTRY MEDAL (QGM) AND GEORGE MEDAL (GM)
DATE OF BRAVERY: 1 AUGUST 1979 – 31 OCTOBER 1979 AND NOT SPECIFIC
GAZETTED: 15 APRIL 1980 AND 16 OCTOBER 1984

Peter Jones is one of only two men to receive the combination of the QGM and GM for his work in Northern Ireland. The award of the GM is traditionally made for bomb-disposal or other life-saving work. However, in Northern Ireland, it was often given as a 'cover' award to protect those involved in undercover intelligence work against the terrorists, which is what happened in Jones's case.

Jones was born in Poole, Dorset, in 1944 and joined the Devonshire and Dorset Regiment in 1962. He served with the regiment for thirteen years until 1975, ending with a tour of duty in Northern Ireland, where he initially worked as an intelligence sergeant and showed an aptitude for engaging with the local community – as the servicemen had been encouraged to do by their commanding officer, Lieutenant Colonel Colin Shortis. In Sir John Wilsey's book, *Ulster Tales* (2009), the author devotes the best part of a chapter to Jones's skills and courage. He writes:

> PJ was a natural 'chatter upper'. He likes the Irish – his wife was local after all – and he understood their colloquialisms and idiosyncrasies. He possessed a friendly, open and, for a British soldier on operations, an unusually easy, relaxed manner. Furthermore he had a remarkable memory for faces and places; he recalled well all those he met and what they had said. Everything he gleaned was passed first to his own headquarters; if significant it then went up the chain of command and sideways to the RUC . . . Unselfconscious and naturally at ease in such a situation, PJ did not find it difficult to blend in.

Soon Jones, who had long hair, a beard and wore civilian clothes, was picking up snippets of information and identifying sources who might be willing to help the Security Forces. Sir John continues:

> PJ kept his wits about him, and patiently over a period of time succeeded in forging a drinking-companionship with one of the many engaging Catholics who frequented the clubs and bars of Belfast. PJ carefully nurtured his contact, sinking pints until the early hours, and over time their relationship matured into one of mutual friendship and trust. At the outset neither PJ nor his companion were to know that one day the latter would occupy a position of trust at the heart of the Provisional IRA. When the potential significance of PJ's contact was appreciated, he was redeployed from his relatively humble job as unit Intelligence

Sergeant to work at a higher level under brigade control. This meant that when his Devon and Dorset colleagues completed their six-month tour and returned to Germany he remained in Belfast. He did so for he relished both the spice of his work and its scope, and he enjoyed the status and responsibility he was now given.

Jones was now working for the Force Research Unit, a branch of the Special Forces which was responsible for gathering intelligence on terrorist suspects. Sir John goes on:

If the relationship between a prospective source and a potential handler is to develop successfully, their chemistry must be right. This was where PJ's personality was so significant for there is something unusual about the man. He has a twinkle in his eye, a casual, unhurried manner and an engaging disrespect for authority. This particularly appeals to those who enjoy mystery and intrigue. PJ's new republican friend, himself unconventional, was attracted from the outset by PJ's rebellious streak. Of course, he would have realised that PJ was not local but, in view of his affinity with all things Irish and the quality of his *craic*, there was nothing to suspect PJ was in the Security Forces, still less a soldier on duty. Moreover, PJ's relaxed manner was unthreatening. He did not talk, act or walk like a soldier; he never asked direct questions or pressed for information, even obliquely. Hence PJ's companion felt under no pressure or obligation. Yet, the man's curiosity was aroused and he became intrigued by his engaging, hard-drinking friend.

Gradually, over their late-night drinks, PJ detected that his new contact, despite being a Catholic republican, was unsympathetic to many of the aims and methods of the Provisional IRA. The contact, who was anything but stupid, eventually twigged that his drinking pal was in the Security Services:

> Like a skilled and patient fisherman, PJ read the river well. He bided his time until, intuitively, he judged the moment right, and cast his fly. He hooked and played his fish which he landed without difficulty.

This achievement would turn out to be the Security Forces' single greatest intelligence breakthrough at the time and, arguably, the Army's most significant single contribution to the campaign – moreover an asset that would run and run. PJ's new agent was given a codename, Kerbstone, to protect his real identity. An agent – especially one as valuable as this – had to be protected so that he or she could continue to provide regular, timely and accurate information.

Jones said, 'In this secret world the relationship between the agent and the handler is a marriage – but a one-sided one. The handler must know everything about his agent: his fears, his personal problems, his concerns about money, how often he has sex, and with whom; his relationship with his wife; who he hates within the IRA, and who he likes.' Gradually, Jones's and Kerbstone's partnership thrived as they met regularly in pre-arranged locations – on foot and in cars – with back-up teams ensuring they were not being followed. Both men knew they were in danger – Kerbstone from the IRA's infamous 'nutting squad', which dealt brutally with 'traitors', while Jones knew he was likely to be the target of an assassination attempt if the Provos discovered his Army role. The brutal interrogation and murder in South Armagh in May 1977 of Captain Robert Nairac, a twenty-nine-year-old Grenadier Guards officer who had been working undercover (and was posthumously awarded the George Cross), brought home the dangers of Jones's work. But, shortly afterwards, the security services had a fortuitous breakthrough – Kerbstone, who had remained above suspicion by his IRA comrades, was promoted from a position on the edge of the movement to one at the heart of it.

In April 1980, by which time Jones was handling other agents in north Belfast, it was announced to a limited number of insiders that Jones had been awarded the QGM. His citation remained secret at the time, although he has been kind enough to provide me with extracts from it:

> Colour Sergeant Jones has probably been handling sources for longer than any other Army handler in the Northern Ireland campaign, and in a particularly hazardous area. He has over the whole period worked extremely long and unsociable hours, which has placed great demands on his health and on his family life.
>
> He has shown a special aptitude for recruiting sources and for developing them as useful sources of information. Before he became a Field Source Controller he worked particularly against the Provisional Irish Republican Army. Colour Sergeant Jones' successes against this target resulted in a number of convictions and the recovery of quantities of arms and ammunition, which effectively reduced the capability of the terrorists.
>
> As a Field Source Controller Colour Sergeant Jones directed the source handling efforts of eight Non-Commissioned Officers, in addition to continuing to run his own sources. His personal example, his powers of leadership and his meticulous planning inspired confidence in these Non-Commissioned Officers and encouraged them to achievements which were well beyond normal expectations.
>
> Colour Sergeant Jones has for three years carried out

innumerable sources meetings, in the full knowledge that the terrorists place great importance on identifying informers in their organisation and on disrupting the activities of the Army's acquisition system. Each meeting carries its own risk of compromise, abduction and death. Colour Sergeant Jones has shown outstanding personal bravery over a protracted period and has never let his personal safety stand in the way of operations. His steady nerve and dedication to duty have impressed and inspired all who have served with him, and his conspicuous and courageous contribution to Army intelligence in Northern Ireland makes him worthy of high recognition.

Promotion followed the official recognition. Jones became detachment commander of a unit assigned to the covert collection of intelligence in South Armagh, notorious as the IRA's heartland. In *Ulster Tales*, Sir John writes: 'As a professional challenge this was the equivalent of leading an assault on Everest with a small, dedicated team: the pinnacle of attainment.' As Nairac's brutal death had shown, South Armagh was the sort of place where a stranger or an unfamiliar vehicle immediately aroused suspicion. Furthermore, given his new responsibilities, Jones had to facilitate the transfer of the running of Kerbstone to a new handler. Kerbstone, despite his animosity to aspects of the IRA, would not accept an RUC handler and so another suitable Army handler had to be found and introduced to the agent. It eventually took six months to achieve a smooth and effective transition.

The dangerous work undertaken by Jones and his team often went unheralded but they provided invaluable intelligence on terrorists and their targets. They found themselves investigating not just the IRA but also the Irish National Liberation Army (INLA), whose leader was the psychopathic Dominic 'Mad Dog'

McGlinchy. It was INLA who, in March 1979, was responsible for the murder of Margaret Thatcher's friend, Airey Neave, by placing a bomb under his car at the House of Commons. Jones successfully targeted INLA and McGlinchy through an informant. However, the INLA informant fell under suspicion and was brought in for questioning by McGlinchy, whose favoured method of getting people to talk was to place them forcibly on two hobs of an electric cooker, which were then switched on. McGlinchy's brutality forced the source to tell him the time and location of the next meeting with his handler.

Fortunately for the Security Forces, they learnt that their agent had been compromised but this did not mean they were out of danger – far from it. Sir John takes up the story of how Jones and his team decided to proceed with the planned meeting with the agent:

> Volunteering for the role of tethered goat, PJ took up position at the appointed spot on the Newry Canal covered by hidden specially selected soldiers. The intention was that Dominic McGlinchy's ambush would itself be ambushed. But this was a high risk operation played for high stakes, and hence had to be authorised at the highest operational level. PJ's life was very much on the line if anything went wrong with his back-up, and he felt distinctly exposed and alone waiting there.

In fact, McGlinchy, perhaps sensing something was amiss, never turned up and the operation was aborted. McGlinchy – at this stage, the most wanted man in Northern Ireland – was eventually arrested south of the border on St Patrick's Day 1984, seized after a shoot-out with the Gardai in which he was wounded. He was extradited to Northern Ireland and, aged thirty, sentenced to life imprisonment after being convicted of the murder of a policeman's mother. This conviction was over-turned in October 1985 on the grounds of insufficient evidence, and McGlinchy was returned to the Republic of Ireland where he was sentenced to ten years' imprisonment on firearms charges. His wife Mary, the mother of his three children, was murdered in Dundalk on 31 January 1987 by fellow members of INLA but McGlinchy was not allowed to attend her funeral. He was released from prison in 1993, but on 10 February 1994 he was making a call from a phonebox in Drogheda when two men got out of a vehicle and shot him fourteen times. No one has ever been charged with his murder and it is not known which group carried out the killing.

As Jones's military career came to an end in 1984, he was honoured once more. The *London Gazette* of 16 October 1984 announced he had been awarded the George Medal. His citation was confidential but, once again, he has allowed me to see and publish extracts from it:

> Warrant Officer Class 2 Jones is now nearing the end of a two-year tour commanding a plain clothes team engaged in the covert collection of intelligence in the highly dangerous area of South Armagh. He had volunteered to return to Northern Ireland after only eighteen months away following an intensive three-year tour in which he earned the Queen's Gallantry Medal for his work.
>
> Since his return, Warrant Officer Class 2 Jones has provided an outstanding example of leadership, courage and skill to the entire unit. Tasked with improvement and expansion of the agent network within the terrorist gangs of South Armagh, he has worked tirelessly and with great success.
>
> Warrant Officer Class 2 Jones has led countless patrols with the aim of improving local contact in the area. In the area where

roulement [major combat] units spent four and a half months this has led to his identification by local terrorists. Despite this he has on innumerable occasions returned to the area covertly and in civilian clothes to meet informers and agents.

Warrant Officer Class 2 Jones personally directed an operation, occasioned by information from his own agent, which resulted in the capture of two terrorists, the subsequent arrest of twelve more terrorists and the recovery of a large quantity of weapons and explosives.

In this period Warrant Officer Class 2 Jones' team produced a number of highly valuable items of pre-emptive intelligence including details of planned targeting of members of the Security Forces, bank robberies and locations of wanted terrorists. As Field Source Controller, Warrant Officer Class 2 Jones was during this period exposed to all sources run by his office, thus greatly increasing the risk to himself.

Throughout his period in command, Warrant Officer Class 2 Jones has inspired his soldiers through his courage, leadership and skill. He has rendered invaluable assistance to local infantry battalions and has earned the admiration and respect of all those with whom he deals. He has made a major contribution to the war against terrorism in Northern Ireland. His conduct is in the highest traditions of his regiment and the Army and richly deserved official recognition.

Jones's twenty-two years of military service came at a price – his time in Northern Ireland cost him his marriage and he admits he was an absent father for too long. On his final day of service, he was invited to the Northern Ireland military headquarters by a senior officer. This resulted in a surprise party to celebrate both his GM and his retirement. From 1984 to 2002 Jones worked as a freelance financial consultant. He then decided on a career switch, taking a job as a postman for six months while also writing poetry. One moving poem is an apology to his daughter for his failed marriage, his long absences and his fondness for alcohol.

As he began to understand and come to terms with his dyslexia, Jones decided to re-educate himself. In 2007, he graduated with an Upper Second in English (creative writing). He now lives in London, where he is planning to take a masters' degree, while at the same time continuing to work as a writer.

STAFF SERGEANT MICHAEL RAYMOND WATSON*

Army (SAS)

AWARDS: QUEEN'S GALLANTRY MEDAL (QGM) AND BRITISH EMPIRE MEDAL (BEM)
DATE OF BRAVERY: BEFORE JULY 1980 AND BEFORE APRIL 1983
GAZETTED: 1 JULY 1980 AND 12 APRIL 1983

Michael Watson played a key role as an undercover operative in ensuring senior IRA leaders were monitored and their arms and explosives were traced and seized. In this way, he undoubtedly saved many lives in Northern Ireland through his dangerous and top-secret work. He spent more than fourteen years in the Army between 1971 and 1985, serving in the Royal Artillery, 14 Intelligence Company and the SAS.

Watson was born in 1950, in Mossend, Lanarkshire, and after being brought up in Scotland, enlisted in the Royal Artillery at Birmingham on 28 September 1971. During the course of the next six years, he completed three tours of duty in Northern

---

* name changed at the request of the medals' recipient.

Ireland as a corporal, as well as tours in Germany, Cyprus, and Canada. In 1977, he underwent selection for 14 Intelligence Company. As an operator with the Belfast Detachment, Watson was involved in the running of dangerous and highly sensitive operations against 'subversive organisations', notably the IRA. He often worked alone and without support, and took part in many operations culminating in 'executive action' being taken.

From 1979 to 1981, Watson was part of the training team of 14 Intelligence Company, serving as a sergeant and being involved in the selection of operators and training them in fitness, map reading, photography, mobile and foot surveillance, rural and urban observation, weapons skills and close-quarter battle situation awareness and close protection.

In 1981 he returned to Northern Ireland for a second tour of duty with the Belfast Detachment, this time as a team leader with the rank of Staff Sergeant. He ran numerous covert operations for the police and military, and also worked in source protection. From 1983 to 1985, he was commanding a team of specialist technicians in Northern Ireland, whose duties included the covert deployment of technical equipment against the IRA in support of police and military operations, with the aim of recovering weapons and explosives, and facilitating arrests. He was responsible during this period for sensitive and secret equipment, and the operational and administrative running of the unit on a daily basis, often giving briefings at the highest levels of command.

His QGM was announced in the *London Gazette* of 1 July 1980 but there were few clues to his activities in the terse, 'For services in Northern Ireland'. When his BEM was announced in the *London Gazette* of 12 April 1983, the wording was the same. However, the accompanying, but unpublished, 'investiture' citation stated:

Sgt M.R. Watson [name changed], Special Air Service. Sergeant Watson is nearing the end of his second two year tour on Special Duties in West Belfast, Northern Ireland. It has been a tour in which he has been in constant unremitting danger. He is very brave and thoroughly steady and has the full trust and respect of his fellow operators. His ability to move unobtrusively, to accurately observe and report, and his deep understanding of the terrorist has set this splendid senior Non Commissioned Officer apart from, and made him an inspiration to, his fellows. He deserves very special recognition. Full citation graded SECRET.

The Prince of Wales sent Watson a telegram on 29 April 1983, which read: 'Having heard the splendid news of your decoration I wanted to send you my warmest congratulations.' At about the same time, the Queen sent an undated, but personally signed, typed note which said: 'I greatly regret that I am unable to give you personally the award [BEM] which you have so well earned. I now send you my congratulations and my best wishes for your future happiness.'

Watson was discharged from the SAS at his own request on 9 December 1985. He left with the assessment that his military conduct was 'exemplary'. His Army testimonial read: 'He is a high grade soldier who expects his own high standards to be achieved by those with whom he comes in contact. His professional attitude has earned him the Queen's Gallantry Medal and the British Empire Medal for services in Northern Ireland. He has a strong sense of humour and ambition; he would be an asset to any employer. His discharge will be a great loss to the service.'

As a fully qualified SAS instructor in the use of all types of domestic and foreign weapons, and being highly trained in the use of covert photography and video, methods of entry and methods of instruction, he went on to enjoy a successful civilian career as a team leader on numerous large-scale corporate surveillance operations, and as a contracted surveillance instructor to an unidentified foreign government. He has worked in Iraq and Africa in the past two decades. Watson, a widower, with a grown-up son, lives in Scotland.

WARRANT OFFICER BRIAN JAMES GREGORY

Army (SAS)
AWARD: QUEEN'S GALLANTRY MEDAL (QGM) AND BAR
DATE OF BRAVERY: 1 MAY 1983 – 30 SEPTEMBER 1983 AND 1 OCTOBER 1987 – 31 MARCH 1988
GAZETTED: 17 APRIL 1984 AND 27 OCTOBER 1992

Brian Gregory was a fearless soldier who, time and time again, operated alone in carrying out undercover surveillance work in the most hostile environments in Northern Ireland. If he had been captured by the IRA, he would almost certainly have been tortured and murdered. Yet he continued, year after year, to thrive in the most arduous and exacting conditions.

Gregory was born in 1945, and enlisted at Preston, Lancashire, on 27 February 1973, aged nineteen, after serving a short apprenticeship as a mechanical engineer. He served in the Parachute Regiment for eight years, reaching the rank of Corporal, and, in 1981, he joined Special Forces and served in the SAS from 1 October 1986 until his discharge on 1 May 1998. The following testimonial is taken from his original Certificate of Service:

> Warrant Officer Class 1 Gregory joined the Parachute Regiment in 1973. After his basic training he attended several tactics and

weaponry courses. He achieved the high standards required and continued to serve as an Infantryman before volunteering for specialist training in 1981. In 1981 Warrant Officer Gregory passed an arduous selection course for plain clothes surveillance work in Northern Ireland. He then deployed to the Province to serve in numerous appointments. His training in close target recognition, surveillance, close quarter battle and advanced driving was rigorously tested in a harsh operational environment. He was widely respected as a thoroughly professional soldier and leader. He has much experience in planning complex and highly sensitive Counter-Terrorist operations. He has been decorated twice with the Queen's Gallantry Medal for bravery; a testament to his courage and ability to operate effectively under the most arduous and exacting conditions.

Gregory's work was highly sensitive and although his QGM was announced in the *London Gazette* of 17 April 1984, the citation provided no details on his undercover work. All it said was: 'In recognition of gallantry in Northern Ireland during the period 1st May 1983 to 30th September 1983'. The Bar to his QGM was announced in the *London Gazette* of 27 October 1992: 'In recognition of gallantry in Northern Ireland during the period 1st October 1987 to 31st March 1988. To be dated 11th October 1988.' It was a common practice for awards to the SAS and other Special Forces not to be published for several years after the actual award had been made.

Gregory received a number of letters of congratulation in late 1988 when it was known within the Army that he had received a Bar to his QGM. Brigadier Michael Rose, the highly decorated Director, Special Forces, wrote on 10 October 1988: 'Many congratulations on getting a Bar to your QGM. I know that this honour was principally for a very important and delicate operation and it is right that you should receive this recognition. I am delighted for you.' Lieutenant Colonel K. Mallett, of the Infantry Training Unit (United Kingdom Land Forces), wrote on 20 October 1988: 'The award was well deserved and very popular with all elements of the SAS Group, particularly those concerned with operations in Northern Ireland.'

Lieutenant General Sir John Waters, from Headquarters, Northern Ireland, wrote on 10 October 1988: 'I am delighted that your outstanding performance whilst serving with your unit on a second tour of duty has been recognised in this way. You have had to work once again in a most demanding area requiring the highest degree of professionalism. Throughout you displayed great coolness and courage in the face of much danger.' Major General Robert Hodges, Commander Land Forces, Headquarters, Northern Ireland, wrote: 'I want to send you my warmest congratulations on this very well deserved award. It reflects the importance of your contribution whilst serving with your unit during your recent tour to the anti-terrorist campaign. You worked in a most demanding environment requiring the highest degree of personal and professional standards, there was no leeway for mistakes. This you coped with very well and achieved a tremendous amount. Several police officers and civilians owe their lives to your actions in particular during the latter part of 1987.'

In his own curriculum vitae, Gregory wrote: 'I served in Northern Ireland for nine years where I worked undercover carrying out close surveillance on terrorist suspects, this involved getting dangerously close to the terrorists whilst working mostly alone. In August 1986 I was awarded the GOC's [General Officer Commanding] Commendation for one such operation. I was formally discharged from the Army on May 01 1998 and from May 1998 to April 1999 I worked in

Colombia SA [South America] as an Area Security Manager for BP. In charge of security on one and sometimes numerous oil rigs in a very hostile environment. In May 1999 I was employed as a Nato Liaison Officer in Albania during the Kosovo conflict. My duties included aid agency security, refugee camp security and Nato liaison on behalf of forty-nine aid agencies. During my twenty-five years of Army service I have spent seventeen years with Special Forces, nine years on covert Surveillance Operations, and eight years instructing covert Surveillance, reaching the rank of Warrant Officer Class 1.'

Gregory was due to take up an appointment as surveillance manager at the US Embassy in Kampala, Uganda, in September 1999 when he suffered a sudden heart attack. He sold his medals at auction in 2000 to pay for a double by-pass operation and, at the same time, gave an interview to the *Sunday People* about the nature of his work: 'Sometimes you'd see reports of huge weapons caches being uncovered and other people taking the credit. We knew it was our boys who'd done all the work and couldn't say a word. But I loved every minute of it. It was obviously an incredibly stressful, high-pressure job.'

Gregory also revealed that his most terrifying moment in Northern Ireland came when he was ambushed by a mob of IRA men wielding baseball bats. He and a colleague were set up by an informer who led them into a trap, claiming they would find an arms dump at a school in West Belfast. Inside, a gang was waiting for them. 'We were surrounded and there was no way out,' he said. The two undercover men were staring death in the face and were forced to draw their 9mm Browning pistols, which were hidden in the waistband of their jeans. Gregory said, 'As they saw our weapons the crowd backed off for a moment. That second or two was enough to allow us to escape. We could hear the IRA men screaming for our blood as we dived into a doorway. We radioed for help and the RUC arrived just as things were about to turn ugly.'

Another SAS source told the newspaper that Gregory had saved many lives and prevented many atrocities through his undercover work. He described Gregory as one of the Army's top undercover operatives in the Province. The source said that Gregory's role had been to spy on terrorist suspects and infiltrate their strongholds.

Other times Brian would spend days, sometimes weeks, hiding in hedges or in freezing, water-filled ditches silently watching his prey. They may not have known it but Brian came within eyeball distance of some of the IRA's top quarter-masters, gunmen and politicians.

Acting on tip-offs from Special Branch, the RUC and regular Army, he and a tight-knit band of colleagues sought out republican arms dumps, safe houses and meeting places. Sometimes they had to break into houses or neighbouring buildings to plant listening devices and eavesdrop on the terrorists' conversations. It was a slow, painstaking slog carried out in the worst possible conditions. But it was vital to build up a comprehensive picture of what the IRA were plotting. Brian was in the heart of their territory and any wrong move could have meant death and disaster. If he was found he would have been executed on the spot . . . In many ways, Brian's role was far more stressful than being under fire. It took a steely nerve and immense courage.

Gregory, who is married with two grown-up children, lives in France.

MICHAEL ASHCROFT

KEITH JOHNSON*
AWARD: MILITARY MEDAL (MM)
DATE OF BRAVERY: 21 FEBRUARY 1984
GAZETTED: **

Keith Johnson remains the only British military operator to
have survived IRA capture – brief though it was. Normally, as
Johnson was only too aware when he was seized, he could have
expected a brutal fate – torture and death. But Johnson was one
of the lucky ones – even though his survival came at a price. He
stopped three bullets in the shoot-out that freed him and later
suffered from emotional problems, which were almost certainly
linked to the stresses associated with his work, in general, and
this incident, in particular. Citations for all Special Forces
awards relating to Northern Ireland remain classified and it is
rare for those who have received decorations to break cover and
tell their story. Johnson, however, is an exception to the rule and
therefore gives a rare insight into life within one of the Army's
most secret units – 14 Intelligence Company.

Johnson first recounted his story – without being identified –
in Peter Taylor's book *Brits: The War Against the IRA*. Taylor
deserves credit for tracking him down, persuading him to talk
and telling his story so well. Johnson recounts how he is
convinced that 14 Intelligence Company, the Det, had an
immense impact on the conflict:

It got to the stage where the IRA couldn't come outside their
front door without being put under surveillance and tracked. We

___

* rank withheld and name changed to protect the safety of the medal's
recipient.
** details withheld to protect the safety of the medal's recipient.

246

knew where they were going, what vehicles they were using, where they were getting their weapons from and where they were hiding them. By the end of the 1980s, they didn't know which way to turn because we were there all the time. Technology gave us the upper hand even more. We were able to watch them from a great distance, photograph what they were doing – and listen to them.

The wall of Johnson's home bears a souvenir of his many years with the Det in Northern Ireland. It is a photograph of four men wearing balaclavas, bomber jackets and trainers emerging from an old VW Passat. They are armed to the teeth with a Browning 9mm revolver, a machine pistol and an HK-53 assault rifle. Written in a circle around them is the Det's unofficial motto: 'Go out into the highways and hedges, and compel them to come in.' The words were originally from the Bible – Luke 14 verse 23 – but its meaning has been somewhat adapted.

Initially, Johnson served with the Queen's Dragoons Guards in Northern Ireland in the late 1970s. However, he became bored and frustrated by his role of 'just wandering around, showing the flag, offering yourself as an occasional target and achieving very little'. He described how he felt like a mushroom – kept in the dark and never really knowing what was going on. He suspected that on the rare occasions when soldiers found a terrorist's weapon, they were led to it by other agencies to boost their morale. Johnson, however, was given a chance to escape the routine of his work when he was selected as part of a close observation platoon, trained by the SAS. This work was more interesting but he still wanted to be nearer the sharp end of the 'war'.

He didn't have long to wait. A few months later an instructor asked him if he would be interested in 'a more specialist job, more cutting edge'. Johnson applied, although at the time he did not know what the job entailed or even the name of the unit that he was seeking to join. When he discussed it with his father, he was told, 'Keep your mouth shut, do your best and get on with it.'

He was summoned to a secret location in England and when he arrived he was shown into a hut. Inside, a blackboard bore some chalked-up words that were not for the timid or faint hearted. 'Basically,' he told Taylor, 'it was a declaration that you gave up all your human rights and they could do with you as they wanted. Your rank meant nothing and your name meant nothing. You were just a number from then on.' He was given a piece of paper to sign, indicating that he had read and understood the conditions of his work, and it was then time to see if he was suitable material for the testing work – his psychological deconstruction began. 'They're only looking for a certain sort of person and they start weeding them out from the word go,' Johnson continued. 'Any Walter Mittys and James Bonds are soon on their way.'

Johnson said the three-week selection process run by the SAS and the Det was the most physically exhausting and mentally draining experience of his life. He said that of the 130 men accepted for possible selection, only thirty passed. They were then sent for 'continuation training' at another Special Forces camp in Wales. That stage took six months and the skills taught ranged from how to remain anonymous in enemy territory to how to survive if your cover is blown. In that situation, the operative could expect no mercy and one of the most harrowing parts of the course was the highly realistic IRA-style interrogation.

The trainees were also instructed on how to survive a firefight – working with a partner they learnt drills until their reactions became second nature. 'We became like Siamese twins,' Johnson said. He was instructed to carry his Browning 9mm pistol at all times. 'Every day we practised drawing from a concealed position and engaging various targets,' he said. If confronted by the IRA, the trainees were encouraged to fight – surrender meant almost certain torture and death. 'You make a decision, go for it and fight your way through,' Johnson said. 'Our training is to ensure that you don't get taken away for interrogation. But, if you are captured, you've got to make sure you stay alive as long as possible to give your back-up time to find you – for the cavalry to come steaming in.'

Of the thirty recruits who passed the original selection, only nine successfully completed continuation training. The reward for Johnson and his eight colleagues was . . . a trip to Northern Ireland at the height of the Troubles.

In *Brits: The War Against the IRA*, Johnson recalls how the Det operated out of three detachments in Northern Ireland – East Det in Belfast, South Det in Armagh and North Det in Derry. Johnson was posted to Derry, which was where some of the IRA's most experienced gunmen and bombers regularly operated. He was asked to blend in with the local community, while at the same time getting to know the main 'players', or targets. He was in search of anonymity, but as a newcomer to the area that was not always easy.

You would wander around Londonderry and see what people were wearing and style yourself to fit in. The same with your vehicles. You went with the fashion. It was during the early eighties so you could wear flares and your hair would be fairly long. At one time, I had a beard. And you could wear plain-glass spectacles. Anything really to disguise what you looked like. Luckily, you could conceal all sorts of things under your flared trousers – your radio and spare [ammunition] magazines and various other things crepe-bandaged around your legs. It was a sad day when flares went out of fashion.

Operators also had to master the local accent – those from the Province were clearly at a much greater advantage than the Brits. He tried to keep the number of words he spoke to locals to a minimum, so as not to arouse suspicion. 'When you were within speaking distance of some fairly well-known characters, the adrenalin was running and your heart was pumping. I must have bumped into the Minister for Education [Martin McGuinness] a few times.' If the situation got too hairy, operators were asked either to radio for a replacement or, if really necessary, get out of the area altogether. Despite – or perhaps even because of – the dangers, he loved his job. 'It was wonderful. Nothing like it. The buzz was fantastic. The best job in the world with a great bunch of people – comradeship you couldn't describe or get anywhere else.' He felt it was on the side of right, too. 'I think I was fighting for the right of people to live a normal life and hopefully defending them from terrorism. We were defending democracy.'

Johnson had nothing but contempt for the IRA. 'They're just a bunch of cowards,' he told Taylor. 'It's a bit rich they actually call themselves an army. They're Irish Republican terrorists and that's about it.' He also despised the terrorists for planting a car bomb outside the Army's married quarters in Londonderry. At the time, most of the soldiers were out on duty and only their wives and children remained on the base. 'The only way to get them out was to keep running backwards and forwards past the bomb before it went off,' he recalled. Just as it seemed the area had been successfully, cleared, one of the women told him that a young child had been left behind. Johnson dashed back, grabbed the baby and got it to safety moments before the bomb exploded. 'It devastated the houses – blew them to bits. They were going to kill wives and babies – and they call themselves soldiers.' The incident led to the RUC Special Branch officers who cleared the area being decorated, while Johnson was mentioned in despatches for saving the young child.

The undercover work of the Det operators made their jobs all the more dangerous, and many feared it was only a matter of time before their cover was blown. On a rainy night in February 1984, Johnson and his partner, Jack, were involved in an undercover operation in the village of Dunloy in North Antrim. They were working on intelligence that a new Active Service Unit (ASU) was being formed in the village. The Det knew the main players and where they lived. Johnson had even sat across the aisle from one of them on a train from Derry as it travelled along the North Antrim coast. More alarmingly, however, the intelligence agencies picked up information that the new ASU was about to commit a major atrocity. Time was short and the Det knew it had to thwart the terrorists before they struck.

On 21 February 1984, Johnson and Jack staked out a house belonging to the family of one of the suspects – Henry Hogan, aged twenty. His family had moved into their new house just three weeks earlier, having been previously intimidated out of two areas by loyalists who, it seemed, knew their staunchly republican credentials. The family lived in a new housing complex on the edge of Dunloy, where other properties were still under construction. Fortunately, at night, the workmen's huts provided reasonable cover for the surveillance team. That night, Johnson and Jack were hiding in the huts about 100 metres from the Hogan house. Although the property had been under surveillance for some time, Johnson had just returned from leave and it was his first night in the huts. According to intelligence reports, the attack was imminent and a car was expected at the house. The weather was harsh – it was pouring with rain and misty. The two operators were wearing donkey jackets and jeans so that if they were spotted locals would dismiss them as thieves come to steal bricks, or yobs.

However, what Johnson and Jack did not know was that the terrorists had found a bug inside one of their weapons, thereby making them fear they were under surveillance. Furthermore, one of the undercover team had been spotted and so Hogan and a second member of the unit, Declan Martin, eighteen, were ordered to check the sighting. At about 8 p.m., having put on their masks and full combat gear, the two armed men set out into the darkness. Hogan was clutching a Vigneron 9mm sub-machine-gun, while Martin was armed with an Armalite assault rifle – the same one that had been used to murder an RUC constable three months earlier. The two terrorists sought to surprise the men in the huts by stalking them from behind. Then, as a car pulled up outside the house, Jack asked Johnson to confirm that it was the right vehicle. Johnson, who had been covering the rear as his training taught him, turned to look at the car just as Hogan and Martin came out of the gloom. Johnson admitted later, 'They got the drop on us. It was bad skills – and bad luck – on our part.'

The terrorists, however, could not be sure they were confronting the British Army and so they were shouting, 'Who the f***ing hell are you?! What are you doing here?!' Johnson recalls, 'They made us stand up with our hands in the air – the classic cowboy position. It seemed a bit bizarre at the time. For a split second, I thought, "My God. This is a realistic training exercise!".' It seemed that the terrorists intended to take their captives away – for interrogation and to meet a grizzly death. 'Looking into the muzzle of an Armalite kind of clears the mind a bit, knowing what it can do,' said Johnson. The two captives looked at each other, knowing that their training told them they must not be taken alive. Standing a metre apart and with the terrorists just three metres away, they chose their moment. 'You practise drawing and firing like in the Old Wild West movies,' said Johnson. 'Jack and I just looked at each other, nodded and went for it.'

The two men whipped their Brownings from their jackets in a single movement and opened fire in the gloom, putting several rounds into Hogan and Martin. As Hogan fell, he fired thirteen shots from his machine-gun. 'Your instinct at the time is survival,' Johnson goes on. 'You have got to make a decision, go for it, put down as much fire as you can and win the firefight. There's no such thing as a draw. I have always thought of it as unlucky thirteen [the shots fired by Hogan]. Three of them hit me. They just went up my body in a line – one through the knee, one through the thigh and one through the back.' Jack was hit by six bullets – two in the neck, two in the trunk, two in the left leg. After Johnson radioed a contact report to his back-up team, he reached across to his partner and said his name. He checked his pulse but could not feel anything and he realised Jack was dead.

Hogan and Martin were on the ground nearby, injured and groaning. Johnson later told how he fired the remaining rounds of his Browning into them, but they were still alive. It was left to the back-up team to finish them off in what Johnson called a 'fire and movement exercise'. He insisted there was no room for sentiment in trying to save their lives. 'They were armed and minutes before had been putting rounds down,' he said. 'You win the firefight. You make sure you're not the one that ends up dead.' He knew that he was lucky to be alive. 'I don't know whether the word "guilt" describes it. I was alive and Jack wasn't. It could so easily have been the other way round. If he'd been on the right and me on the left, he'd have been alive and I'd have been dead. It's as simple as that.' Johnson was taken to Coleraine hospital in a car to save time waiting for an ambulance. He later recalled being in a bad way 'with blood squirting out and with one of the operators with his fingers in the holes'.

Martin's family did not even know he was in the IRA until they were told of his death. Untypically, Johnson felt a tinge of regret for the two young terrorists: 'On reflection, I felt a bit sorry for them. At least they were dressed as "soldiers". Those who sent them out were responsible for their deaths. They should never have been out there. They should have been at home with their mummies, watching TV. I wasn't sad for them. They tried to kill us and we killed them. That's the way that armies work.'

Johnson spent a year recovering in hospital during which his first marriage, which was already under pressure, ended. He then left the Army but struggled to lead a normal working life. As his second marriage started to fail and he became severely stressed, Johnson went to an Army medical centre and sought psychiatric help. He suffered a nervous breakdown, but eventually recovered. 'The problem is they [the Army] build you up and fine-tune you into a killing machine – and then they drop you,' he said. However, he has no regrets about his choice of career, or even his experiences in Northern Ireland. 'When the time came to leave the Army, I was mortified. To this day, I've never handed in my ID card. I'd have carried on and on if I'd been able to.'

Johnson left the Army with a testimonial that praised his twenty-two years of service and his talents as a soldier and sportsman. 'He is trained, and trained others, in advanced surveillance, photography, weapon handling and close target reconnaissance. He is also a police trained driving instructor. His service with Special Forces is best summarised by his award of the Military Medal for conspicuous gallantry . . . as Johnson [rank withheld and name changed] is a capable and intelligent man. Professionally he has much experience at leadership, man management and the organisation of operational tasks. He is also a fit and active man who, in addition to his adventure training and Special Forces skills, demonstrates a good deal of business acumen and is a service funds accountant. I can wholeheartedly recommend Johnson [rank withheld and name changed] to any future employment.'

Johnson's whereabouts today are not known.

WARRANT OFFICER JOHN McALEESE

Army (SAS)
AWARD: MILITARY MEDAL (MM)
DATE OF BRAVERY: NOT SPECIFIC
GAZETTED: CIRCA JUNE 1989

In his book *The Complete History of the SAS: The Story of the World's Most Feared Special Forces*, Nigel McCrery describes McAleese as 'one of the Regiment's most famous sons, without anyone really knowing who he is'. He added that 'he epitomizes the image of an SAS soldier'. McCrery also wrote: 'He is highly intelligent (more than capable of completing *The Times* crossword in a few minutes), thoughtful and calm, but with an air of menace that most members of the Regiment seem to possess and retain . . .' During an interview with McCrery, McAleese told the author that he knew the SAS was for him when he first visited the camp in Hereford and saw soldiers drinking beer while basking in the sun on old settees. But he didn't pass selection first time, because he failed to complete the final fitness test by just a few minutes, which was probably due to him breaking an ankle halfway around the course. The Regiment very sensibly kept him on, and he completed selection second time around.

McAleese, who was born in Stirling, Scotland, in 1949, enlisted in the Army on 9 February 1970. He was awarded the MM for some highly dangerous and secret missions in Northern Ireland. Most of his work has remained, and will continue to remain, confidential, but it is known, however, that McAleese was involved in a shoot-out in 1988 when three senior IRA men were killed in an ambush at Drumnakilly, Co. Tyrone. The victims were Gerard Harte, twenty-nine, the leader of the IRA in mid-Tyrone, his brother Martin, twenty-two, and Brian Mullin, twenty-five. This incident is detailed by Peter Taylor in his book *Brits: The War Against the IRA*. He says the three men had been placed under surveillance from 14 Intelligence Company, and an MI5 bug had been placed in one of their houses. The security forces established that the IRA intended to kill an Ulster Defence Regiment (UDR) man, who drove an easily recognised lorry around the area. Taylor writes:

> A carefully planned ambush was set up. An SAS soldier, bearing some resemblance to the driver, took over the wheel as a decoy and for a couple of days followed the UDR man's usual route to lure the IRA into a trap. On 30 August, the SAS decoy stopped the vehicle at a pre-arranged spot on a country lane near Drumnakilly, knowing that the IRA was unlikely to ignore such an obvious opportunity for a 'kill'. He acted as if his vehicle had broken down and pretended to be attending to the wheel. The Harte brothers and Mullin drove up in a white Sierra, planning to kill the driver of the truck who they believed to be the off-duty UDR soldier. They were wearing blue overalls and black

masks and [were] armed with two AK-47s and a Webley .38 revolver.

Around a dozen SAS soldiers were lying in wait, some of them manning a heavy machine-gun as they had done at Loughgall the previous year [when an IRA unit was ambushed and wiped out by the SAS as it attacked a police station]. The army said the IRA opened fire first and the SAS returned it as the 'decoy' dived for cover over a wall. A local farmer working in a field a few hundred yards away told a different story. He did not see the shooting but heard the first burst of firing, describing it as loud and rapid, which would suggest the SAS machine-gun . . . The IRA fired 16 shots. The SAS fired 236. The IRA never stood a chance. The subsequent inquest did not reach any conclusion about who fired first. There is no doubt that the SAS soldier changing the wheel was an *agent provocateur* and a very brave one at that.

Margaret Thatcher, the then prime minister, made it clear two days after the inquest that she had little sympathy for the three dead IRA men. 'When you are faced with terrorism, you obviously do not let the terrorists know precisely what steps you are taking to counter their terrorism. Nor shall we. But my message to them is this: do not doubt our resolve to defeat terrorism.'

McAleese, who was one of those firing on the three IRA men, had even less sympathy for his victims. Interviewed by Jack Ramsay for his book *SAS: The Soldiers' Story*, McAleese, who is prone to use colourful language, calls the three terrorists 'bad f***ing people'. He describes the operation in detail:

During the night we discussed final operational details and before first light we moved into position along the hedgeway beside the road where the lorry was due to 'break down'. There were two parallel roads and we placed blokes from the Det out actually covering the road junctions, so as to be able to give us advance warning of the arrival of the hit squad. Plus we had three cars up and about, driving around looking for the enemy. Finally, there was a quick-reaction force of covert police also in the area, ready to move in and provide assistance if needed.

Geordie [a colleague] was the substitute. He looked a bit like the coalman, being a similar size and shape. Once we were in position we gave the okay via the radio and Geordie drove the lorry to our location. We were all wearing the green kit: a camouflage top and bottom, which looked funny, given that some of us had really long hair and beards and all sorts. We also wore a special brassard [badge on the arm] which you could flick down to reveal a coloured band which was our ID. We were in communication with Geordie, who was using a covert radio, so we were chatting away to him while he was on his way and when he first arrived. He was disguised as the coalman, wearing one of those leather jackets like a mat. When he arrived, to my surprise, four more of our lads emerged from the back of his lorry and also positioned themselves along the ditch, in under the hedgerow. We still didn't know if anything was actually going to happen.

I positioned myself right under the truck and chatted to Geordie from time to time. We were aware that our base could hear everything we said (and that it was being tape-recorded) and that our boss and some very senior anti-terrorist police officers were also monitoring our operation. We'd been in position for more than an hour. Suddenly the radio crackled to life with a voice I hadn't heard before that moment. 'X-Ray One spotted.' And then, after a few seconds, 'Heading over your way. Over.'

This was our target. A grungy orange car appeared in the road coming directly towards our position. Geordie was working on the offside front wheel, looking as if he was repairing a flat tyre. As the car approached, it slowed right down. It was f***ing obvious. I remember thinking, 'Here we go.' But you can't do anything. We knew they were f***ing bad bastards but you can't just shoot them. They weren't doing anything wrong. They drove right up and had a good look at Geordie. They carried on up the lane and then, still in full view of our position, turned around and came back towards us. I thought, 'This is it. Something's going to happen.' Gerard [Harte], the older brother, was driving, his brother was in the back and the big fat f***er [Brian Mullin] was in the passenger seat. They drove past us and off the way they had originally come. The c***s disappeared. They went through a couple of checkpoints and disappeared.

Over the next half hour, three or four cars stopped beside Geordie to ask him if he needed a hand. He was polite to them but said no, he didn't need them. Of course, each time a car slowed down we were all ready because we didn't know if they were going to use a different car for the attack. And if they had appeared, we didn't want anyone else around for fear of them getting caught in the crossfire.

After several hours in position, we were talking over the situation with Control. Geordie seemed to have been changing a wheel for more than two hours and it was starting to look a bit f***ing obvious. It doesn't take that long. We agreed that we would stay for just half an hour more. So Geordie started taking the wheel off again. Suddenly the radio came to life. 'There's a white Ford Sierra just pulled into the farm not far from your position.' They gave us continual updates on all the movements in the area. A few minutes later the same white car reappeared with our three targets in it. They had been waiting in this farm to hijack the car. The radio continued, 'Yep, white Sierra approaching the junction. It has now turned right towards you.'

I'd been lying under the truck, face down between the two front wheels. When I knew they were coming for the actual attack, I crawled to the back of the truck and stood up behind it in order to have some cover and also to be able to get a clear line of fire. 'Still coming, still coming,' the radio warned. There was a dip in the road and the car was temporarily out of sight. Just as it came back into view, about 100 metres away, this dick-head was hanging out of the back window f***ing shooting off bursts of automatic fire, from an AK-47, which slammed into the lorry. They were approaching at about forty miles an hour. Geordie was f***ing funny. He hot-footed it round the back of the truck like a cartoon character. He wasn't running properly. More kind of lurching. He dived head-first into the bushes behind me to get out of the way.

We were using Heckler & Koch G3s. As the car came level with me, I put a burst into it. The weapon does ride up a bit as you fire, so I had to put a good line up the side of the car. As this was happening, I honestly thought to myself, 'There's no way they are going to f***ing stop.' But after the car had only gone another ten metres, it stopped. I couldn't believe it. I had put about nine rounds through it. I didn't know if I had hit anybody. The next second the rest of the guys opened up from their positions in the hedge. It was nice. Very nice . . . As the others were firing, I stepped into the middle of the road and pumped rounds into the back of the f***ing car. It was all over in seconds.

In 1980 – and nearly halfway through his Army service – McAleese played a prominent part in the SAS's storming of the Iranian Embassy in London after a six-day siege (see Peter Winner page 171). He was eventually discharged from the

Army on 8 February 1992, after twenty-two years' service, more than seventeen of them in the SAS.

After leaving the SAS, McAleese did a variety of jobs, including running a pub in Hereford and helping to make a television series. McAleese, who is married with four children and lives in Herefordshire, now works as a tactical firearms instructor and also in the security business.

CORPORAL ROBERT DUNCAN
Army
AWARD: DISTINGUISHED CONDUCT MEDAL (DCM)
DATE OF BRAVERY: 13 DECEMBER 1989
GAZETTED: 6 NOVEMBER 1990

Robert 'Bobby' Duncan showed his bravery in what has been described as one of the most spectacular and audacious attacks ever launched by the IRA. His action was immortalised for his regiment – the King's Own Scottish Borderers – in a painting by David Rowlands, the military artist. Duncan and seven colleagues came under an assault of terrifying ferocity from about a dozen terrorists belonging to the South Fermanagh Brigade of the IRA.

Duncan's DCM was announced in the *London Gazette* of 6 November 1990 in a joint citation with Corporal B. Harvey:

On 13 December 1989 the IRA mounted a highly coordinated, sophisticated direct assault on the permanent vehicle checkpoint at Derryard, close to the Fermanagh/Monaghan border, intending to kill all eight men and blow up the base. Concealed in a heavily armoured lorry, twelve terrorists armed with machine-guns, automatic rifles, an RPG 7 rocket launcher, a flamethrower, fragmentation grenades and using a van packed with 500 lbs of explosives, drove to the checkpoint and launched their attack. The base commander was Corporal R.B. Duncan. Corporal I.B. Harvey was commanding a 4 man patrol on task to the North of the checkpoint.

Having seen his road sentry killed, with his observational sentry wounded and incapacitated and the off-duty soldiers pinned down inside the accommodation Portakabins, Corporal Duncan single-handedly held the terrorists at bay. The enemy smashed through the gates of the base in the lorry and drove in the van bomb. In an inferno of point blank fire, grenade and flame attacks, Corporal Duncan fought to save the base and to muster his men. During this action Lance Corporal M.J. Paterson was also killed, being posthumously Mentioned in Despatches.

Moving rapidly across country towards the checkpoint, Corporal Harvey engaged the enemy in the lorry outside the base, instantly drawing a mass of machine-gun and rifle fire. By controlled and skilful movement, he continually engaged the terrorists and led his men through withering fire across open ground, eventually fighting his way to the checkpoint and forcing the enemy to withdraw.

Conscious that the base was in dire peril, Corporal Duncan fought to repel the enemy onslaught and rally his men. In an act of aggressive and decisive intervention, Corporal Harvey forced the enemy to call off their assault. With no regard for their own safety, the conduct of both men under the sternest battle conditions was a model of leadership and personal gallantry.

During what became known as the Battle of Derryard, Duncan had been called on by the IRA to surrender and he was told, if he obeyed, his life would be spared. However, later – as he prepared for duty in the First Gulf War – he told how he refused to comply with the IRA and eventually held out long enough for help to arrive. 'At first I was shocked by the attack but I soon got over it,' he said. 'It didn't put me off then, and it doesn't put me off now. I'm going to the Gulf. It's my job and I'll do it to the best of my ability.'

Duncan's whereabouts today are not known.

FRANK COLLINS
Army (SAS)
AWARD: NOT SPECIFIC
DATE OF BRAVERY: NOT RELEVANT
GAZETTED: NOT RELEVANT

Frank Collins is one of only three of the forty-four people highlighted in this book who was never given a specific gallantry award. Yet he enjoyed a distinguished SAS career during which time he served in Northern Ireland and the Falklands War, and he was the first man through the roof during the Iranian Embassy siege. In short, he is more than deserving of a place in these pages. At the end of his time in the SAS, he found God and was eventually ordained as a Church of England minister. Many of his SAS colleagues mocked him, others respected his views, but his conversion meant he ended up with the affectionate nickname of 'Padre Two Zero'.

Collins told the story of his life in his autobiography *Baptism of Fire*, first published in 1997, in which he uses the book's acknowledgements to thank his old friend Andy McNab, the SAS hero turned author, for his help. It was McNab's own Gulf War mission and later a best-selling book, *Bravo Two Zero*, that inadvertently gave Collins his nickname after he discovered his religious faith.

In the prologue to his book – recorded here in full – Collins conjures up a wonderful image of a dangerous situation that SAS members had to encounter frequently in the Province:

We're in the heart of the Northern Ireland countryside. A Provisional IRA hit team is planning to shoot a man as he leaves his farmhouse. There's only one place to hide: a small group of bushes outside the house. We don't know if the terrorists are already in these bushes. 'Er, what shall we do?' asks my lance-corporal.

I say, 'I'll go. You stay here and cover me.'

'Frank . . .' He starts to argue, but I get out of the car and walk towards the bushes. They are 300 metres away across open ground. In there, perhaps, lurks a terrorist. His gun is trained on me, his safety catch is off, his finger is ready to make the tiny movement needed to kill a man and that man is me. He doesn't want to do it yet. He's waiting until the last possible moment.

Perhaps I appear unafraid. Perhaps he thinks I don't know he's there. He's sweating. He must kill me and probably be killed himself. It isn't easy to murder, even if you're a terrorist. He's crouching in his bush, perhaps shaking, his heart thudding.

I am afraid. I am afraid that he'll shoot me in the face. With every step my body waits, my face waits. My eyes are fixed on the bush and, although I know I'm moving towards it, I feel frozen with anticipation. I'm waiting to die, he's waiting to kill me. Long, long seconds, as long as a lifetime.

I am afraid of dying but I am not afraid of death. I'm a Christian and that means I'm ready for whatever's waiting for me. The prospect is even exciting. I'm about to embark on the greatest adventure. I'm about to see God.

I reach the bushes. I stretch towards them and part the branches. Any man here, reluctant to shoot, sizing up the situation, waiting, waiting to kill, can wait no longer. I brace myself for the impact of the bullet.

Collins, one of five children, was born in Newcastle upon Tyne, the son of a hard-drinking ship's carpenter. His family moved to Whitley Bay when he was a youngster. As a schoolboy at Whitley Bay Grammar School, Collins had wanted to be a soldier and he joined the Army Cadet Force. Later, he joined the Royal Corps of Signals, aged sixteen. He failed a fitness test to join the Parachute Regiment but then, at nineteen, switched his ambitions, becoming a member of the SAS after a troop sergeant told him, 'The SAS is the cream of the British Army. The élite. They're highly trained, mate, to a degree you can't imagine. Shooting, demolitions, medicine, hostage rescue, jungle warfare . . . proper soldiering, the best.'

After his failure to join the Paras, Collins's comrades mocked his chances of joining the Regiment. However, this time he trained hard – running ten miles each night with an 8olb rucksack on his back. He was accepted into the SAS Signals, just as Harold Wilson, the prime minister, announced he was sending the SAS to Ireland in retaliation for the Kingsmill Massacre by the Provos in 1974. The IRA responded by issuing posters of Wilson and Merlyn Rees, the home secretary, holding pistols and looking menacing. Underneath the two men, it read: 'SAS – State Authorized Slaughter. An SAS man will dance with your daughter, deliver milk, drive your taxi. Trust no one. Talk to no one.'

After training in Hereford, Collins was sent to South Armagh. One largely event-free tour of the Province was followed by another – this time more exciting. 'There are car chases and close-target surveillance ambushes and shoot-outs. The signallers have to be able to deal with fast, abbreviated communications,' Collins wrote in his autobiography. By now, Collins was determined to become a fully fledged SAS man – not just a signaller – and he resumed his brutal training regime.

It paid off. In December 1978, aged twenty-two, he was 'badged'. Collins later wrote of his thoughts at that time: 'I've made it. I am in the Regiment. The undistinguished, unpromoted boy signaller from apprentice college has joined the cream of the British Army. No one is more surprised than me. I look in the mirror and someone else, someone new, someone in an unfamiliar beret, stares back at me. I know I'm still me, I don't feel any different. But the uniform says I am different.'

In May 1980, Collins was part of the SAS team at the Iranian Embassy siege (see Peter Winner page 171) and the next year he got married – the bride, Claire, and groom wore jeans and jumpers and had three friends as witnesses, including one, Paul, who wore a suit. 'The registrar keeps trying to marry Claire to Paul,' Collins wrote later. He and his wife, who shared Collins's passion for free-fall parachuting, later had four children together. It was while training in Germany, and encouraged by an American soldier called Larry, that Collins started to develop a religious faith. He started to believe that soldiers are 'God's agents', whose role is to carry out God's punishment on evil-doers. 'For the first time in my life, I have a sense of God. He is there,' Collins later wrote.

Back serving in Northern Ireland, Collins was a member of a sniper team. One job was to monitor a road where intelligence reports indicated that an IRA team was planning to murder a UDR (Ulster Defence Regiment) man. Looking through the sights of his gun, Collins became convinced he had located the getaway car for the hit team. He even thought he recognised the driver as a player – a terrorist. In his autobiography, Collins graphically described the dilemma he – and many other SAS men at that time – faced:

I want to shoot. But do I know for sure, for 100 per cent, that this is a terrorist? It's unlikely, but possible, that it's a civilian waiting for someone. The car remains there for fifteen minutes and for fifteen minutes I agonise. Of course, I don't get the command over the radio to shoot. No one wants responsibility for a shot like this. The other sniper [his comrade] isn't the kind of guy who would work on his own initiative. Should I?

I lie on my hillside weighing up my problem. If he's a civilian he might have a wife and family. That would be a terrible mistake. I would get ten years for murder, but I'd be out in five. What about my own wife and family in that situation? What about my career? But if he's a terrorist shooting him would be the right thing to do. I believe this as a soldier and a Christian. Shooting him might prevent many more deaths.

Eventually, the car drove off without the sniper firing. Collins learnt later that day that he had indeed been observing an IRA hit team in the car, with the two gunmen hidden under blankets on the back seat. Fifteen minutes after driving off, the same men – after deciding to switch targets – went to a factory in Belfast and shot dead a UDR man before abandoning their car – the very vehicle Collins had been watching earlier. 'Working in Northern Ireland, our actions hampered by rules which wouldn't apply in a real war, is frustrating,' Collins wrote. Days later, his best friend and SAS colleague, Alastair Slater, was killed in a shoot-out with the IRA. At the time Collins, a corporal, and Slater had been planning to leave the Regiment to set up their own security company.

Shortly afterwards, Collins decided to leave the SAS in order to take up security work. At different times, he worked for Mohamed al-Fayed, the owner of Harrods, and Sir Ralph Halpern, the head of the Burton group. However, he tired of this and, instead, embarked on a three-year course to be ordained as a Church of England minister. After qualifying, he became curate of St Peter's Church in Hereford – home to the SAS – and its daughter church, St James's. In 1995, Collins rejoined the Army as a chaplain to the Parachute Regiment.

Collins's autobiography closed with the words: 'It's difficult to end a book about your life when life keeps rolling on. I want a lot more to happen to me, but my route so far has been so unpredictable that I can't even guess what's next. I just trust in God to show me the path.' But Collins's life did not keep rolling on. The Ministry of Defence took a dim view of his book – for its insight into the SAS – and Collins was forced to give up his role as an Army chaplain shortly before the book came out. The following year, in June 1998, he took his own life and was found in his fume-filled car in a friend's garage in Hampshire. He had been calmly reading Leo Tolstoy's *War and Peace* as he died and had left a suicide note, called 'The Final Chapter', on his laptop. Collins, who was just forty-one when he died, left a widow and four children under sixteen.

6

THE FALKLANDS WAR,
THE FIRST GULF WAR,
SIERRA LEONE AND
THE SECOND GULF WAR

The Falklands War

On 2 April 1982, Argentina invaded the Falkland Islands, the South Atlantic territories that had been under British sovereignty since 1833. The next day the separate British dependency of South Georgia, 800 miles away, was also invaded, although it had been occupied by Argentinian scrap metal dealers the previous month. Britain's team of Foreign Office ministers, headed by Lord Carrington, resigned after being caught wrong-footed by Argentina's claim to 'liberate' the 'Malvinas'. The Falkland Islands were 8,000 miles from the UK but it was soon resolved by Margaret Thatcher, the prime minister, that they would have to be recaptured – if necessary by force.

Lieutenant Colonel Michael Rose, then the commanding officer of 22 SAS, first learnt about the invasion through a BBC news flash. He immediately told D Squadron to be ready to move. Rose then telephoned Brigadier Julian Thompson, in charge of 3 Commando Brigade – the likely spearhead of any British counterattack – and offered the services of the SAS. The day after the invasion, D Squadron was assembled at the Regiment's headquarters. The following day – 4 April – the men were given a general briefing about the conditions they were likely to encounter in the Falklands. One officer, with typical understatement, described it as 'just like the Brecon Beacons in a wet winter'. The truth was that the SAS were going to have to go to war in the wet and bitter cold of the Falklands or the numbing blizzards of South Georgia.

Both Peter de la Billière, then a Brigadier, and Lieutenant Colonel Rose argued forcibly for the SAS to be included in the task force that would be sent to the Falklands, and by early April, members of D and G Squadrons were on their way to the South Atlantic. B Squadron and members of the SBS also became involved. The Special Forces deployed repeatedly and effectively against the enemy – there was even an aborted SAS mission to attack military targets in Argentina. Twenty SAS members were killed during the Falklands War, including Captain John Hamilton, who was awarded a posthumous Military Cross for his courage on West Falkland when, despite being heavily outnumbered, he fought a spirited gun battle after his observation post above Port Howard was discovered. Hamilton, who had been in the SAS for just over a year, died from severe gunshot injuries on 10 June 1982.

Argentina's military government, led by General Leopoldo Galtieri, had totally misjudged Britain's determination to keep the Falkland Islands, and surrendered on 14 June 1982. The conflict had lasted seventy-four days during which more than 900 people were killed and 1,800 injured on both sides. Neither side had formally declared war on the other.

SERGEANT THOMAS COLLINS
Royal Marines (SBS)
AWARD: MILITARY MEDAL (MM)
DATE OF BRAVERY: MAY 1982
GAZETTED: 8 OCTOBER 1982

It was, in Sergeant Tom Collins's own words, 'a classic SBS operation', which took place way in advance of the large-scale operations to retake the Falkland Islands. The four-man team had been dropped into the heart of enemy territory after a 250-mile journey from their troop ship in a Sea King helicopter. They flew at no more than fifty feet to prevent detection from enemy radar. At one point, they realised they were being chased by a 'hostile' – Argentinian – helicopter, but it peeled off, apparently in the mistaken belief that the Sea King was a 'friendly' aircraft. They were eventually dropped in the dead of night with enough food for three weeks, an armoury of weapons and a clear mission – to recce the area around San Carlos Bay to see if it was the right site for British forces to land with the aim of recapturing the Falkland Islands. The drop-off point, where the men had first to unload their kit and then drop ten feet to the ground from the hovering Sea King, was at Campito, high above San Carlos Bay in the north-western area of East Falkland.

Born in Preston, Lancashire, in 1943, Collins had enjoyed an unorthodox military career, not joining the Royal Marines until he was aged twenty-eight in 1971. Before then, he had worked for thirteen years as a carpenter, having left school at fifteen. Within two years of signing up with 4/5 Commando, he was seeking selection for the SBS, eventually joining in 1973, aged thirty. Now, nine years later, in May 1982, Collins's training, skills and nerve would be put to the ultimate test. He was in charge of the team that would spend an estimated three weeks gathering information on enemy positions and possible landing sites in and around San Carlos Bay. Their only contact with the main British force was to be through morse code. Lengthy daily messages were not an option, in case they were intercepted by Argentinian listening posts. Instead, they sent just the signal 'Tango Charlie' (Collins's initials) twice a day to the British base on Ascension Island to indicate they were alive and well. 'It was a daunting task. Our role was to gather intelligence and assess whether this was a good place to start the invasion,' Collins told me. 'When we landed we expected trouble, but in the end we didn't have any firefights.' The four-man team was equipped with rocket launchers, rifles, handguns and hand grenades.

They suffered a major setback early on in their mission when the BBC – in an act of astonishing stupidity and recklessness – reported that Special Forces were on East Falkland, apparently disguised as local farmers. This led to a huge increase in Argentinian patrols all over the island but still the men remained undetected. The SBS team also heard, but could not see, HMS *Sheffield*, a type-42 guided missile destroyer, being hit by an enemy Exocet missile on 4 May 1982 – the ship finally foundered on 10 May. At the time, the SBS team thought, and hoped, an Argentinian ship had been hit, but they heard on the BBC's World Service that the ship was British, and the loss was a major setback for the task force.

Their own mission had, in fact, almost ended before it had begun. On the first night, they found a small, cramped cave and camouflaged the entrance by putting plants on top of chicken wire. But at first light the next day, an Argentinian helicopter hovered just feet above their hide-out and was so low that one of the SBS men could read the serial numbers on the chopper's rockets.

'The down draught from the enemy helicopter was causing the camouflage material on the front of the OP [observation post] to come adrift,' Collins said. 'Fortunately, it left before causing any serious risk of seeing us.'

From their base in the cave, the four-man team went out with cameras, and also used sketches and written descriptions to build up a picture of the area. According to Collins, 'The first day was very dry and fine, but things changed for the worse from then on. For the first week we didn't have a dry day. Although the OP was in the perfect position for viewing the whole of San Carlos Water, the high winds drove the constant rain directly into our position. I suppose the best way to describe the area was the South Atlantic's version of Dartmoor.'

After more than two weeks – and following another increase in enemy patrols – they radioed asking to be picked up from a pre-arranged spot at nearby Rookery Point. 'Things were getting a bit hot. We decided to get out so that we didn't lose [by being killed or captured] the information we had gathered. Also, to have got into a firefight might have compromised any invasion plans,' Collins said. They waited to be picked up in a new hide-out, beneath a grassy bank in the middle of a penguin colony. Now down to their final food supplies, even the birds began to look appetising. The SBS team went to the pick-up spot every night at an agreed time but it was not until their third visit, with all their kit each time, that the Sea King came in and lifted them to safety. In the end, San Carlos Bay *was* chosen as the invasion point on East Falkland for 3 Brigade Commando on 21 May 1982.

After the war, during which the SBS team carried out other missions, Collins and his team were nicknamed the 'Interflora Squad' by first their comrades and later the media. This was because they spent so much time picking fresh foliage – each night they went out to search for new plants to place on their hide-out so they would blend in with the landscape. The bravery of Collins was recognised when it was announced he had been awarded the MM, but he regrets that the courage of the rest of the team was not officially acknowledged.

Collins left the SBS in 1993 after more than twenty-two years' service. Today he is married with five grown-up children, and lives in Sturminster Newton, Dorset. Collins recently retired from his job as a budget manager for the Ministry of Defence.

SERGEANT THOMAS HARLEY

Army

AWARD: MILITARY MEDAL (MM)
DATE OF BRAVERY: 28 MAY 1982
GAZETTED: 8 OCTOBER 1982

Sergeant Thomas Harley, who served with the 2nd Battalion, the Parachute Regiment, displayed outstanding bravery during fierce fighting at Goose Green, shortly after Argentinian troops had killed Colonel H. Jones in the encounter for which he would eventually receive a posthumous Victoria Cross.

Harley's bravery was fully recognised when his MM was announced in the *London Gazette* on 8 October 1982:

> In the early hours of Friday 28th May 1982, the 2nd Battalion the Parachute Regiment launched an attack on enemy positions in the area of Darwin and Goose Green settlements on the island of East Falkland. The enemy was thought to be entrenched in Battalion strength. In the event their numbers were far greater. Fierce fighting ensued all day. Cpl Harley was a Section Commander in the assault at Goose Green. During the day, in repeated attacks on the enemy, Cpl Harley constantly distinguished himself in action. Leading his section, he and his men assaulted and destroyed three separate positions. Amidst ferocious fighting, he ignored enemy fire to encourage, steady and direct his men in inflicting casualties on the enemy. Throughout, his distinguished conduct and leadership were of the highest order.

At the end of the hard-fought victory at Goose Green, Harley claimed the sword of Lieutenant Roberto Estevez as a trophy of war. Estevez was the only Argentinian officer to be killed in the battle and it had been his machine-gunners who had killed

Colonel H. Jones. Estevez, like Jones, received his country's highest gallantry award when he was later awarded a posthumous Cruz La Nacion.

When Harley left the Army in March 1994, he reclaimed the sword, which for nearly twelve years had been displayed in the Sergeants' Mess. He was later photographed with the sword outside the Imperial War Museum in London. I am now immensely proud to have the very same sword displayed on the mantelpiece of my office in London.

Harley is understood to be working in the security industry.

CORPORAL JULIAN BURDETT
Royal Marines
AWARD: DISTINGUISHED CONDUCT MEDAL (DCM)
DATE OF BRAVERY: 11/12 JUNE 1982
GAZETTED: 8 OCTOBER 1982

Corporal Julian Burdett was awarded his DCM for a Special Forces-style operation while working in conjunction with the SAS. He was serving in the Royal Marines as part of 3 Commando Brigade at the time of a major offensive during the Falklands War. At the time, 3 Para, 42 Commando and 45 Commando – in which Burdett served – had been asked to carry out a three-pronged attack on East Falkland. The first two battle units were tasked with taking Mounts Longdon and Harriet respectively while Burdett's section was assigned the large craggy hill feature called the Two Sisters.

Burdett and his fellow Marines had already completed an eighty-mile, two-day march to reach Teal Inlet in readiness for the attack. By the time they arrived at the bottom of the Two Sisters, they were facing a daunting task – weather conditions were appalling and the enemy was well dug in on high ground. The Argentinian troops, including some Special

Forces units, were protected by well-concealed machine-guns and minefields and the steep incline gave an impregnable feel to their position.

The unit set about gaining intelligence on precise enemy positions with a view to mounting a night-time attack. The information was gathered by small parties of Marines, Paras and SAS soldiers and, armed with this new intelligence, it was decided to launch a combined attack on the night of 11/12 June.

Burdett and his comrades in 3 Commando were faced with a fearsome 300-metre ascent. The pace of their advance was severely restricted by the need to carry heavy Milan missile launchers with them as they climbed up the hillside. The terrain was so harsh that many men were knocked unconscious by falls. Just as the order was given for a final push, the Marines were hit by a devastating artillery and mortar barrage.

The ferocity of the battle, and Burdett's own courage, are apparent from the citation for his DCM announced on 8 October 1982:

> On the night of 11/12 June 1982, on the island of East Falkland, 45 Commando Royal Marines launched a silent night attack against strongly held enemy positions on the craggy hill feature of the Two Sisters, ten kilometres to the west of Port Stanley. As Section Commander, Corporal Burdett was leading his Section when they came under heavy fire from enemy mortars. Two of his men were killed instantly and he himself severely wounded. Despite these setbacks, he continued to steady and encourage his Section as they moved forward. Ignoring his wounds, Corporal Burdett also continued to pass further important reports of enemy positions. Simultaneously, he organised the evacuation of his wounded colleagues until he himself was carried from the

scene of fighting. Despite serious losses, Burdett's selfless and distinguished leadership inspired his men to continue their advance.

The final push for the summit was accomplished by Z Company, which dashed in amid enemy flares and machine-gun fire. By 14.30 hours on 12 June, the Colonel commanding operations was able to radio Brigade Headquarters that – after a fierce two-hour firefight – the position was in his hands.

Burdett's whereabouts today are not known.

The First Gulf War

The First Gulf War, or Persian War, was a seven-month conflict between Iraq, led by the military dictator President Saddam Hussein, and a coalition of thirty-four countries authorised by the United Nations. It lasted from 2 August 1990, when Kuwait was invaded by Iraq, to 28 February 1991, after the Iraqi army was routed by the coalition forces, led by the United States. The aim was to restore the Emir of Kuwait to power and to prevent Iraq's further aggression in the Middle East.

The UN Security Council authorised the use of force to eject Iraq from Kuwait on 30 November 1990. The Iraqis were later ordered to leave the Emirate by 15 January 1991 or face the inevitable consequences. For the first few weeks of the conflict, the SAS was frustrated – it was trained in desert warfare but military commanders could find no obvious role for the men of the Regiment. General Norman Schwarzkopf, the commander-in-chief of the Allied Forces in the Gulf, was not a fan of the Special Forces, preferring to rely on conventional warfare. However, Lieutenant General Sir Peter de la Billière, a decorated SAS hero and the British commander in the Gulf, knew their worth. At one point, ambitious plans were studied to try to simultaneously rescue the 3,500 western hostages in Iraq using Special Forces. Yet, with the hostages split into several groups, such a task was impossible and, in December 1990, most hostages were released.

Initially, Schwarzkopf had hoped Iraqi missiles – hybrids adapted from Soviet-built scuds – would be detected by satellite technology before they were even fired but, from missile testing by the Iraqis on their own land in December 1990, this proved to be unrealistic. Schwarzkopf then hoped that the coalition's vastly superior air power would be able to destroy the missile launchers. However, this too proved impossible – some mobile launchers were moved around Iraq while others were protected by reinforced bunkers. The coalition, therefore, decided to use Special Forces – notably the SAS – to tackle the missile threat. The entire Regiment – other than G Squadron – was committed to the Gulf in the biggest SAS combined operation since the Second World War. They were supported by the SBS and a select team of RAF Special Forces crew. The force that assembled in late December 1990 and early January 1991 included its own signals and headquarters teams and consisted of more than 700 personnel. Of these, more than 300 were SAS soldiers, mainly from A, B and D Squadrons.

As the coalition built up its forces in the Gulf, Saddam Hussein saw that his army would be unable to match the firepower of his enemy in a land battle. When the coalition forces started their air bombardment of Iraq in the early hours of 17 January 1991, Saddam's worst fears came true and he realised his forces were vastly inferior to those of the coalition. On 18 January, Iraq started firing scud missiles into Israel in an attempt to bring the Jewish nation into the war. He hoped that other Arab nations would start supporting Iraq if Israel became part of the coalition.

It was time for the SAS to go into action. Over the next two weeks, several SAS units were dropped, or made their way, deep behind enemy lines. Some were tasked with attacking targets, others with reconnaissance duties so that the mobile scuds could be destroyed from the air. As de la Billière later noted: 'The main lesson we learned with Special Forces is you can't beat a pair of eyes on the ground'. He also later wrote: 'Their {the SAS's} prime operational task was to counter the threat of Iraqi Scud missiles. This objective was achieved with outstanding success.'

The first units sent into Iraq were three patrols from B Squadron with call signs Bravo One Zero, Bravo Two Zero and Bravo Three Zero. These eight-man patrols landed behind enemy lines to gather intelligence on the movements of mobile missile launchers and to target the fibre-optic communications that lay in pipelines. It was Bravo Two Zero, led by Sergeant Andy McNab, that was to go down in SAS folklore. The story of the mission was later turned into a best-selling book and a film after three men were killed, four were captured and tortured, and one made it over the Iraqi-Syrian border to safety. The British offensive in Iraq was codenamed Operation Granby.

The full-scale ground war began early on 24 February 1991. Coalition forces swept into Iraq and, later, Kuwait. As Iraqi forces fled from Kuwait they started setting fire to oil wells but by 27 February the Emirate had been liberated. Just ten hours after Operation Desert Storm had begun, President George Bush declared a ceasefire on 28 February. Coalition fatalities totalled 358, including four members of the SAS. Up to 100,000 Iraqi servicemen are estimated to have died.

In his book Who Dares Wins: The Story of the SAS, 1950–1992, *Tony Geraghty is in no doubt that the SAS prevented an escalation of the war by locating the scud missile launchers – and forestalling Israel entering the war.*

> *The escalation did not happen because the SAS, in its finest hour of geopolitical warfare, kept the lid on the Scud threat just enough to deter an Israeli response either with its ground forces, who were preparing a full-scale invasion of the areas from which the missiles were being fired, or with its nuclear weapons. Had nuclear weapons melted down Baghdad the consequences for world peace would have been incalculable. Yet, as General Schwarzkopf was generously to acknowledge after the war, air power alone could not cope with the threat. Nor could any other formation in the Alliance except the SAS.*

REGIMENTAL SERGEANT MAJOR (LATER MAJOR) PETER RATCLIFFE

Army (SAS)

AWARD: DISTINGUISHED CONDUCT MEDAL (DCM)
DATE OF BRAVERY: JANUARY – MARCH 1991
GAZETTED: 13 MAY 1997

CORPORAL (LATER STAFF SERGEANT) KENNETH PHILLIPS*

Army (SAS)

AWARD: MILITARY MEDAL (MM)
DATE OF BRAVERY: JANUARY – MARCH 1991
GAZETTED: 13 MAY 1997

On a late summer's day in 1991, Peter 'Billy' Ratcliffe went secretly to Buckingham Palace with other members of the SAS. The occasion was not publicised so as to protect the identities of those serving in the Regiment who were to be decorated. In the Throne Room and as the Queen was about to present him with his DCM, she said that serving in the Gulf War must have been very frightening. 'Actually, Your Majesty, I quite enjoyed it,' came the unexpected reply. 'Oh,' said the Queen before presenting the medal to Ratcliffe and moving swiftly on.

Peter Ratcliffe was born into a working-class family in Salford, Greater Manchester in 1951. He was the second of five children and the son of a bread-delivery man, who had served in the Royal Navy during the Second World War, and a Roman Catholic mother. The passionate young Manchester United supporter was a rebellious youngster and left home for good at sixteen. He initially worked as an apprentice plasterer in

---

* name changed to protect the security of the medal's recipient.

Preston, Lancashire, but became disillusioned with his job. He enlisted in the Army in January 1970. Later that year he joined the 1st Battalion, the Parachute Regiment, having passed out as top recruit of his intake. He served with the Paras in Northern Ireland before, in 1972, applying for SAS selection, which he passed at the first attempt. Over the next twenty-five years, he served with the Regiment in Oman, Northern Ireland, the Falklands and the Middle East – as well as mainland Britain.

On 5 April 1982, three days after Argentina had invaded the Falkland Islands, the SAS was on its way to war. Ratcliffe, by now a sergeant, was among those flown to the war zone. At the time, he had been stationed in Birmingham on a two-year posting to 23 SAS, one of the Regiment's two Territorial Army units, as a staff instructor, but as a Spanish speaker he was sent to join D Squadron when it flew on a VC-10 to Ascension Island, a thirty-four-square mile mound of volcanic rock in the South Atlantic. 'In a sense it was a flight into the unknown because we didn't know at the time that we were off to a real scrap,' Ratcliffe later wrote in his autobiography, *Eye of the Storm: Twenty-five Years in Action with the SAS*. Later, once the task force had caught up, the squadron was split among three warships. Ratcliffe went on board HMS *Plymouth* for what turned out to be a ten-day voyage to South Georgia, which was quickly recaptured. 'During the fighting that was to come she [HMS *Plymouth*] was bombed three times by the Argentinian Air Force, on the last occasion being hit by no fewer than three 1,000-pound bombs, which caused severe damage, although the crew eventually managed to put out the fires and patch her up so that she was at least still seaworthy,' Ratcliffe later wrote.

It was in June 1982, towards the end of the Falklands War, that Ratcliffe was tasked with the mission of establishing an observation post (OP) at Fox Bay, on the east coast of enemy-occupied West Falkland. His comrade, Captain John Hamilton, was to establish a similar position some twelve miles to the north-east on the same coast. Carrying 90lb packs, Ratcliffe's four-man team inadvertently strayed on to the airfield at Fox Bay and were forced to lie low in a marsh and then dig in to a sloping bank. When it was light, they found themselves just 200 yards from the enemy and right on the edge of their forward position. 'And the beauty of it was that they had no idea we were there,' Ratcliffe later wrote. 'I thought, Hell, a few more feet and we would have been sharing their trenches . . . From the OP we had a clear view of Fox Bay. The area was bristling with enemy soldiers and their gear. They were at least a battalion strong – perhaps as many as 1,000 men – supported by artillery pieces and plenty of gear.' All this information and more was being regularly radioed back to HMS *Intrepid*.

The team remained there for five days until Ratcliffe decided it was becoming too dangerous and their job had been completed. They moved further away but were still able to send radio reports on the enemy's positions and strength. In turn, they heard over the radio that Captain Hamilton had been killed at Port Howard – they later learnt he had been discovered by the enemy and was shot dead while trying to flee, and another member of the four-man team was captured. Hamilton was later awarded a posthumous Military Cross (MC) – his bravery had enabled the other two men in his team to escape.

On 12 June, their seven-day mission up and their food supplies virtually gone, they received a radio message: 'Stay in your location. Helicopter arrival to be advised soon.' It was to be another five days, however, before the unit – by now frozen and hungry – was picked up by a Sea King helicopter. By 28 June, with the war won, Ratcliffe was back in the UK and preparing to train for his county squash tournament. On 11 October 1982, he was mentioned in despatches for his command of the SAS undercover patrol. Three days earlier, after learning the news privately, the Prince of Wales sent Ratcliffe a telegram, which read: 'Having heard of your Mention in Despatches I wanted to send you my warmest congratulations. I have immense admiration for the way in which you carried out your duty in such conditions and upheld the gallant traditions of the Regiment.'

After Kuwait was invaded by Iraq on 2 August 1990, and the West feared Saddam Hussein's army would sweep through Saudi Arabia and beyond, it soon became clear that the SAS was going to war. Their enemy were battle-hardened veterans of the eight-year Iran–Iraq war, who were not afraid to use nerve and poison gas to achieve their objectives. It was decided that, with the exception of G Squadron (which remained on counter-terrorism duties), the entire Regiment would be deployed to the Gulf between 27 December 1990 and 3 January 1991. Ratcliffe, by now Regimental Quartermaster Sergeant, was deployed on 30 December to Abu Dhabi, one of seven emirates comprising the United Arab Emirates (UAE). Between midnight and dawn on 17 January, 671 Allied sorties were launched against Iraq. By midnight on 17 January, a quarter of the SAS's force had been moved to the frontline. But what would they do?

This question was quickly answered. On 18 January, Iraq fired the first of its antiquated scud missiles on Dhahran in Saudi Arabia. The same day, from mobile launchers in the western Iraq desert, Saddam's forces fired seven scud missiles at Israel in an attempt to turn the war into an Israeli-Arab conflict. The Allies were desperate to keep Israel out of the war but first the hidden – fixed and mobile – scud launchers had to be found and destroyed. This, even General Schwarzkopf agreed, was a job for the SAS. In no time, A and D Squadrons, in four mobile

units totalling 128 men, were preparing to enter enemy
territory.

Ratcliffe later wrote:

> By midnight on 20 January the first four fighting units were
> heading across the border. The SAS was officially at war. In the
> space of just forty-eight hours, the Regiment had gone from
> having no part to play in the Gulf War, to being responsible for
> taking out the greatest single threat to Allied victory. We had
> been hurled in at the deep end with a vengeance . . . It seemed
> almost as though we had suddenly been placed on a countdown
> to save the world . . . We were the best hit-and-run outfit in the
> world, the purpose for which the SAS had been founded. Now
> we were to take on the role once again.

Initially, Ratcliffe was not assigned to any one of the four units
but when the commander of one – Alpha One Zero – seemed
reluctant to enter Iraq, Ratcliffe was asked to join and bolster
the mission. 'To join one of the fighting patrols behind enemy
lines was more than I could have hoped for in my wildest
dreams, and to say that I was surprised would be a huge understatement.' When the actions of Alpha One Zero later became
even more erratic, Ratcliffe was given authority – in the form of
a letter – to take command of the unit. The letter addressed to
the A Squadron commander read: 'You are to comply with this
order. You are to hand over your command to the RSM. He can
take whatever action is necessary to ensure that you leave your
present location. You are to get onboard the helicopter. You are
to speak to no one and to report to me directly on your return.'
It was signed 'Commanding Officer, 22 SAS.'

Soon Ratcliffe was flying deep into enemy territory by
helicopter.

As I approached the gaping rear doors of the huge, twin-engined, twin-rotor Boeing Chinook, I was acutely aware that I was about to become the central character in a piece of regimental history. This was the first time that an SAS squadron commander had been relieved of his command in the field, and also the first time that the RSM had been sent in on active service to replace an officer . . . Furthermore, my destination lay behind enemy lines, so quite apart from any problems that might arise with men whose patrol commander I was to replace, or with informing that officer that, in effect, his career was in tatters, I was also having to adjust to the recognition that, from this night on, every move I made could lead to an incident that might well become a matter of life and death. Nor was it just my life or death; I was about to become responsible for not only the successful outcome of a vital mission, but also for the lives and well-being of thirty-three soldiers, most of whom were married and had children.

After the Chinook landed deep in Iraq to rendezvous with Alpha One Zero, the officer accepted that he was being relieved of his command. He hugged his number two and boarded the helicopter to return to Saudi Arabia. 'I am in charge now, and that means a whole new ball game,' Ratcliffe told his second-in-command. Some men resented his presence, but Ratcliffe was determined to do things his way.

Alpha One Zero had eight Land Rover Defender 110s, three motorcycles and a Unimog (a Mercedes Benz 4 x 4 light truck) at its disposal. When Ratcliffe took over command, Alpha One Zero was seventy kilometres behind enemy lines and the men had been behind those lines for four days. The terrain was bumpy, however, and on the first night the unit could only cover a maximum of twenty kilometres an hour. The next day – at

1600 hours – Ratcliffe gave his men a pep talk and late that afternoon they set out with the intention of meeting up with Alpha Three Zero, another SAS team behind enemy lines. The unit had radio contact with Army headquarters in Al Jouf. At 0400 hours on 30 January, Alpha One Zero met up with Captain Guy, a representative from Alpha Three Zero, as planned, having driven all through the evening and night averaging some fifteen kilometres an hour. Guy had earmarked an LUP (lying-up place) for them, two kilometres north. Once there, Ratcliffe spelt out the aim of the mission to his men: 'First, to locate and destroy scud missiles and their launch sites. Second, to gather intelligence. And third, to take offensive action. Which means dealing with enemy forces or enemy locations that we come across.' Then he added: 'Tonight we will head north another fifty kilometres. Which means that our LUP in the morning will be the centre of our operations.'

By the next morning – 31 January – the unit had driven for three nights in a row and was 200 kilometres into Iraq. Alpha One Zero was now given its first specific mission – a recce of the Mudaysis airfield some twenty kilometres west of the main supply route. A two-man forward team arrived above it at 0200 on the morning of 2 February. The men discovered it was a virtual ghost airfield, with just a couple of light aircraft, but they located a heavily protected fibre-optic cable. That same night, Ratcliffe got permission from HQ to cut it and took two men with him, one an explosives expert, Corporal Kenneth Phillips. In his book, *Eye of the Storm*, Ratcliffe refers to Phillips by the pseudonym 'Ken'.

Phillips – like Ratcliffe – had served with distinction in the Falklands and had also been mentioned in despatches. Born in 1959, he had enlisted in the Army on 18 November 1976, aged seventeen. The *London Gazette* of 8 October 1982 recognised the

talents he displayed while serving with the Parachute
Regiment:

> During the night attack in the battle for Port Darwin and Goose
> Green on 28/29 May 1982, Lance Corporal Phillips [name
> changed] showed outstanding leadership skills and courage in
> the hand-to-hand fighting as the enemy positions were cleared
> trench by trench. At first light B Company was pinned down by
> a strong enemy bunker. Lance Corporal Phillips realising this,
> and on his own initiative, stood up under enemy fire, and from
> a range of 150 metres, calmly fired a light anti-tank rocket into
> the bunker. This action undoubtedly saved the lives of several
> soldiers and allowed the Company to reorganise in safety and
> continue to advance. After neutralising the enemy bunker Lance
> Corporal Phillips returned to his section and continued to
> display the same standards of leadership, coolness and courage
> until the end of the battle.

In short, for his mission that night in Iraq, Ratcliffe had, in
Phillips, a highly professional and courageous soldier as a
comrade – and he immediately recognised it. In his book,
Ratcliffe describes him as a 'cheerful sort' and 'a first-class
demolition man', adding, 'I had him marked down as very
"wilco", meaning that he had a positive attitude and was likely
to do anything I asked him to do quickly and competently.'

That night, in the Iraqi desert, the three men located two
manhole covers and set timed charges below, only to find they
had triggered an alarm. Three enemy vehicles were soon heading for them, just a kilometre away, but they avoided contact
and, just minutes later, the first charge blew, followed by the
second. 'Saddam won't be launching any more scuds using that
command line. Well done lads,' Ratcliffe told his men.

A Chinook helicopter brought new supplies for Alpha One Zero and a new second-in-command. Ratcliffe now decided to move his men in daylight, as well as during the night, and to carry out operations in daylight wherever possible. On the morning of 6 February, after successfully following orders to find a suitable airstrip that could be used in enemy territory, HQ radioed a coded signal to Ratcliffe. Alpha One Zero was tasked with penetrating and destroying a microwave scud-control station known as Victor Two – and by no later than 0600 on 8 February, which was less than thirty-nine hours away. The unit was also ordered to render unusable the fibre-optic cables and communications 'switching gear' located in a fortified underground bunker. It was thought the target was protected by about thirty soldiers. Ratcliffe later wrote: 'I had a gut feeling from the very outset that we would be walking into a heavily defended location, from which perhaps not all of us could expect to walk away. It was almost certain that we were being sent into a situation that must result in a firefight.'

He decided to attack at night, but remained convinced that there was likely to be contact with the enemy before the explosives could be detonated. Pulling out after any firefight presented still more worries. In a radio conversation with HQ, Ratcliffe learnt that the main target – a bunker of about forty square metres – was protected by an eight-feet-high wall of prefabricated concrete slabs slotted into concrete posts. Between this wall and the target was a six-feet-high, chain-link fence. At the main building were steps leading to three underground concrete bunkers. Nearby was a second target – a 250-foot-high mast. The targets were some thirty-five kilometres from their LUP. He decided to use three 'demolitionists' – explosives experts, each backed up by two men. This meant there would be a nine-man team, including Ratcliffe and Phillips, in the target area backed up by the remainder of the half squadron. A swiftly made model was used to plan the attack.

A final recce showed the SAS unit was outnumbered and, possibly, outgunned by enemy soldiers. 'I knew that, ideally, I could have done with the whole Regiment to handle this attack, instead of just thirty-four of us – a number that included the few doubtful types who thought the whole mission was suicidal,' Ratcliffe later wrote. 'I had no other choice than to make the most of what I'd been given. None the less, I remained certain of my objective: this mission was going ahead as ordered. Calling it off was simply not an option.' The unit had also discovered the main target consisted of two bunkers, not one. The intention was to take out both using different anti-tank weapons. His final orders to his men were: 'Let's keep it quiet for as long as possible. I don't want those bunkers being taken out unless it goes "noisy" – and preferably not until the first charges go off when we break through the outer wall. Then Pat [his former second-in-command] and the rest of you can hit them with everything you've got and hope it either scares, confuses or occupies them enough so that we can get out without suffering too much damage.'

When Ratcliffe, Phillips and another man reached the target area, they discovered it had already been hit at some point earlier by Allied bombs. The staircase to the three underground rooms and the rooms themselves were buried beneath rubble. There was also no 'switching gear' left to destroy and, initially, Ratcliffe felt a sense of anti-climax. He decided to blow the mast and get out of the area. Three 35lb explosive charges were attached to the mast's three legs, each with a two-minute time delay. Ratcliffe later wrote:

At which point our good fortune took a nose dive. We were through the tangled fence and close to the gap in the wall [their exit route] when all hell broke loose. There were several single shots followed by a burst of automatic fire, then the enormous whoosh of a Milan [anti-tank missile] going in and, seconds later, a huge explosion as the missile struck home. Then everyone seemed to let rip together. Rounds were zipping overhead and we could hear them smacking into the other side of the wall.

There were bullets flying everywhere, riddling the sheeting covering the gap while, above, tracers created amazing patterned arches. We were safe enough on our side of the wall, but not for long. Behind us, no more than ten metres away, was over a hundred pounds of high-explosive getting ready to blow in less than ninety seconds . . .

Surging forward, we spread out like the three-quarter line in a rugby game and belted towards the dark, looming mass of the north end of the berm [manmade sandbank]. Though I swear not even the finest line-up ever made it from one end of the rugby pitch to the other at the speed we travelled that night . . . We were halfway between the wall and the jumping-off point when the first explosive charge blew, followed seconds later by another boom and, almost immediately afterwards, by a third.

None of us stopped to watch the effects, however, because there were bullets whistling all around us. As I ran I looked to the left. The bunker was gushing flames and smoke from its gun slits and entrance, which meant the Milan had done its job.

As they reached their support team, Ratcliffe could see his comrades to the other side of the target were involved in a firefight with Iraqi troops. Later, at the debrief, Ratcliffe learnt that a bleary Iraqi truck driver had stumbled on part of the party. He had been shot dead but that had alerted the enemy, who opened fire, and the SAS soldier operating the LAW 80 anti-tank weapon sent a missile straight into the bunker. The soldier who had been in charge of the anti-tank weapon was not able to fire it himself because he had been leapt on by another Iraqi driver, who emerged from a truck and tried to strangle him. The Iraqi fought hard but was eventually clubbed on the head by an SAS man, using a rifle-butt. There was no time to set up the LAW 80 again before the men had to pull out. As Ratcliffe's team regrouped and started to drive off, they came under heavy fire from the berm – two bullets passed through the clothing of one of the explosives experts and other bullets narrowly missed other SAS men, but all thirty-four were reunited, and the backslapping and hugging began.

> Even for the SAS, the end of a mission brings a tremendous release of tension, made up partly of relief and partly of pleasure at having performed well in a difficult and dangerous task. By some incredible miracle, and against far greater odds than we could have anticipated, we had managed to get in and out of the enemy stronghold with every member of the unit present and unwounded. In doing so we had undoubtedly killed and wounded numbers of Iraqi troops, as well as firing the demolition charges on the mast. We had also thoroughly alarmed and confused the enemy.

The mast crumbled to the ground a short time later. It had been a 'perfect mission' –targets destroyed and zero casualties.

For the next two weeks, Alpha One Zero carried out various recces and gathered valuable intelligence behind enemy lines. At one point, Ratcliffe, aware of just how many SAS men were deep in enemy territory, decided to call and chair a Sergeants' Mess meeting, a monthly event normally held in their barracks.

This time it would be held in a *wadi* – a valley or dried-up water hole – 150 kilometres behind enemy lines. At first, his idea was ridiculed but he wanted to show that the Regiment had style. Ratcliffe later wrote:

> At 12.00 hours that day, 16 February 1991, thirty-five members of the Sergeants' Mess, including myself as Chairman and Gary [a comrade] as President, met on the rocky slope. The other sergeants and warrant officers sat in a line two deep, and Gary and I stood facing them to conduct our business. Apart from the setting, and the fact that every man had his rifle with him, it ran much like a mess meeting back at Stirling Lines [Hereford]. After the usual votes of thanks we came up with our main proposal, which was to spend over £20,000 on new leather furniture for the mess over the next two years. It was then agreed that the next mess dinner would take place in April, and that there would be a Christmas function which members would attend in mess dress, but without medals, and with no guests present. There were various minor decisions about mess facilities agreed and noted, and minutes were kept of the whole meeting, scribbled in an exercise book to be taken back to Hereford and typed up properly.

Every proposal agreed was eventually acted upon and, much later, the minutes of the meeting were signed by General Sir Peter de la Billière and General Norman Schwarzkopf.

On 23 February Ratcliffe received orders to take his unit south to the Saudi Arabian border and then return to Al Jouf for 'rest and recuperation'. That same day the coalition launched its land offensive against Iraqi forces in Kuwait. By chance, the war was almost over. The conflict had claimed the lives of four SAS men behind enemy lines. Ratcliffe returned to Britain on the day of the Cheltenham Gold Cup in March 1991, before the SAS started planning events to mark the fiftieth anniversary of its founding in 1941. He was awarded the DCM for his leadership of his mobile patrol.

Field Marshal Lord Bramall, then the Director, Special Forces, wrote Ratcliffe a letter on 29 June 1991: 'I was delighted to see you were awarded a DCM in the recent Op. Granby Honours List. Your leadership in the face of the enemy was exemplary and ensured that your half squadron overcame its earlier setbacks and contributed significantly to the strategic aim.' He added that Ratcliffe's 'determinedly aggressive leadership, presence of mind and conspicuous personal bravery are worthy of national recognition.'

In 1992, Ratcliffe was commissioned to the rank of captain and went to Germany on detachment for six months. He then spent two years as a quartermaster with 21 SAS, based in London, followed by a further two years with 23 SAS, based in Birmingham. He left the Army in November 1997, as a major. Three years later, he published his account of his life and Army career. Ratcliffe was in no doubt that his time in the Army, especially his years in the Special Forces, was the making of him. In his book, he wrote:

> Thirty years ago, no one would have figured me for a soldier. At the time, I was a scarcely educated, often dishonest, streetwise kid from a poverty-stricken slum home – in the end, a broken home – in the depressed industrial north-west of England. Almost without prospects, I joined the army for all the wrong reasons: to get away from a miserable dead-end existence as a manual labourer, and because I had been thwarted in my efforts to emigrate to Australia. I owe to my Regiments – first the Parachute Regiment, then, for twenty-five years, the Special Air

Service Regiment – the fact that I am not still a manual labourer in a dead-end job, or even worse, in prison. I owe a great deal more than that, however, most of which I could not put into words, and all of it priceless . . . What I do know is that I gained from the SAS a sense of self-worth and confidence while soldiering with the best in any army, anywhere in the world.

Ratcliffe, who is married with a grown-up daughter, ran a guesthouse for a time but now lives and works abroad.

Phillips also enjoyed a long and distinguished Army career, being discharged in December 1999. He left with this Army testimonial:

Staff Sergeant Phillips [name changed] MM has given twenty-two years' exemplary service to the British Army. During this time he has worked at various employments and roles including active service on sensitive operations abroad. He was Mentioned in Despatches during the Falklands Conflict and in 1991 he was awarded the Military Medal for bravery during the Gulf War. Staff Sergeant Phillips MM is a highly motivated man who has a pleasant, friendly manner and disposition. He is very well-experienced at managing men and resources which, added to his personal skills, makes him an excellent team leader. He is a very personable man who can identify with objectives and, with his enthusiastic approach to all tasks, ensures that they are completed to the best of his ability. He mixes easily in professional and personal situations. Staff Sergeant Phillips' commitment and dedication throughout his service has been outstanding. His inherent qualities of self-discipline, trustworthiness and loyalty will make him an immense asset to any future employer.

Phillips's whereabouts today are not known.

MAJOR JOHN POTTER
Army
AWARD: MILITARY CROSS (MC)
DATE OF BRAVERY: FEBRUARY 1991
GAZETTED: 29 JUNE 1991

Major John Potter did not serve in the Special Forces but he developed SAS-style skills during his many years of service in Northern Ireland. Furthermore, he had earlier shown outstanding bravery in the Gulf War and, photographed in the thick of the action, was responsible for some of the most memorable images of the 1991 conflict. I therefore have no hesitation in including the exploits of this outstanding soldier in this book.

Potter was born in Hamilton, Scotland, where he was brought up. He attended Glasgow University, where he joined the Officer Training Corps. After leaving university, he joined the Royal Highland Fusiliers. During the Gulf War, Potter commanded B Company of 1 Royal Scots Battle Group, and kept a diary of his and his men's exploits, extracts of which were published in Laurie Milner's book *Royal Scots in the Gulf: 1st Battalion, The Royal Scots (The Royal Regiment) on Operation Granby 1990–1991.*

In November 1990, it was announced that the Royal Scots were to join 4th Brigade in the Gulf. Potter wrote:

> As soon as we heard that a British contingent was going to be sent, I was in no doubt that we would go. We, as a battalion, would go to the Gulf and fight a war. That was really drummed in to me by somebody I used to work for at the Ministry of Defence, who was a Company Commander in the Falklands. His abiding words of wisdom [were] 'If ever a conflict blows up somewhere in the world, and we're going to send troops there,

always assume that you will go and always assume that you will fight. If you believe that and believe it one hundred percent you'll never be disappointed,' and it was hard initially to put that across to my men.

Potter later wrote:

We had four weeks to get operationally ready, there was no time to fart about with floppy hats and desert boots and all that sort of stuff. We had to train with a singleness of purpose. Everything that we did, everything that we trained for, was geared towards one object and that was the eventual engagement and destruction of the Iraqi ground forces. To some people it came as a bit of a shock that we took things so very seriously. There was a [staff officer] who thought that we were taking it too seriously. He commented that I had too rigid, too spartan a regime for my men. I told him to f*** off!

On 18 January, while training in the Gulf, Potter wrote of a serious accident:

It was just about that time that our O/C [officer commanding] Fire Support Company was shot by accident on one of the hill firing ranges. My Company was waiting to go on next and we were really more concerned with getting him out of the way so that we could carry on training than if he lived or died actually. It was like that, just get the helicopter in and get him out of there so we can crack on. Then we realized that our attitudes had hardened to such a point that preparation for the war or training was paramount and nothing would be allowed to get in the way. By that stage we were absolutely committed to going all out for it.

As the ground war began, British troops feared they would be subjected to a chemical attack by the Iraqis but this did not materialise. However, the 'train hard, fight easy' philosophy – supported so vigorously by Potter and others – was quickly reaping dividends. After just three hours of bombardment from 120mm guns and machine-guns, it looked as though some Iraqi units were willing to surrender.

> There were really two options open, that we could get out and clear through the bunkers one by one, at night, or we could try and persuade them to come out with their hands up, and I ordered my driver and indeed 5 Platoon to flash their headlights, really to show them where we were. It was such a pitch black night, although we could look through our Image Intensifiers, they couldn't see us. You've got to be able to surrender to something. Anybody who has got the balls to flash their headlights 100 metres away from a defensive position has an air of superiority about them, and you can surrender to someone like that. It was just to give the message: 'Do we go on? You either surrender or you die, and that is your choice!'

Some Iraqis surrendered immediately, others after further tank and mortar fire. One Iraqi prisoner tried to embrace Potter but he was mindful that an American soldier had been killed by a prisoner with a Claymore mine concealed in his clothing. Potter later wrote:

> We were more frightened of that, of the suicide bomber. This bloody man decided to leap forward and hug me as I turned to talk to someone. I was biting and clawing and scratching and butting and everything and he went down very quickly. The top of his nose was well-dented by my helmet and I was about to

shoot him when I realized what it was, that he was not a suicide bomber, he was just so grateful and expressing his gratitude in the way Arabs do, they embrace. It just wasn't the right time or the right person to embrace!

Potter's modesty prevented him recording his own courage during the first forty-eight hours of the ground war. Suffice to say he led his men with unstinting bravery and showed little or no regard for his own safety. As a result he was awarded the MC. The *London Gazette* of 29 June 1991 recorded his gallantry:

Major Potter commanded B Company in 1 Royal Scots Battle Group during the campaign. The Battle Group was in contact with the enemy for the majority of the time and B company was left in front throughout. 1 Royal Scots attacked three major objectives and Major Potter's Company was heavily involved. Wherever his Company was, his vehicle could always be seen in the midst of the action. He moved around constantly encouraging, leading, directing, and chastising, without regard for enemy fire or mines.

The first engagement for the Battle Group in Southern Iraq began with tanks engaging an enemy artillery battery. The night was pitch dark and rain obscured the image intensification sights of the Warrior Armoured Personnel Carrier. B Company moved forward to either force a surrender or to complete the destruction of the enemy. There were reports of mines in the area and the enemy had been engaged just to the North.

Major Potter coordinated a violent concentration of fire onto the objective and shortly after, the enemy began to surrender, Major Potter used headlights to encourage the others and soon the position was secured. Later, at another position, after a surrender, Major Potter gave clear instructions for the tending of enemy wounded and the burial of the dead. Under pressure to press on, he ensured the worst of the wounded were carried forward with the Battle Group.

During the Battle Group attack on yet another position, Major Potter led his Company through a turmoil of dust, direct and indirect fire, to execute a classic rolling up operation. His awareness and steadiness helped him ease his company into position to exert an unsurvivable concentration of firepower. He executed the operation with ruthless efficiency and quickly redeployed to cover A Company's impending attack.

Following a further four attacks, and during a Battle Group replenishment, Major Potter's Company observed another enemy position which it immediately attacked and soon overcame. By this time Major Potter's Company had been in action or on the move for forty-eight hours and had had little sleep.

Major Potter's leadership was outstanding. He was cool under fire, calm in contact, resolute in danger and pursued the enemy with clinical ruthlessness. He was an example to all who knew him.

Potter featured heavily in some of the most memorable photographs from the war. One shows him, with his bayoneted rifle in his right hand, about to search Iraqi prisoners taken after a battle. Another shows him, with his left arm raised aloft, smiling and giving a victory salute as the Royal Scots Battle Group entered Kuwait on 27 February 1991.

It was while serving in Northern Ireland some years later that Potter's intelligence and innovation were again publicly recognised – and his skills in Special Forces-style combat became apparent. He was mentioned in despatches in the *London Gazette* of 12 October 1993 at the end of an eventful six-month tour serving as company commander in Crossmaglen, in the heart of South Armagh's 'bandit country'.

His unpublished recommendation for a gallantry award did justice to the officer's forward-thinking talents:

> Major Potter completed a six-month tour in South Armagh between 1992 and March 1993. On this, his second tour in Northern Ireland, he was Company Commander in Crossmaglen, controlling this most difficult area with a much expanded company under his command. Crossmaglen is notorious as a difficult area to operate in, and a soldier had been shot dead only 400 yards from the Army base a month before Major Potter and his company arrived. Under such circumstances it would have been easy to listen to the police and his predecessor and adopt a safety-first approach to operations.
>
> In practice Major Potter took a different approach. With intelligence and great energy he set himself and his company to move them from a largely defensive posture, to one which might wrest the initiative from the terrorist. He changed patrol patterns and tactics, altered the equipment-carrying requirements, experimented successfully with a number of deployment techniques to keep the opposition guessing, and in every way possible sought to keep the momentum of counter-terrorism going.
>
> During the tour there were a total of seven attacks in the Crossmaglen area, resulting in the death of an RUC constable and, on two occasions, significant damage to bases. Major Potter's command never faltered, and the whole of his company reflected his calm and professional determination in the face of the most serious terrorist attack.
>
> Despite the commitment required to sustain his efforts Major Potter found time to develop new ideas. Patrols remained flexible and innovative throughout the tour, and he did a great

deal of work on intelligence gathering and surveillance. At the same time, he managed to create an excellent relationship with the Royal Ulster Constabulary in Crossmaglen and with other agencies based there.

Throughout the tour Major Potter displayed the highest standards of professionalism as a commander and as a soldier. He was dedicated and determined in his approach to operations, quick to react to incidents and at all times had a full grasp on his command. The standard of patrolling which he engendered in his troops was consistently the highest in the battalion and the drills and procedures he imposed within the bases undoubtedly saved lives when the bases were attacked.

During the whole tour Major Potter never ceased to be an inspiration to his soldiers and those around him. He is richly deserving of official recognition for such a magnificent effort.

When I tracked Potter down to his new home in Canada, he told me that he and his men had adopted an unusual tactic whereby those on patrol in South Armagh would not wash or shave for a week or more. 'This was to give the impression that they were living "rough" in the countryside and therefore cast doubts in the minds of the IRA. If they couldn't see any patrol's presence, but the appearance of unshaven, unwashed soldiers on patrol indicated they must be there, the IRA would be unwilling to make any moves of equipment, or set up an attack, for fear of compromise or capture.'

Potter was again gazetted on 9 May 1996, this time receiving the Queen's Commendation for Valuable Service (QCVS) after a successful two-year command of the 5th Battalion, Royal Irish Regiment, based in Londonderry. Potter was discharged from the Army on 14 November 1997. He is twice divorced with five daughters from the two marriages. Potter now lives in Montreal, where he heads the programme management office of a major aerospace company.

Sierra Leone

In August 2000, a British Army patrol was captured in war-torn Sierra Leone by a notorious criminal militia gang called the West Side Boys (WSB). At this time, the WSB were subjecting the country to a reign of robbery, rape and murder. Eleven members of the Royal Irish Regiment were held by the ill-disciplined rebel group, who assaulted some of their captives and threatened them with death. British forces were in Sierra Leone because on 7 May 2000 the UK launched Operation Palliser and deployed a task force to evacuate British, EU and Commonwealth passport holders from Freetown, the capital of the troubled West African country.

After lengthy negotiations, five of the Royal Irish Regiment captives were released but the situation looked increasingly grim for the remaining six men and the Sierra Leone Army (SLA) liaison officer who was with them. As the situation deteriorated, Prime Minister Tony Blair ordered a rescue mission. Operation Barras was the codename given to the planned mission involving 1 Para, the SAS and the SBS. However, the daring operation had – in the words of one military veteran – 'plenty of scope for things to go wrong'.

COLOUR SERGEANT JAMES DRUMMOND CARNEGIE
Army
AWARD: NOT SPECIFIC
DATE OF BRAVERY: NOT RELEVANT
GAZETTED: NOT RELEVANT

After emerging from the jungle, the British Army patrol arrived in the run-down village of Magbeni. There were eleven soldiers in three Land Rovers but, in the mid-afternoon sun, they were taken by surprise when their vehicles were surrounded by a twenty-five-strong armed gang, many of whom had been smoking strong ganja since late morning. Initially, however, the situation remained calm as the members of the Royal Irish Regiment, all armed with SA80 5.56mm rifles, climbed from their vehicles and started chatting with the West Side Boys (WSB). Major Alan Marshall, the patrol commander, was asked by one of the gang to wait for the return of their twenty-four-year-old leader, 'Brigadier' Foday Kallay, a former sergeant in the Sierra Leone Army.

However, when Kallay arrived, the atmosphere quickly became more hostile. Having been summoned from the nearby village of Gberi Bana, Kallay was angry that there had been no request from British troops to visit Magbeni, a village some 100 kilometres east of the capital of Freetown that he regarded as part of his territory. He was also disillusioned that his group – also known as the West Side Soldiers – was starting to disintegrate. The patrol first watched as their road south was blocked by a four-tonne truck with a twin heavy machine-gun mounted upon it. Then they observed Marshall, their thirty-three-year-old commander, being surrounded and beaten to the ground by rifle-butts and heavy fists. The soldier mounting the Browning heavy machine-gun on one of the Land Rovers was unable to shoot because it would have led to a massacre first of the WSB then, provided the gang had time to retaliate, of the patrol themselves. Within minutes, the patrol had been overwhelmed and stripped down to their olive T-shirts and underwear. Kallay also stole their wedding rings and watches before transporting the men in two motorised canoes across Rokel Creek to Gberi Bana, the militia's main base near a deserted palm oil plantation. At some point during or after the capture, a radio from one of the Land Rovers was unbolted and taken to Gberi Bana. It was 25 August 2000 and soon the British Government knew it had a crisis on its hands.

The British Government insisted the eleven-man patrol, accompanied by a Sierra Leone Army (SLA) liaison officer, had been on a legitimate mission to see the Jordanian peacekeepers at Masiaka. However, the United Nations Mission in Sierra Leone (UNAMSIL) rejected this claim and suggested the British had been wrong to encroach into territory controlled by the WSB. UNAMSIL, which had been set up in 1999, looked upon the crisis as a not untypical 'hostage and ransom' situation. Meanwhile, at Howe Barracks in Canterbury, Kent – the UK headquarters of 1 Royal Irish – the families of the captured soldiers gathered and waited for news of their loved ones. A Downing Street spokesman said Tony Blair had been briefed on the situation on his return from holiday. 'Whenever British forces are held against their will, anywhere in the world, it is something the government takes very seriously,' he said.

In Freetown, Dr Julius Spencer, the Minister of Information, was in no doubt of the seriousness of the situation and he described the WSB as 'unpredictable bandits'. It is understood that the early contact between the WSB (who, incidentally, included a large number of women soldiers) and the Benguema Training Centre (BTC) in Sierra Leone came in brief exchanges over the patrol's radio. Soon, however, there were face-to-face negotiations between Lieutenant Colonel Simon Fordham, commanding officer 1 Royal Irish, a gruff but shrewd 'soldier's soldier', and the rebels, who arrived armed and in large numbers.

The meetings took place at the top of a track leading down to Magbeni, where the patrol had been captured. Unseen further down the track were two men from the Metropolitan Police's Hostage and Crisis Negotiation Unit. The two men advised

Fordham on his strategy as well as briefing and debriefing him before and after the meetings. From early on, the aim was to avoid 'direct action' – an attack to rescue the hostages. However, from early on, too, plans were being made for a direct assault on the WSB if the situation worsened – particularly if one or more hostages were killed. Human intelligence and electronic surveillance were used to try to locate the exact positions of the WSB's forces.

At a meeting on 27 August, two days after the hostages were seized, the WSB demanded the release from detention of Foday Sankoh, whom they referred to as General Papa, along with food and medicine. In return, they said, the troops would be freed. The next day, Kofi Annan, the UN Secretary General, speaking at the group's headquarters in New York, said the hostages would be released 'in the near future'.

On 29 August, the Regimental Signals Officer (RSO) was brought by 'Brigadier' Foday Kallay, the WSB leader, to meet Lieutenant Colonel Simon Fordham and the hostage negotiation team at the UN base in Masiaka. The officer assured the British negotiators that the captives were being well treated. More importantly, before being taken back to rejoin his fellow hostages, he was able to hand over – hidden in a ballpoint pen – a map of the WSB base where they were still being held.

The next day, five of the soldiers from the Royal Irish – formed in 1992 and the youngest regiment in the British Army – were released in return for a satellite phone and medical supplies. Six men – officers and NCOs – and the SLA liaison officer were still being held.

The five freed soldiers were flown to Freetown for debriefing and they told how Kallay visited the hostages every day, demanding to know why they had driven to his camp. 'Explain your mission or I will shoot you!' he said. The five also described how their CO had been beaten. For the seven remaining hostages, the situation soon deteriorated and the SLA liaison officer was subjected to an even more serious assault. In his book *Operation Barras: The SAS Rescue Mission: Sierra Leone 2000*, William Fowler gives an eyewitness account of how the six soldiers were marched to the 'Dead Zone' and tied to wooden poles about a metre apart. The rebels lined up their AK-47 assault rifles and waited for Kallay's order to fire. As Major Alan Marshall tried to reason with the rebel leader, Kallay shouted, 'I will kill you! I will kill you!' Eventually, however, Marshall's gentle reasoning won the day after half-an-hour of tense discussions. 'We just came to see you, to tell you to forget fighting. We did not come with any bad intentions. If you kill us, it will not be for any reason,' Marshall said.

The batteries on the satellite phone given to the WSB eventually ran out but not before it had enabled the British to pinpoint the exact position of the rebels' camp.

On 31 August, British officials in London insisted that negotiation was still the best course but they added, more worryingly, that the situation had become 'delicate' and 'volatile'. On the same day, a message reached 1 Para's Connaught Barracks headquarters in Dover, Kent, that they might soon become involved in a joint operation with Special Forces in Sierra Leone. The broad plan was that, if required, the Paras would tie down the WSB in a firefight while the Special Forces rescued the hostages. The Parachute Regiment – the nearest the British Army has to 'shock troops' – had exercised with the SAS and many men from the two fighting units knew each other.

A planning group from 1 Para flew to Dakar, the Sengalese capital, on the morning of Sunday, 3 September. In Dakar, intelligence gathered by the SAS – who had patrols operating close to the WSB base – was studied, along with maps and photographs of the area. The village of Magbeni was identified as the target for the 1 Para company group. The biggest threat to any attack was from the heavy machine-gun in the village, which was capable of bringing down a helicopter that was trying to land either at Magbeni or across the river at Gberi Bana. The planning group decided that it would have to be destroyed by Lynx attack helicopters at the start of any assault.

The arrival of the Paras in the region did not go unreported but it also distracted attention from any Special Forces operations that were going on at the same time. In fact, SAS four-man teams had already concealed themselves in swamps that were just 250 metres from Kallay's base at Gberi Bana, where an estimated fifty to 100 WSB were based. A similar number of rebels were in nearby Magbeni. Both groups were heavily armed. By now, much of the detailed planning was taking place in Seaview House, the British military head-quarters situated on a hillside above the British High Commission in Freetown. Maps, aerial photographs and models were all used to plan the rescue.

It is believed that there were some twenty-five SAS soldiers in the force deployed to attack Gberi Bana. They were told that, after an initial 'shock and awe' attack on the WSB, they would have just sixty seconds to rescue the hostages. After that time had passed, the WSB would be in a position to fight back. It was felt that some of the WSB might try to hide among the hostages and therefore it was decided that anyone seized – unless they were a recognisable British soldier – should be secured with 'plasticuffs'.

Lynx helicopters and Chinook helicopters were deployed to a small airfield at Hastings Battle Camp at the southern end of the Freetown peninsula. (At the request of senior Ministry of

Defence officials, the number of helicopters deployed is not detailed here, even though there has been informed speculation in the media and in two books.) Two possible helicopter landing sites were identified – one at the eastern end of Magbeni and the other to the south-west of the village. The attack was planned to take place shortly before dawn and the soldiers were to wear helmets and combat body armour. Two SAS negotiators were sent to support Lieutenant Colonel Fordham and his team. To complicate an already fraught situation, the WSB – buoyed by their success in seizing the British hostages – were carrying out attacks on rival armed groups, even using their captured Royal Irish Land Rovers for the forays. This led to fears that the Gbethis and Kapras groups might hit back against the WSB, thereby endangering the lives of the British soldiers still further.

As negotiations continued to stall, the decision to put the plan into action and rescue the hostages was taken on the morning of Saturday, 9 September. One official told author William Fowler: 'It became clear that Kallay had no intention of releasing the men.' Instead, there was a growing feeling that it was only a matter of time before some, or even all, of the hostages were executed. Tony Blair, who was at his country home in Chequers, was updated on the crisis on Saturday afternoon and was told that the rescue operation would start at first light the next day. President Kabbah authorised British forces to strike against the WSB on his soil.

By 5 a.m. on Sunday, 10 September, the young paratroopers from A Company and their SAS colleagues were making final checks on their equipment, after which they clambered into the waiting Chinook helicopters and Operation Barras was on its way. At 6.40 a.m., the attack commenced – the Lynx gunship fitted with night-vision equipment led the way. Shortly behind were the Chinooks carrying the SAS hostage-snatch and fire teams. It was not long before the WSB at Gberi Bana opened fire but the expertise of the pilots won the day and they reached the first designated landing site. With the attack teams safely on the ground, using their 'fast-roping' techniques, the helicopters swung away to safety. As soon as the WSB opened fire, the SAS patrol lying just fifty-five metres from Gberi Bana surged from their jungle hiding point and burst into the huts where the captives were being held. Following a fierce firefight, just two of the WSB emerged alive from the huts. One of them was their leader, Kallay, who was found hiding under dead bodies and blankets. His wife, 'Mamma Kallay', was more heroic, and was shot dead with her gun in her hand. It was believed to be during this initial onslaught that Trooper Bradley Tinnion was fatally wounded by a 7.62mm round that passed though his body, exiting through his shoulder.

One SAS trooper described the action as a 'bit like "Gunfight at the OK Corral" '. Less than twenty minutes after the first shot was fired, all the hostages had been successfully liberated, rounded up and delivered to the waiting Chinook.

At the second landing point, another Chinook had dropped more men, but the land was far more marshy than had been expected. This meant what should have been a sprint to the tree line became a slog of between 100 and 150 metres through the mud with their weapons held aloft. As they reached the tree line – by now under a heavy fire – the ground became firmer. The small Special Forces team across the river in Gberi Bana was able to hold off the militia men. A Lynx helicopter swept in overhead and attacked the WSB position in Magbeni, concentrating the attack on the rebels' heavy machine-gun.

Once again the fighting was fierce and prolonged, and for most of the Paras it was their first experience of a sustained firefight. Corporal Simon Dawes, from Basingstoke, Hampshire, said later: 'I don't like to talk about that sort of situation but it was scary. But once we got into the fighting the training took over.' Some of the WSB fled but others stood their ground. A loud explosion took place in front of 1 Para Company HQ as they tried to move forward to join 2 Platoon. Seven of the soldiers were injured, including a major who received shrapnel wounds to his legs. A radio operator transmitted a casualty evacuation request and a Chinook, taking off from the Gberi Bana side of the creek, came to the aid of the injured men. Displaying bravery and skill, the crew landed the helicopter on the track running through the village despite coming under heavy fire. The wounded reached the operating theatre aboard *Sir Percivale*, the support ship moored in Freetown harbour, within twenty minutes of being hit. By 8 a.m., after further fierce fighting, Magbeni was secure.

In his book about Operation Barras, William Fowler writes:

> It was the first year of the twenty-first century, but the scene was timeless – as the flames crackled and the columns of smoke rose above the jungle, the victors surveyed the scene of their triumph. For many of the young Paras, after the pre-dawn start and a day of combat, there was a feeling of relief to be alive, accompanied by creeping fatigue.

The WSB had put up more of a resistance than many had expected. One war veteran told the *Observer* newspaper that the young battle-hardened militiamen did not understand the rules of war – 'No one ever told them that war is not like a Rambo video, about how soldiers should behave, when to be scared, so they just stand there and blast away.'

Another SAS veteran said of the attack: 'This was not a clinical, black balaclava, Prince's Gate-type [the Iranian

Embassy siege] operation. It was a very grubby, green operation with lots of potential for things to go wrong.' Operation Barras had resulted in one death and twelve injuries, only one of them serious, for the British forces. Across the river in Gberi Bana, fifteen male and three female prisoners had been captured – their wrists secured, as had been planned, with the white plasticuffs. Officially, twenty-four WSB died during the raid, including three women. However, blood trails into the jungle suggested that the final death toll would have been much higher. Twenty-two Sierra Leoneans, who had been held prisoner by the WSB for weeks or months, were also freed. These included five women who had been forced to become 'bush wives' for the WSB soldiers, while the men had been used as forced labour.

Slowly, it emerged how badly the British hostages had been treated. Militia commanders said one of the forced labourers had often pointed his gun at the captured Royal Irish soldiers and threatened to kill them if a rescue operation was attempted. The self-styled 'Lieutenant Colonel' Contobie forced his captives to bow down each day and say 'Good morning, Commandant.' The hostages had to ask for permission to eat and drink, and had been forced to treat the wounds of injured militiamen using cheap, local gin as an antiseptic. The hostages were regularly surrounded by drug and alcohol-fuelled child fighters, some just ten years old, from the Small Boys' Unit.

It was reported that a coded note had been smuggled to the hostages during one of the negotiation meetings, which said: 'Sally and Sarah send their regards and so does Dawn', meaning the SAS would attack at dawn. As they suffered in silence, the hostages were apparently hopeful after receiving the coded message that the SAS would arrive at first light. However, the accuracy of this story is in doubt.

By coincidence, General Sir Charles Guthrie, the Chief of the Defence Staff and someone who had been heavily involved in the discussions about how to free the hostages, had long been due to appear in a live interview on *Breakfast with Frost*. He arrived at BBC Television Centre in west London in his chauffeur-driven car later than planned and switched off his secure mobile phone. 'I'm sorry I'm late. There's been a bit of trouble in Africa,' he said with James Bond-style understatement. However, he was soon on air, telling Sir David Frost that the hostages were apparently safe but he added that 'the situation is still very confused'. At a press conference at the Ministry of Defence later the same day, the General added, 'This kind of operation is never without risk. We are not playing some stupid arcade game . . . The West Side Boys were not a pushover. They fought very hard. We did not want to do this, but the clock started turning [ticking].'

However, it was *The Democrat*, a daily newspaper in Sierra Leone, that summed up the story with its front-page headline: 'BRITS KICK ASS IN WEST SIDE'. The Sierra Leone Government was as thrilled by the outcome as was its British counterpart – the rule of law and the elected government had been boosted in the war-torn west African nation, while the WSB had been weakened, particularly by Kallay's capture. Operation Barras had hit one of eight WSB bases. Yet by 22 September, a total of 371 WSB disenchanted militiamen had surrendered or been disarmed, including fifty-seven child combatants.

Damien Lewis ends his book, *Operation Certain Death: The Inside Story of the SAS's Greatest Battle*:

> The men of the Operation Barras assault force had done more than simply rescue the British and Sierra Leonean hostages. They

had, in effect, brought about an end to ten years of terrible civil war and appalling suffering in Sierra Leone. One mindless, murderous rebel group had been removed from the scene, and then the others had basically surrendered. Which meant that the people of that suffering country could finally breathe a little more easily. There would be no more lopping off of the limbs of babies, no more gang rapes of children, no more rebel Russian roulette or 'sex the child' games. Those British soldiers who had risked their lives – *and sacrificed their lives* – on Operation Certain Death had not done so in vain.

One of the soldiers from 1 Para to take part in the assault on the WSB was Colour Sergeant James 'Jim' Carnegie. Born in Bedford in 1972, he had joined the Parachute Regiment in June 1989 and two years later was posted to Northern Ireland for the first time, returning there as part of Operation Banner Tour in 1994. He embarked for Sierra Leone with other members of 1 Para on 4 September 2000 and was not injured during the fierce fighting. Mission accomplished, Carnegie returned to Britain on 12 September. He was then posted once again to Northern Ireland before being sent to Lithuania in 2001. On 12 September 2003, he was posted to Kuwait and took part in the Allied invasion of Iraq. A further posting to Northern Ireland followed. Despite enjoying a distinguished career, he is one of just three men featured in this book who was never awarded a gallantry medal.

The Ministry of Defence announced on 6 April 2001 that various decorations had been awarded for Operation Barras. Two SAS soldiers were awarded the Conspicuous Gallantry Cross (CGC), a new award, second only to the Victoria Cross. Four Military Crosses (MCs) were also awarded to members of the rescue team, three from Special Forces and one to a captain from

A Company 1 Para. Tinnion, the only named SAS soldier – identified because of his untimely death – was mentioned in despatches. Five helicopter crewmen received the Distinguished Flying Cross (DFC).

The British Government announced on 1 September 2001 that the final short-term training team deployed to Sierra Leone would leave the country at the end of the month, having completed its task. Lieutenant Colonel Peter Davies, commanding the 2nd Battalion Light Infantry, said: 'We have set standards of discipline and basic skills that will make the SLA [Sierra Leone Army] able to defend themselves against rebel activity in this country. It will be a very different army from the one we found.' The SAS's legacy to the nation's people was helping to set up a company-strength Special Forces Unit in Sierra Leone, which goes by the name of the Force Reconnaissance Unit (FRU).

The Second Gulf War

The Second Gulf War was fought in 2003 with the aim of overthrowing the Iraqi dictator, Saddam Hussein. The US forces called the initiative to topple Saddam Operation Iraqi Freedom, while the British called it Operation Telic. The controversial justification for the war was that Iraq had been producing weapons of mass destruction (WMDs) in violation of a 1991 agreement. Intelligence supporting this notion was later criticised and eventually weapons inspectors found no evidence of WMDs.

On 20 March 2003, the US led an invasion of Iraq by a multi-national force comprising troops from the US and the UK, supported by contingents from other nations including Australia, Denmark and Poland. The invasion led to the rapid defeat of the Iraqi military and the flight of Saddam. He was captured in December 2003 and executed by order of the Iraqi courts in December 2006. The US-led coalition set up a 'democratic' government in Iraq, which has not yet been able to establish any sort of lasting peace. There has been prolonged violence against coalition forces and also among various sectarian groups, particularly Sunni and Shia Iraqis. Al-Qaeda operations in Iraq have also led to an escalation in the deaths. The war is ongoing, while estimates of the number of people killed during the conflict range from over 150,000 to more than a million.

GUARDSMAN LEE WHEELER

Army

AWARD: QUEEN'S GALLANTRY MEDAL (QGM)
DATE OF BRAVERY: 10 APRIL 2003
GAZETTED: 7 SEPTEMBER 2004

And, finally, as they say on *News at Ten*, a gallantry medal that, although strictly speaking nothing to do with the Special Forces, is so rare that I am going to include it as my final story. A relatively small number of bravery medals were awarded for the Second Gulf War and most of them remain with the recipients. The medal awarded to Guardsman Lee Wheeler is one of the very few to become available for sale.

Wheeler, who was born in Birmingham in 1983, and another Guardsman, Lance Corporal Simon Campbell, both serving with the Irish Guards, received the QGM after they defied enemy fire to save the life of their section commander, who had been hit by snipers during the fall of Basra in April 2003. The Irish Guards had borne the brunt of some of the fiercest fighting during the Second Gulf War – just two days before the shooting of the section commander two Irish Guards had been killed by sniper fire.

Wheeler's gallantry award was announced in the *London Gazette* of 7 September 2004. A Ministry of Defence press release issued at the time said:

Irish Guards Lance Corporal Simon Campbell and Guardsman Lee Wheeler receive the Queen's Gallantry Medal for their bravery whilst on patrol in Basra on 10 April 2003. As their section came under heavy machine-gun fire, Lance Corporal Campbell and Guardsman Wheeler crossed open ground to save their Section Commander who had been critically wounded by sniper fire. Their swift actions, bravery and professionalism helped save their Section Commander's life.

Wheeler now lives with his girlfriend in Birmingham. His modest comments on learning of his gallantry award are typical of those uttered by so many brave men over the years. He said simply, 'We really weren't expecting a medal.'

SELECTED BIBLIOGRAPHY

Arthur, Max, *Forgotten Voices of the Second World War*, Ebury Press, London, 2004.

Ashcroft, Michael, *Victoria Cross Heroes*, Headline Review, London, 2006.

Asher, Michael, *The Regiment: The Real Story of the SAS*, Viking, London, 2007.

Burn, Michael, *Turned Towards The Sun: An Autobiography*, Michael Russell, Norwich, 2003.

Chant-Sempill, Stuart, *St Nazaire Commando*, John Murray, London, 1985.

Collins, Frank, *Baptism of Fire*, Doubleday, London, 1997.

Connor, Ken, *Ghost Force: The Secret History of the SAS*, Weidenfeld & Nicolson, London, 1998.

Davies, Barry, *Fire Magic*, Bloomsbury, London, 1994.

Davies, Barry, *Heroes of the SAS*, Virgin, London, 2000.

Dorrian, James, *Saint-Nazaire: Operation Chariot – 1942*, Pen and Sword, Barnsley, 2006.

Dorrian, James, *Storming St Nazaire: The Gripping Story of the Dock-Busting Raid, March* 1942, Leo Cooper, London, 1998. (By courtesy of Pen and Sword Books Ltd.)

Falconer, Duncan, *First Into Action*, Little Brown, London, 1998.

Fleming, Jon, and Faux, Ronald, *Soldiers on Everest*, Her Majesty's Stationery Office, London, 1977.

Ford, Ken, *St Nazaire 1942: The Great Commando Raid*, Osprey Publishing Ltd, Oxford, 2001.

Fowler, William, *Operation Barras: The SAS Rescue Mission: Sierra Leone 2000*, Cassell, London, 2004.

Geraghty, Tony, *Who Dares Wins: The Special Air Service, 1950 to the Gulf War*, Little Brown, London, 1980.

Harnden, Toby, *Bandit Country: The IRA and South Armagh*, Hodder & Stoughton, London, 1999.

Hoe, Alan, *David Stirling: The Authorised Biography of the Creator of the SAS*, Little Brown, London, 1992.

Howarth, David, *Dawn of D-Day*, Collins, London, 1959.

Kennedy, Michael Paul, *Soldier I: SAS*, Bloomsbury, London, 1989.

Keyes, Elizabeth, *Geoffrey Keyes: V.C., M.C., Croix de Guerre*, George Newnes Limited, London, 1956.

Lane, Bronco, *Military Mountaineering: A History of Services Mountaineering, 1945–2000*, Hayloft, Kirby Stephen (Cumbria), 2000.

Lewis, Damien, *Operation Certain Death: The Inside Story of the SAS's Greatest Battle*, Century, London, 2004.

Lindsay, Oliver, *Once A Grenadier . . . The Grenadier Guards 1945–1995*, Leo Cooper, London, 1996. (Reprinted by permission of The Random House Group Ltd.)

Lucas Phillips, C.E., *The Greatest Raid of All*, Heinemann, London Melbourne Toronto, 1958.

McCrery, Nigel, *The Complete History of the SAS*, Carlton Books, London, 2003.

Milner, Laurie, *Royal Scots in the Gulf: 1st Battalion, The Royal Scots (The Royal Regiment) on Operation Granby 1990–1991*, Leo Cooper, London, 1994. (By courtesy of Pen and Sword Books Ltd.)

Morgan, Mike, *The SAS Story*, Sutton Publishing, Stroud, 2008.

Perrault, Gilles, *The Secrets of D-Day*, Arthur Barker Limited, London, 1965.

Ramsay, Jack, *SAS: The Soldiers' Story*, Macmillan, London, 1996. (Reprinted by permission of ITV Global Entertainment)

Ratcliffe, Peter, *Eye of the Storm: Twenty-five Years in Action with the SAS*, Michael O'Mara Books, London, 2000. (Reproduced by permission of the author and the publishers. Copyright © Peter Ratcliffe 2000.)

Ryder, Commander R.E.D., *VC, The Attack on St Nazaire*, John Murray, London, 1947.

Scholey, Pete, *SAS Heroes: Remarkable Soldiers, Extraordinary Men*, Osprey Publishing, Oxford, 2008.

Seymour, William, *British Special Forces*, Pen and Sword, Barnsley, 1985. (By courtesy of Pen and Sword Books Ltd.)

Sparks, William with Munn, Michael, *The Last of the Cockleshell Heroes: A World War Two Memoir*, Leo Cooper, London, 1992. (By courtesy of Pen and Sword Books Ltd.)

Sparks, Bill, *Cockleshell Commando: The Memoirs of Bill Sparks DSM*, Leo Cooper, Barnsley, 2002. (By courtesy of Pen and Sword Books Ltd.)

Stilwell, Alexander, *Special Forces in Action*, Pen and Sword, Barnsley, 2007.

Taylor, Peter, *Brits: The War Against the IRA*, Bloomsbury, London, 2001.

Urban, Mark, *Big Boys' Rule*, Faber and Faber, London, 1992.

Windmill, Lorna Almonds, *Gentleman Jim: The Wartime Story of a Founder of the SAS and Special Forces*, Constable and Robinson, London, 2001 (new edition).

INDEX

'WW1' and 'WW2' denote World Wars One and Two, '(P)' a posthumous award. An asterisk (*) appended to a name denotes an alias. For consistency, ranks are not given unless this is the only qualifier.